Bison - The Yacc-compatible Parser Generator

A catalogue record for this book is available from the Hong Kong Public Libraries.

Published in Hong Kong by Samurai Media Limited.

Email: info@samuraimedia.org

ISBN 978-988-8381-37-1

Table of Contents

Introduction

Bison is a general-purpose parser generator that converts an annotated context-free grammar into a deterministic LR or generalized LR (GLR) parser employing LALR(1) parser tables. As an experimental feature, Bison can also generate IELR(1) or canonical LR(1) parser tables. Once you are proficient with Bison, you can use it to develop a wide range of language parsers, from those used in simple desk calculators to complex programming languages.

Bison is upward compatible with Yacc: all properly-written Yacc grammars ought to work with Bison with no change. Anyone familiar with Yacc should be able to use Bison with little trouble. You need to be fluent in C or C++ programming in order to use Bison or to understand this manual. Java is also supported as an experimental feature.

We begin with tutorial chapters that explain the basic concepts of using Bison and show three explained examples, each building on the last. If you don't know Bison or Yacc, start by reading these chapters. Reference chapters follow, which describe specific aspects of Bison in detail.

Bison was written originally by Robert Corbett. Richard Stallman made it Yacc-compatible. Wilfred Hansen of Carnegie Mellon University added multi-character string literals and other features. Since then, Bison has grown more robust and evolved many other new features thanks to the hard work of a long list of volunteers. For details, see the THANKS and ChangeLog files included in the Bison distribution.

This edition corresponds to version 3.0.4 of Bison.

Conditions for Using Bison

The distribution terms for Bison-generated parsers permit using the parsers in nonfree programs. Before Bison version 2.2, these extra permissions applied only when Bison was generating LALR(1) parsers in C. And before Bison version 1.24, Bison-generated parsers could be used only in programs that were free software.

The other GNU programming tools, such as the GNU C compiler, have never had such a requirement. They could always be used for nonfree software. The reason Bison was different was not due to a special policy decision; it resulted from applying the usual General Public License to all of the Bison source code.

The main output of the Bison utility—the Bison parser implementation file—contains a verbatim copy of a sizable piece of Bison, which is the code for the parser's implementation. (The actions from your grammar are inserted into this implementation at one point, but most of the rest of the implementation is not changed.) When we applied the GPL terms to the skeleton code for the parser's implementation, the effect was to restrict the use of Bison output to free software.

We didn't change the terms because of sympathy for people who want to make software proprietary. **Software should be free.** But we concluded that limiting Bison's use to free software was doing little to encourage people to make other software free. So we decided to make the practical conditions for using Bison match the practical conditions for using the other GNU tools.

This exception applies when Bison is generating code for a parser. You can tell whether the exception applies to a Bison output file by inspecting the file for text beginning with "As a special exception...". The text spells out the exact terms of the exception.

GNU GENERAL PUBLIC LICENSE

Version 3, 29 June 2007

Copyright © 2007 Free Software Foundation, Inc. http://fsf.org/

Everyone is permitted to copy and distribute verbatim copies of this
license document, but changing it is not allowed.

Preamble

The GNU General Public License is a free, copyleft license for software and other kinds of works.

The licenses for most software and other practical works are designed to take away your freedom to share and change the works. By contrast, the GNU General Public License is intended to guarantee your freedom to share and change all versions of a program—to make sure it remains free software for all its users. We, the Free Software Foundation, use the GNU General Public License for most of our software; it applies also to any other work released this way by its authors. You can apply it to your programs, too.

When we speak of free software, we are referring to freedom, not price. Our General Public Licenses are designed to make sure that you have the freedom to distribute copies of free software (and charge for them if you wish), that you receive source code or can get it if you want it, that you can change the software or use pieces of it in new free programs, and that you know you can do these things.

To protect your rights, we need to prevent others from denying you these rights or asking you to surrender the rights. Therefore, you have certain responsibilities if you distribute copies of the software, or if you modify it: responsibilities to respect the freedom of others.

For example, if you distribute copies of such a program, whether gratis or for a fee, you must pass on to the recipients the same freedoms that you received. You must make sure that they, too, receive or can get the source code. And you must show them these terms so they know their rights.

Developers that use the GNU GPL protect your rights with two steps: (1) assert copyright on the software, and (2) offer you this License giving you legal permission to copy, distribute and/or modify it.

For the developers' and authors' protection, the GPL clearly explains that there is no warranty for this free software. For both users' and authors' sake, the GPL requires that modified versions be marked as changed, so that their problems will not be attributed erroneously to authors of previous versions.

Some devices are designed to deny users access to install or run modified versions of the software inside them, although the manufacturer can do so. This is fundamentally incompatible with the aim of protecting users' freedom to change the software. The systematic pattern of such abuse occurs in the area of products for individuals to use, which is precisely where it is most unacceptable. Therefore, we have designed this version of the GPL to prohibit the practice for those products. If such problems arise substantially in other domains, we stand ready to extend this provision to those domains in future versions of the GPL, as needed to protect the freedom of users.

Finally, every program is threatened constantly by software patents. States should not allow patents to restrict development and use of software on general-purpose computers, but in those that do, we wish to avoid the special danger that patents applied to a free program could make it effectively proprietary. To prevent this, the GPL assures that patents cannot be used to render the program non-free.

The precise terms and conditions for copying, distribution and modification follow.

TERMS AND CONDITIONS

0. Definitions.

   "This License" refers to version 3 of the GNU General Public License.

   "Copyright" also means copyright-like laws that apply to other kinds of works, such as semiconductor masks.

   "The Program" refers to any copyrightable work licensed under this License. Each licensee is addressed as "you". "Licensees" and "recipients" may be individuals or organizations.

   To "modify" a work means to copy from or adapt all or part of the work in a fashion requiring copyright permission, other than the making of an exact copy. The resulting work is called a "modified version" of the earlier work or a work "based on" the earlier work.

   A "covered work" means either the unmodified Program or a work based on the Program.

   To "propagate" a work means to do anything with it that, without permission, would make you directly or secondarily liable for infringement under applicable copyright law, except executing it on a computer or modifying a private copy. Propagation includes copying, distribution (with or without modification), making available to the public, and in some countries other activities as well.

   To "convey" a work means any kind of propagation that enables other parties to make or receive copies. Mere interaction with a user through a computer network, with no transfer of a copy, is not conveying.

   An interactive user interface displays "Appropriate Legal Notices" to the extent that it includes a convenient and prominently visible feature that (1) displays an appropriate copyright notice, and (2) tells the user that there is no warranty for the work (except to the extent that warranties are provided), that licensees may convey the work under this License, and how to view a copy of this License. If the interface presents a list of user commands or options, such as a menu, a prominent item in the list meets this criterion.

1. Source Code.

   The "source code" for a work means the preferred form of the work for making modifications to it. "Object code" means any non-source form of a work.

   A "Standard Interface" means an interface that either is an official standard defined by a recognized standards body, or, in the case of interfaces specified for a particular programming language, one that is widely used among developers working in that language.

The "System Libraries" of an executable work include anything, other than the work as a whole, that (a) is included in the normal form of packaging a Major Component, but which is not part of that Major Component, and (b) serves only to enable use of the work with that Major Component, or to implement a Standard Interface for which an implementation is available to the public in source code form. A "Major Component", in this context, means a major essential component (kernel, window system, and so on) of the specific operating system (if any) on which the executable work runs, or a compiler used to produce the work, or an object code interpreter used to run it.

The "Corresponding Source" for a work in object code form means all the source code needed to generate, install, and (for an executable work) run the object code and to modify the work, including scripts to control those activities. However, it does not include the work's System Libraries, or general-purpose tools or generally available free programs which are used unmodified in performing those activities but which are not part of the work. For example, Corresponding Source includes interface definition files associated with source files for the work, and the source code for shared libraries and dynamically linked subprograms that the work is specifically designed to require, such as by intimate data communication or control flow between those subprograms and other parts of the work.

The Corresponding Source need not include anything that users can regenerate automatically from other parts of the Corresponding Source.

The Corresponding Source for a work in source code form is that same work.

2. Basic Permissions.

All rights granted under this License are granted for the term of copyright on the Program, and are irrevocable provided the stated conditions are met. This License explicitly affirms your unlimited permission to run the unmodified Program. The output from running a covered work is covered by this License only if the output, given its content, constitutes a covered work. This License acknowledges your rights of fair use or other equivalent, as provided by copyright law.

You may make, run and propagate covered works that you do not convey, without conditions so long as your license otherwise remains in force. You may convey covered works to others for the sole purpose of having them make modifications exclusively for you, or provide you with facilities for running those works, provided that you comply with the terms of this License in conveying all material for which you do not control copyright. Those thus making or running the covered works for you must do so exclusively on your behalf, under your direction and control, on terms that prohibit them from making any copies of your copyrighted material outside their relationship with you.

Conveying under any other circumstances is permitted solely under the conditions stated below. Sublicensing is not allowed; section 10 makes it unnecessary.

3. Protecting Users' Legal Rights From Anti-Circumvention Law.

No covered work shall be deemed part of an effective technological measure under any applicable law fulfilling obligations under article 11 of the WIPO copyright treaty adopted on 20 December 1996, or similar laws prohibiting or restricting circumvention of such measures.

When you convey a covered work, you waive any legal power to forbid circumvention of technological measures to the extent such circumvention is effected by exercising rights under this License with respect to the covered work, and you disclaim any intention to limit operation or modification of the work as a means of enforcing, against the work's users, your or third parties' legal rights to forbid circumvention of technological measures.

4. Conveying Verbatim Copies.

You may convey verbatim copies of the Program's source code as you receive it, in any medium, provided that you conspicuously and appropriately publish on each copy an appropriate copyright notice; keep intact all notices stating that this License and any non-permissive terms added in accord with section 7 apply to the code; keep intact all notices of the absence of any warranty; and give all recipients a copy of this License along with the Program.

You may charge any price or no price for each copy that you convey, and you may offer support or warranty protection for a fee.

5. Conveying Modified Source Versions.

You may convey a work based on the Program, or the modifications to produce it from the Program, in the form of source code under the terms of section 4, provided that you also meet all of these conditions:

   a. The work must carry prominent notices stating that you modified it, and giving a relevant date.

   b. The work must carry prominent notices stating that it is released under this License and any conditions added under section 7. This requirement modifies the requirement in section 4 to "keep intact all notices".

   c. You must license the entire work, as a whole, under this License to anyone who comes into possession of a copy. This License will therefore apply, along with any applicable section 7 additional terms, to the whole of the work, and all its parts, regardless of how they are packaged. This License gives no permission to license the work in any other way, but it does not invalidate such permission if you have separately received it.

   d. If the work has interactive user interfaces, each must display Appropriate Legal Notices; however, if the Program has interactive interfaces that do not display Appropriate Legal Notices, your work need not make them do so.

A compilation of a covered work with other separate and independent works, which are not by their nature extensions of the covered work, and which are not combined with it such as to form a larger program, in or on a volume of a storage or distribution medium, is called an "aggregate" if the compilation and its resulting copyright are not used to limit the access or legal rights of the compilation's users beyond what the individual works permit. Inclusion of a covered work in an aggregate does not cause this License to apply to the other parts of the aggregate.

6. Conveying Non-Source Forms.

You may convey a covered work in object code form under the terms of sections 4 and 5, provided that you also convey the machine-readable Corresponding Source under the terms of this License, in one of these ways:

a. Convey the object code in, or embodied in, a physical product (including a physical distribution medium), accompanied by the Corresponding Source fixed on a durable physical medium customarily used for software interchange.

b. Convey the object code in, or embodied in, a physical product (including a physical distribution medium), accompanied by a written offer, valid for at least three years and valid for as long as you offer spare parts or customer support for that product model, to give anyone who possesses the object code either (1) a copy of the Corresponding Source for all the software in the product that is covered by this License, on a durable physical medium customarily used for software interchange, for a price no more than your reasonable cost of physically performing this conveying of source, or (2) access to copy the Corresponding Source from a network server at no charge.

c. Convey individual copies of the object code with a copy of the written offer to provide the Corresponding Source. This alternative is allowed only occasionally and noncommercially, and only if you received the object code with such an offer, in accord with subsection 6b.

d. Convey the object code by offering access from a designated place (gratis or for a charge), and offer equivalent access to the Corresponding Source in the same way through the same place at no further charge. You need not require recipients to copy the Corresponding Source along with the object code. If the place to copy the object code is a network server, the Corresponding Source may be on a different server (operated by you or a third party) that supports equivalent copying facilities, provided you maintain clear directions next to the object code saying where to find the Corresponding Source. Regardless of what server hosts the Corresponding Source, you remain obligated to ensure that it is available for as long as needed to satisfy these requirements.

e. Convey the object code using peer-to-peer transmission, provided you inform other peers where the object code and Corresponding Source of the work are being offered to the general public at no charge under subsection 6d.

A separable portion of the object code, whose source code is excluded from the Corresponding Source as a System Library, need not be included in conveying the object code work.

A "User Product" is either (1) a "consumer product", which means any tangible personal property which is normally used for personal, family, or household purposes, or (2) anything designed or sold for incorporation into a dwelling. In determining whether a product is a consumer product, doubtful cases shall be resolved in favor of coverage. For a particular product received by a particular user, "normally used" refers to a typical or common use of that class of product, regardless of the status of the particular user or of the way in which the particular user actually uses, or expects or is expected to use, the product. A product is a consumer product regardless of whether the product has substantial commercial, industrial or non-consumer uses, unless such uses represent the only significant mode of use of the product.

"Installation Information" for a User Product means any methods, procedures, authorization keys, or other information required to install and execute modified versions of a covered work in that User Product from a modified version of its Corresponding Source.

The information must suffice to ensure that the continued functioning of the modified object code is in no case prevented or interfered with solely because modification has been made.

If you convey an object code work under this section in, or with, or specifically for use in, a User Product, and the conveying occurs as part of a transaction in which the right of possession and use of the User Product is transferred to the recipient in perpetuity or for a fixed term (regardless of how the transaction is characterized), the Corresponding Source conveyed under this section must be accompanied by the Installation Information. But this requirement does not apply if neither you nor any third party retains the ability to install modified object code on the User Product (for example, the work has been installed in ROM).

The requirement to provide Installation Information does not include a requirement to continue to provide support service, warranty, or updates for a work that has been modified or installed by the recipient, or for the User Product in which it has been modified or installed. Access to a network may be denied when the modification itself materially and adversely affects the operation of the network or violates the rules and protocols for communication across the network.

Corresponding Source conveyed, and Installation Information provided, in accord with this section must be in a format that is publicly documented (and with an implementation available to the public in source code form), and must require no special password or key for unpacking, reading or copying.

7. Additional Terms.

"Additional permissions" are terms that supplement the terms of this License by making exceptions from one or more of its conditions. Additional permissions that are applicable to the entire Program shall be treated as though they were included in this License, to the extent that they are valid under applicable law. If additional permissions apply only to part of the Program, that part may be used separately under those permissions, but the entire Program remains governed by this License without regard to the additional permissions.

When you convey a copy of a covered work, you may at your option remove any additional permissions from that copy, or from any part of it. (Additional permissions may be written to require their own removal in certain cases when you modify the work.) You may place additional permissions on material, added by you to a covered work, for which you have or can give appropriate copyright permission.

Notwithstanding any other provision of this License, for material you add to a covered work, you may (if authorized by the copyright holders of that material) supplement the terms of this License with terms:

  a. Disclaiming warranty or limiting liability differently from the terms of sections 15 and 16 of this License; or

  b. Requiring preservation of specified reasonable legal notices or author attributions in that material or in the Appropriate Legal Notices displayed by works containing it; or

  c. Prohibiting misrepresentation of the origin of that material, or requiring that modified versions of such material be marked in reasonable ways as different from the original version; or

    d. Limiting the use for publicity purposes of names of licensors or authors of the material; or

    e. Declining to grant rights under trademark law for use of some trade names, trademarks, or service marks; or

    f. Requiring indemnification of licensors and authors of that material by anyone who conveys the material (or modified versions of it) with contractual assumptions of liability to the recipient, for any liability that these contractual assumptions directly impose on those licensors and authors.

All other non-permissive additional terms are considered "further restrictions" within the meaning of section 10. If the Program as you received it, or any part of it, contains a notice stating that it is governed by this License along with a term that is a further restriction, you may remove that term. If a license document contains a further restriction but permits relicensing or conveying under this License, you may add to a covered work material governed by the terms of that license document, provided that the further restriction does not survive such relicensing or conveying.

If you add terms to a covered work in accord with this section, you must place, in the relevant source files, a statement of the additional terms that apply to those files, or a notice indicating where to find the applicable terms.

Additional terms, permissive or non-permissive, may be stated in the form of a separately written license, or stated as exceptions; the above requirements apply either way.

8. Termination.

You may not propagate or modify a covered work except as expressly provided under this License. Any attempt otherwise to propagate or modify it is void, and will automatically terminate your rights under this License (including any patent licenses granted under the third paragraph of section 11).

However, if you cease all violation of this License, then your license from a particular copyright holder is reinstated (a) provisionally, unless and until the copyright holder explicitly and finally terminates your license, and (b) permanently, if the copyright holder fails to notify you of the violation by some reasonable means prior to 60 days after the cessation.

Moreover, your license from a particular copyright holder is reinstated permanently if the copyright holder notifies you of the violation by some reasonable means, this is the first time you have received notice of violation of this License (for any work) from that copyright holder, and you cure the violation prior to 30 days after your receipt of the notice.

Termination of your rights under this section does not terminate the licenses of parties who have received copies or rights from you under this License. If your rights have been terminated and not permanently reinstated, you do not qualify to receive new licenses for the same material under section 10.

9. Acceptance Not Required for Having Copies.

You are not required to accept this License in order to receive or run a copy of the Program. Ancillary propagation of a covered work occurring solely as a consequence of using peer-to-peer transmission to receive a copy likewise does not require acceptance.

However, nothing other than this License grants you permission to propagate or modify any covered work. These actions infringe copyright if you do not accept this License. Therefore, by modifying or propagating a covered work, you indicate your acceptance of this License to do so.

10. Automatic Licensing of Downstream Recipients.

Each time you convey a covered work, the recipient automatically receives a license from the original licensors, to run, modify and propagate that work, subject to this License. You are not responsible for enforcing compliance by third parties with this License.

An "entity transaction" is a transaction transferring control of an organization, or substantially all assets of one, or subdividing an organization, or merging organizations. If propagation of a covered work results from an entity transaction, each party to that transaction who receives a copy of the work also receives whatever licenses to the work the party's predecessor in interest had or could give under the previous paragraph, plus a right to possession of the Corresponding Source of the work from the predecessor in interest, if the predecessor has it or can get it with reasonable efforts.

You may not impose any further restrictions on the exercise of the rights granted or affirmed under this License. For example, you may not impose a license fee, royalty, or other charge for exercise of rights granted under this License, and you may not initiate litigation (including a cross-claim or counterclaim in a lawsuit) alleging that any patent claim is infringed by making, using, selling, offering for sale, or importing the Program or any portion of it.

11. Patents.

A "contributor" is a copyright holder who authorizes use under this License of the Program or a work on which the Program is based. The work thus licensed is called the contributor's "contributor version".

A contributor's "essential patent claims" are all patent claims owned or controlled by the contributor, whether already acquired or hereafter acquired, that would be infringed by some manner, permitted by this License, of making, using, or selling its contributor version, but do not include claims that would be infringed only as a consequence of further modification of the contributor version. For purposes of this definition, "control" includes the right to grant patent sublicenses in a manner consistent with the requirements of this License.

Each contributor grants you a non-exclusive, worldwide, royalty-free patent license under the contributor's essential patent claims, to make, use, sell, offer for sale, import and otherwise run, modify and propagate the contents of its contributor version.

In the following three paragraphs, a "patent license" is any express agreement or commitment, however denominated, not to enforce a patent (such as an express permission to practice a patent or covenant not to sue for patent infringement). To "grant" such a patent license to a party means to make such an agreement or commitment not to enforce a patent against the party.

If you convey a covered work, knowingly relying on a patent license, and the Corresponding Source of the work is not available for anyone to copy, free of charge and under the terms of this License, through a publicly available network server or other readily accessible means, then you must either (1) cause the Corresponding Source to be so available, or (2) arrange to deprive yourself of the benefit of the patent license for this particular work, or (3) arrange, in a manner consistent with the requirements of this License, to extend the patent license to downstream recipients. "Knowingly relying" means you have actual knowledge that, but for the patent license, your conveying the covered work in a country, or your recipient's use of the covered work in a country, would infringe one or more identifiable patents in that country that you have reason to believe are valid.

If, pursuant to or in connection with a single transaction or arrangement, you convey, or propagate by procuring conveyance of, a covered work, and grant a patent license to some of the parties receiving the covered work authorizing them to use, propagate, modify or convey a specific copy of the covered work, then the patent license you grant is automatically extended to all recipients of the covered work and works based on it.

A patent license is "discriminatory" if it does not include within the scope of its coverage, prohibits the exercise of, or is conditioned on the non-exercise of one or more of the rights that are specifically granted under this License. You may not convey a covered work if you are a party to an arrangement with a third party that is in the business of distributing software, under which you make payment to the third party based on the extent of your activity of conveying the work, and under which the third party grants, to any of the parties who would receive the covered work from you, a discriminatory patent license (a) in connection with copies of the covered work conveyed by you (or copies made from those copies), or (b) primarily for and in connection with specific products or compilations that contain the covered work, unless you entered into that arrangement, or that patent license was granted, prior to 28 March 2007.

Nothing in this License shall be construed as excluding or limiting any implied license or other defenses to infringement that may otherwise be available to you under applicable patent law.

12. No Surrender of Others' Freedom.

    If conditions are imposed on you (whether by court order, agreement or otherwise) that contradict the conditions of this License, they do not excuse you from the conditions of this License. If you cannot convey a covered work so as to satisfy simultaneously your obligations under this License and any other pertinent obligations, then as a consequence you may not convey it at all. For example, if you agree to terms that obligate you to collect a royalty for further conveying from those to whom you convey the Program, the only way you could satisfy both those terms and this License would be to refrain entirely from conveying the Program.

13. Use with the GNU Affero General Public License.

    Notwithstanding any other provision of this License, you have permission to link or combine any covered work with a work licensed under version 3 of the GNU Affero General Public License into a single combined work, and to convey the resulting work. The terms of this License will continue to apply to the part which is the covered work, but the special requirements of the GNU Affero General Public License, section 13, concerning interaction through a network will apply to the combination as such.

14. Revised Versions of this License.

The Free Software Foundation may publish revised and/or new versions of the GNU General Public License from time to time. Such new versions will be similar in spirit to the present version, but may differ in detail to address new problems or concerns.

Each version is given a distinguishing version number. If the Program specifies that a certain numbered version of the GNU General Public License "or any later version" applies to it, you have the option of following the terms and conditions either of that numbered version or of any later version published by the Free Software Foundation. If the Program does not specify a version number of the GNU General Public License, you may choose any version ever published by the Free Software Foundation.

If the Program specifies that a proxy can decide which future versions of the GNU General Public License can be used, that proxy's public statement of acceptance of a version permanently authorizes you to choose that version for the Program.

Later license versions may give you additional or different permissions. However, no additional obligations are imposed on any author or copyright holder as a result of your choosing to follow a later version.

15. Disclaimer of Warranty.

    THERE IS NO WARRANTY FOR THE PROGRAM, TO THE EXTENT PERMITTED BY APPLICABLE LAW. EXCEPT WHEN OTHERWISE STATED IN WRITING THE COPYRIGHT HOLDERS AND/OR OTHER PARTIES PROVIDE THE PROGRAM "AS IS" WITHOUT WARRANTY OF ANY KIND, EITHER EXPRESSED OR IMPLIED, INCLUDING, BUT NOT LIMITED TO, THE IMPLIED WARRANTIES OF MERCHANTABILITY AND FITNESS FOR A PARTICULAR PURPOSE. THE ENTIRE RISK AS TO THE QUALITY AND PERFORMANCE OF THE PROGRAM IS WITH YOU. SHOULD THE PROGRAM PROVE DEFECTIVE, YOU ASSUME THE COST OF ALL NECESSARY SERVICING, REPAIR OR CORRECTION.

16. Limitation of Liability.

    IN NO EVENT UNLESS REQUIRED BY APPLICABLE LAW OR AGREED TO IN WRITING WILL ANY COPYRIGHT HOLDER, OR ANY OTHER PARTY WHO MODIFIES AND/OR CONVEYS THE PROGRAM AS PERMITTED ABOVE, BE LIABLE TO YOU FOR DAMAGES, INCLUDING ANY GENERAL, SPECIAL, INCIDENTAL OR CONSEQUENTIAL DAMAGES ARISING OUT OF THE USE OR INABILITY TO USE THE PROGRAM (INCLUDING BUT NOT LIMITED TO LOSS OF DATA OR DATA BEING RENDERED INACCURATE OR LOSSES SUSTAINED BY YOU OR THIRD PARTIES OR A FAILURE OF THE PROGRAM TO OPERATE WITH ANY OTHER PROGRAMS), EVEN IF SUCH HOLDER OR OTHER PARTY HAS BEEN ADVISED OF THE POSSIBILITY OF SUCH DAMAGES.

17. Interpretation of Sections 15 and 16.

    If the disclaimer of warranty and limitation of liability provided above cannot be given local legal effect according to their terms, reviewing courts shall apply local law that most closely approximates an absolute waiver of all civil liability in connection with the Program, unless a warranty or assumption of liability accompanies a copy of the Program in return for a fee.

END OF TERMS AND CONDITIONS

How to Apply These Terms to Your New Programs

If you develop a new program, and you want it to be of the greatest possible use to the public, the best way to achieve this is to make it free software which everyone can redistribute and change under these terms.

To do so, attach the following notices to the program. It is safest to attach them to the start of each source file to most effectively state the exclusion of warranty; and each file should have at least the "copyright" line and a pointer to where the full notice is found.

```
one line to give the program's name and a brief idea of what it does.
Copyright (C) year name of author

This program is free software: you can redistribute it and/or modify
it under the terms of the GNU General Public License as published by
the Free Software Foundation, either version 3 of the License, or (at
your option) any later version.

This program is distributed in the hope that it will be useful, but
WITHOUT ANY WARRANTY; without even the implied warranty of
MERCHANTABILITY or FITNESS FOR A PARTICULAR PURPOSE.  See the GNU
General Public License for more details.

You should have received a copy of the GNU General Public License
along with this program.  If not, see http://www.gnu.org/licenses/.
```

Also add information on how to contact you by electronic and paper mail.

If the program does terminal interaction, make it output a short notice like this when it starts in an interactive mode:

```
program Copyright (C) year name of author
This program comes with ABSOLUTELY NO WARRANTY; for details type 'show w'.
This is free software, and you are welcome to redistribute it
under certain conditions; type 'show c' for details.
```

The hypothetical commands 'show w' and 'show c' should show the appropriate parts of the General Public License. Of course, your program's commands might be different; for a GUI interface, you would use an "about box".

You should also get your employer (if you work as a programmer) or school, if any, to sign a "copyright disclaimer" for the program, if necessary. For more information on this, and how to apply and follow the GNU GPL, see http://www.gnu.org/licenses/.

The GNU General Public License does not permit incorporating your program into proprietary programs. If your program is a subroutine library, you may consider it more useful to permit linking proprietary applications with the library. If this is what you want to do, use the GNU Lesser General Public License instead of this License. But first, please read http://www.gnu.org/philosophy/why-not-lgpl.html.

1 The Concepts of Bison

This chapter introduces many of the basic concepts without which the details of Bison will not make sense. If you do not already know how to use Bison or Yacc, we suggest you start by reading this chapter carefully.

1.1 Languages and Context-Free Grammars

In order for Bison to parse a language, it must be described by a *context-free grammar*. This means that you specify one or more *syntactic groupings* and give rules for constructing them from their parts. For example, in the C language, one kind of grouping is called an 'expression'. One rule for making an expression might be, "An expression can be made of a minus sign and another expression". Another would be, "An expression can be an integer". As you can see, rules are often recursive, but there must be at least one rule which leads out of the recursion.

The most common formal system for presenting such rules for humans to read is *Backus-Naur Form* or "BNF", which was developed in order to specify the language Algol 60. Any grammar expressed in BNF is a context-free grammar. The input to Bison is essentially machine-readable BNF.

There are various important subclasses of context-free grammars. Although it can handle almost all context-free grammars, Bison is optimized for what are called LR(1) grammars. In brief, in these grammars, it must be possible to tell how to parse any portion of an input string with just a single token of lookahead. For historical reasons, Bison by default is limited by the additional restrictions of LALR(1), which is hard to explain simply. See Section 5.7 [Mysterious Conflicts], page 116, for more information on this. As an experimental feature, you can escape these additional restrictions by requesting IELR(1) or canonical LR(1) parser tables. See Section 5.8.1 [LR Table Construction], page 118, to learn how.

Parsers for LR(1) grammars are *deterministic*, meaning roughly that the next grammar rule to apply at any point in the input is uniquely determined by the preceding input and a fixed, finite portion (called a *lookahead*) of the remaining input. A context-free grammar can be *ambiguous*, meaning that there are multiple ways to apply the grammar rules to get the same inputs. Even unambiguous grammars can be *nondeterministic*, meaning that no fixed lookahead always suffices to determine the next grammar rule to apply. With the proper declarations, Bison is also able to parse these more general context-free grammars, using a technique known as GLR parsing (for Generalized LR). Bison's GLR parsers are able to handle any context-free grammar for which the number of possible parses of any given string is finite.

In the formal grammatical rules for a language, each kind of syntactic unit or grouping is named by a *symbol*. Those which are built by grouping smaller constructs according to grammatical rules are called *nonterminal symbols*; those which can't be subdivided are called *terminal symbols* or *token types*. We call a piece of input corresponding to a single terminal symbol a *token*, and a piece corresponding to a single nonterminal symbol a *grouping*.

We can use the C language as an example of what symbols, terminal and nonterminal, mean. The tokens of C are identifiers, constants (numeric and string), and the various keywords, arithmetic operators and punctuation marks. So the terminal symbols of a grammar for C include 'identifier', 'number', 'string', plus one symbol for each keyword, operator or punctuation mark: 'if', 'return', 'const', 'static', 'int', 'char', 'plus-sign', 'open-brace', 'close-brace', 'comma' and many more. (These tokens can be subdivided into characters, but that is a matter of lexicography, not grammar.)

Here is a simple C function subdivided into tokens:

```
int                 /* keyword 'int' */
square (int x)      /* identifier, open-paren, keyword 'int',
                       identifier, close-paren */
{                   /* open-brace */
  return x * x;     /* keyword 'return', identifier, asterisk,
                       identifier, semicolon */
}                   /* close-brace */
```

The syntactic groupings of C include the expression, the statement, the declaration, and the function definition. These are represented in the grammar of C by nonterminal symbols 'expression', 'statement', 'declaration' and 'function definition'. The full grammar uses dozens of additional language constructs, each with its own nonterminal symbol, in order to express the meanings of these four. The example above is a function definition; it contains one declaration, and one statement. In the statement, each 'x' is an expression and so is 'x * x'.

Each nonterminal symbol must have grammatical rules showing how it is made out of simpler constructs. For example, one kind of C statement is the **return** statement; this would be described with a grammar rule which reads informally as follows:

A 'statement' can be made of a 'return' keyword, an 'expression' and a 'semicolon'.

There would be many other rules for 'statement', one for each kind of statement in C.

One nonterminal symbol must be distinguished as the special one which defines a complete utterance in the language. It is called the *start symbol*. In a compiler, this means a complete input program. In the C language, the nonterminal symbol 'sequence of definitions and declarations' plays this role.

For example, '1 + 2' is a valid C expression—a valid part of a C program—but it is not valid as an *entire* C program. In the context-free grammar of C, this follows from the fact that 'expression' is not the start symbol.

The Bison parser reads a sequence of tokens as its input, and groups the tokens using the grammar rules. If the input is valid, the end result is that the entire token sequence reduces to a single grouping whose symbol is the grammar's start symbol. If we use a grammar for C, the entire input must be a 'sequence of definitions and declarations'. If not, the parser reports a syntax error.

1.2 From Formal Rules to Bison Input

A formal grammar is a mathematical construct. To define the language for Bison, you must write a file expressing the grammar in Bison syntax: a *Bison grammar* file. See Chapter 3 [Bison Grammar Files], page 51.

A nonterminal symbol in the formal grammar is represented in Bison input as an identifier, like an identifier in C. By convention, it should be in lower case, such as **expr**, **stmt** or **declaration**.

The Bison representation for a terminal symbol is also called a *token type*. Token types as well can be represented as C-like identifiers. By convention, these identifiers should be upper case to distinguish them from nonterminals: for example, INTEGER, IDENTIFIER, IF or RETURN. A terminal symbol that stands for a particular keyword in the language should be named after that keyword converted to upper case. The terminal symbol error is reserved for error recovery. See Section 3.2 [Symbols], page 57.

A terminal symbol can also be represented as a character literal, just like a C character constant. You should do this whenever a token is just a single character (parenthesis, plus-sign, etc.): use that same character in a literal as the terminal symbol for that token.

A third way to represent a terminal symbol is with a C string constant containing several characters. See Section 3.2 [Symbols], page 57, for more information.

The grammar rules also have an expression in Bison syntax. For example, here is the Bison rule for a C return statement. The semicolon in quotes is a literal character token, representing part of the C syntax for the statement; the naked semicolon, and the colon, are Bison punctuation used in every rule.

```
stmt: RETURN expr ';' ;
```

See Section 3.3 [Syntax of Grammar Rules], page 59.

1.3 Semantic Values

A formal grammar selects tokens only by their classifications: for example, if a rule mentions the terminal symbol 'integer constant', it means that *any* integer constant is grammatically valid in that position. The precise value of the constant is irrelevant to how to parse the input: if 'x+4' is grammatical then 'x+1' or 'x+3989' is equally grammatical.

But the precise value is very important for what the input means once it is parsed. A compiler is useless if it fails to distinguish between 4, 1 and 3989 as constants in the program! Therefore, each token in a Bison grammar has both a token type and a *semantic value*. See Section 3.4 [Defining Language Semantics], page 61, for details.

The token type is a terminal symbol defined in the grammar, such as INTEGER, IDENTIFIER or ','. It tells everything you need to know to decide where the token may validly appear and how to group it with other tokens. The grammar rules know nothing about tokens except their types.

The semantic value has all the rest of the information about the meaning of the token, such as the value of an integer, or the name of an identifier. (A token such as ',' which is just punctuation doesn't need to have any semantic value.)

For example, an input token might be classified as token type INTEGER and have the semantic value 4. Another input token might have the same token type INTEGER but value 3989. When a grammar rule says that INTEGER is allowed, either of these tokens is acceptable because each is an INTEGER. When the parser accepts the token, it keeps track of the token's semantic value.

Each grouping can also have a semantic value as well as its nonterminal symbol. For example, in a calculator, an expression typically has a semantic value that is a number. In a compiler for a programming language, an expression typically has a semantic value that is a tree structure describing the meaning of the expression.

1.4 Semantic Actions

In order to be useful, a program must do more than parse input; it must also produce some output based on the input. In a Bison grammar, a grammar rule can have an *action* made up of C statements. Each time the parser recognizes a match for that rule, the action is executed. See Section 3.4.6 [Actions], page 64.

Most of the time, the purpose of an action is to compute the semantic value of the whole construct from the semantic values of its parts. For example, suppose we have a rule which says an expression can be the sum of two expressions. When the parser recognizes such a sum, each of the subexpressions has a semantic value which describes how it was built up. The action for this rule should create a similar sort of value for the newly recognized larger expression.

For example, here is a rule that says an expression can be the sum of two subexpressions:

```
expr: expr '+' expr    { $$ = $1 + $3; } ;
```

The action says how to produce the semantic value of the sum expression from the values of the two subexpressions.

1.5 Writing GLR Parsers

In some grammars, Bison's deterministic LR(1) parsing algorithm cannot decide whether to apply a certain grammar rule at a given point. That is, it may not be able to decide (on the basis of the input read so far) which of two possible reductions (applications of a grammar rule) applies, or whether to apply a reduction or read more of the input and apply a reduction later in the input. These are known respectively as *reduce/reduce* conflicts (see Section 5.6 [Reduce/Reduce], page 113), and *shift/reduce* conflicts (see Section 5.2 [Shift/Reduce], page 108).

To use a grammar that is not easily modified to be LR(1), a more general parsing algorithm is sometimes necessary. If you include %glr-parser among the Bison declarations in your file (see Section 3.1 [Grammar Outline], page 51), the result is a Generalized LR (GLR) parser. These parsers handle Bison grammars that contain no unresolved conflicts (i.e., after applying precedence declarations) identically to deterministic parsers. However, when faced with unresolved shift/reduce and reduce/reduce conflicts, GLR parsers use the simple expedient of doing both, effectively cloning the parser to follow both possibilities. Each of the resulting parsers can again split, so that at any given time, there can be any number of possible parses being explored. The parsers proceed in lockstep; that is, all of them consume (shift) a given input symbol before any of them proceed to the next. Each of the cloned parsers eventually meets one of two possible fates: either it runs into a parsing error, in which case it simply vanishes, or it merges with another parser, because the two of them have reduced the input to an identical set of symbols.

During the time that there are multiple parsers, semantic actions are recorded, but not performed. When a parser disappears, its recorded semantic actions disappear as well, and are never performed. When a reduction makes two parsers identical, causing them to merge, Bison records both sets of semantic actions. Whenever the last two parsers merge, reverting to the single-parser case, Bison resolves all the outstanding actions either by precedences given to the grammar rules involved, or by performing both actions, and then calling a designated user-defined function on the resulting values to produce an arbitrary merged result.

1.5.1 Using GLR on Unambiguous Grammars

In the simplest cases, you can use the GLR algorithm to parse grammars that are unambiguous but fail to be LR(1). Such grammars typically require more than one symbol of lookahead.

Consider a problem that arises in the declaration of enumerated and subrange types in the programming language Pascal. Here are some examples:

```
type subrange = lo .. hi;
type enum = (a, b, c);
```

The original language standard allows only numeric literals and constant identifiers for the subrange bounds ('lo' and 'hi'), but Extended Pascal (ISO/IEC 10206) and many other Pascal implementations allow arbitrary expressions there. This gives rise to the following situation, containing a superfluous pair of parentheses:

```
type subrange = (a) .. b;
```

Compare this to the following declaration of an enumerated type with only one value:

```
type enum = (a);
```

(These declarations are contrived, but they are syntactically valid, and more-complicated cases can come up in practical programs.)

These two declarations look identical until the '..' token. With normal LR(1) one-token lookahead it is not possible to decide between the two forms when the identifier 'a' is parsed. It is, however, desirable for a parser to decide this, since in the latter case 'a' must become a new identifier to represent the enumeration value, while in the former case 'a' must be evaluated with its current meaning, which may be a constant or even a function call.

You could parse '(a)' as an "unspecified identifier in parentheses", to be resolved later, but this typically requires substantial contortions in both semantic actions and large parts of the grammar, where the parentheses are nested in the recursive rules for expressions.

You might think of using the lexer to distinguish between the two forms by returning different tokens for currently defined and undefined identifiers. But if these declarations occur in a local scope, and 'a' is defined in an outer scope, then both forms are possible— either locally redefining 'a', or using the value of 'a' from the outer scope. So this approach cannot work.

A simple solution to this problem is to declare the parser to use the GLR algorithm. When the GLR parser reaches the critical state, it merely splits into two branches and pursues both syntax rules simultaneously. Sooner or later, one of them runs into a parsing error. If there is a '..' token before the next ';', the rule for enumerated types fails since it cannot accept '..' anywhere; otherwise, the subrange type rule fails since it requires a '..' token. So one of the branches fails silently, and the other one continues normally, performing all the intermediate actions that were postponed during the split.

If the input is syntactically incorrect, both branches fail and the parser reports a syntax error as usual.

The effect of all this is that the parser seems to "guess" the correct branch to take, or in other words, it seems to use more lookahead than the underlying LR(1) algorithm actually allows for. In this example, LR(2) would suffice, but also some cases that are not LR(k) for any k can be handled this way.

In general, a GLR parser can take quadratic or cubic worst-case time, and the current Bison parser even takes exponential time and space for some grammars. In practice, this rarely happens, and for many grammars it is possible to prove that it cannot happen. The present example contains only one conflict between two rules, and the type-declaration context containing the conflict cannot be nested. So the number of branches that can exist at any time is limited by the constant 2, and the parsing time is still linear.

Here is a Bison grammar corresponding to the example above. It parses a vastly simplified form of Pascal type declarations.

```
%token TYPE DOTDOT ID

%left '+' '-'
%left '*' '/'

%%
type_decl: TYPE ID '=' type ';' ;

type:
  '(' id_list ')'
| expr DOTDOT expr
;

id_list:
  ID
| id_list ',' ID
;

expr:
  '(' expr ')'
| expr '+' expr
| expr '-' expr
| expr '*' expr
| expr '/' expr
| ID
;
```

When used as a normal LR(1) grammar, Bison correctly complains about one reduce/reduce conflict. In the conflicting situation the parser chooses one of the alternatives, arbitrarily the one declared first. Therefore the following correct input is not recognized:

```
type t = (a) .. b;
```

The parser can be turned into a GLR parser, while also telling Bison to be silent about the one known reduce/reduce conflict, by adding these two declarations to the Bison grammar file (before the first '%%'):

```
%glr-parser
%expect-rr 1
```

No change in the grammar itself is required. Now the parser recognizes all valid declarations, according to the limited syntax above, transparently. In fact, the user does not even notice when the parser splits.

So here we have a case where we can use the benefits of GLR, almost without disadvantages. Even in simple cases like this, however, there are at least two potential problems to beware. First, always analyze the conflicts reported by Bison to make sure that GLR splitting is only done where it is intended. A GLR parser splitting inadvertently may cause problems less obvious than an LR parser statically choosing the wrong alternative in a conflict. Second, consider interactions with the lexer (see Section 7.1 [Semantic Tokens], page 129) with great care. Since a split parser consumes tokens without performing any actions during the split, the lexer cannot obtain information via parser actions. Some cases of lexer interactions can be eliminated by using GLR to shift the complications from the lexer to the parser. You must check the remaining cases for correctness.

In our example, it would be safe for the lexer to return tokens based on their current meanings in some symbol table, because no new symbols are defined in the middle of a type declaration. Though it is possible for a parser to define the enumeration constants as they are parsed, before the type declaration is completed, it actually makes no difference since they cannot be used within the same enumerated type declaration.

1.5.2 Using GLR to Resolve Ambiguities

Let's consider an example, vastly simplified from a C++ grammar.

```
%{
  #include <stdio.h>
  #define YYSTYPE char const *
  int yylex (void);
  void yyerror (char const *);
%}

%token TYPENAME ID

%right '='
%left '+'

%glr-parser

%%

prog:
  %empty
| prog stmt   { printf ("\n"); }
;

stmt:
  expr ';'  %dprec 1
| decl      %dprec 2
;
```

```
expr:
  ID                 { printf ("%s ", $$); }
| TYPENAME '(' expr ')'
                     { printf ("%s <cast> ", $1); }
| expr '+' expr    { printf ("+ "); }
| expr '=' expr    { printf ("= "); }
;

decl:
  TYPENAME declarator ';'
                     { printf ("%s <declare> ", $1); }
| TYPENAME declarator '=' expr ';'
                     { printf ("%s <init-declare> ", $1); }
;

declarator:
  ID                 { printf ("\"%s\" ", $1); }
| '(' declarator ')'
;
```

This models a problematic part of the C++ grammar—the ambiguity between certain declarations and statements. For example,

```
T (x) = y+z;
```

parses as either an `expr` or a `stmt` (assuming that 'T' is recognized as a `TYPENAME` and 'x' as an `ID`). Bison detects this as a reduce/reduce conflict between the rules `expr : ID` and `declarator : ID`, which it cannot resolve at the time it encounters x in the example above. Since this is a GLR parser, it therefore splits the problem into two parses, one for each choice of resolving the reduce/reduce conflict. Unlike the example from the previous section (see Section 1.5.1 [Simple GLR Parsers], page 21), however, neither of these parses "dies," because the grammar as it stands is ambiguous. One of the parsers eventually reduces `stmt : expr ';'` and the other reduces `stmt : decl`, after which both parsers are in an identical state: they've seen 'prog stmt' and have the same unprocessed input remaining. We say that these parses have *merged*.

At this point, the GLR parser requires a specification in the grammar of how to choose between the competing parses. In the example above, the two `%dprec` declarations specify that Bison is to give precedence to the parse that interprets the example as a `decl`, which implies that x is a declarator. The parser therefore prints

```
"x" y z + T <init-declare>
```

The `%dprec` declarations only come into play when more than one parse survives. Consider a different input string for this parser:

```
T (x) + y;
```

This is another example of using GLR to parse an unambiguous construct, as shown in the previous section (see Section 1.5.1 [Simple GLR Parsers], page 21). Here, there is no ambiguity (this cannot be parsed as a declaration). However, at the time the Bison parser encounters x, it does not have enough information to resolve the reduce/reduce conflict

(again, between x as an expr or a declarator). In this case, no precedence declaration
is used. Again, the parser splits into two, one assuming that x is an expr, and the other
assuming x is a declarator. The second of these parsers then vanishes when it sees +, and
the parser prints

```
x T <cast> y +
```

Suppose that instead of resolving the ambiguity, you wanted to see all the possibilities.
For this purpose, you must merge the semantic actions of the two possible parsers, rather
than choosing one over the other. To do so, you could change the declaration of stmt as
follows:

```
stmt:
    expr ';'   %merge <stmtMerge>
|  decl        %merge <stmtMerge>
;
```

and define the stmtMerge function as:

```
static YYSTYPE
stmtMerge (YYSTYPE x0, YYSTYPE x1)
{
  printf ("<OR> ");
  return "";
}
```

with an accompanying forward declaration in the C declarations at the beginning of the
file:

```
%{
  #define YYSTYPE char const *
  static YYSTYPE stmtMerge (YYSTYPE x0, YYSTYPE x1);
%}
```

With these declarations, the resulting parser parses the first example as both an expr and
a decl, and prints

```
"x" y z + T <init-declare> x T <cast> y z + = <OR>
```

Bison requires that all of the productions that participate in any particular merge have
identical '%merge' clauses. Otherwise, the ambiguity would be unresolvable, and the parser
will report an error during any parse that results in the offending merge.

1.5.3 GLR Semantic Actions

The nature of GLR parsing and the structure of the generated parsers give rise to certain
restrictions on semantic values and actions.

1.5.3.1 Deferred semantic actions

By definition, a deferred semantic action is not performed at the same time as the associated
reduction. This raises caveats for several Bison features you might use in a semantic action
in a GLR parser.

In any semantic action, you can examine yychar to determine the type of the lookahead
token present at the time of the associated reduction. After checking that yychar is not set
to YYEMPTY or YYEOF, you can then examine yylval and yylloc to determine the lookahead

token's semantic value and location, if any. In a nondeferred semantic action, you can also modify any of these variables to influence syntax analysis. See Section 5.1 [Lookahead Tokens], page 107.

In a deferred semantic action, it's too late to influence syntax analysis. In this case, yychar, yylval, and yylloc are set to shallow copies of the values they had at the time of the associated reduction. For this reason alone, modifying them is dangerous. Moreover, the result of modifying them is undefined and subject to change with future versions of Bison. For example, if a semantic action might be deferred, you should never write it to invoke yyclearin (see Section 4.8 [Action Features], page 103) or to attempt to free memory referenced by yylval.

1.5.3.2 YYERROR

Another Bison feature requiring special consideration is YYERROR (see Section 4.8 [Action Features], page 103), which you can invoke in a semantic action to initiate error recovery. During deterministic GLR operation, the effect of YYERROR is the same as its effect in a deterministic parser. The effect in a deferred action is similar, but the precise point of the error is undefined; instead, the parser reverts to deterministic operation, selecting an unspecified stack on which to continue with a syntax error. In a semantic predicate (see Section 1.5.4 [Semantic Predicates], page 26) during nondeterministic parsing, YYERROR silently prunes the parse that invoked the test.

1.5.3.3 Restrictions on semantic values and locations

GLR parsers require that you use POD (Plain Old Data) types for semantic values and location types when using the generated parsers as C++ code.

1.5.4 Controlling a Parse with Arbitrary Predicates

In addition to the %dprec and %merge directives, GLR parsers allow you to reject parses on the basis of arbitrary computations executed in user code, without having Bison treat this rejection as an error if there are alternative parses. (This feature is experimental and may evolve. We welcome user feedback.) For example,

```
widget:
  %?{  new_syntax } "widget" id new_args  { $$ = f($3, $4); }
| %?{ !new_syntax } "widget" id old_args  { $$ = f($3, $4); }
;
```

is one way to allow the same parser to handle two different syntaxes for widgets. The clause preceded by %? is treated like an ordinary action, except that its text is treated as an expression and is always evaluated immediately (even when in nondeterministic mode). If the expression yields 0 (false), the clause is treated as a syntax error, which, in a nondeterministic parser, causes the stack in which it is reduced to die. In a deterministic parser, it acts like YYERROR.

As the example shows, predicates otherwise look like semantic actions, and therefore you must be take them into account when determining the numbers to use for denoting the semantic values of right-hand side symbols. Predicate actions, however, have no defined value, and may not be given labels.

There is a subtle difference between semantic predicates and ordinary actions in nondeterministic mode, since the latter are deferred. For example, we could try to rewrite the previous example as

```
widget:
  { if (!new_syntax) YYERROR; }
    "widget" id new_args  { $$ = f($3, $4); }
| { if (new_syntax) YYERROR; }
    "widget" id old_args  { $$ = f($3, $4); }
;
```

(reversing the sense of the predicate tests to cause an error when they are false). However, this does *not* have the same effect if `new_args` and `old_args` have overlapping syntax. Since the mid-rule actions testing `new_syntax` are deferred, a GLR parser first encounters the unresolved ambiguous reduction for cases where `new_args` and `old_args` recognize the same string *before* performing the tests of `new_syntax`. It therefore reports an error.

Finally, be careful in writing predicates: deferred actions have not been evaluated, so that using them in a predicate will have undefined effects.

1.5.5 Considerations when Compiling GLR Parsers

The GLR parsers require a compiler for ISO C89 or later. In addition, they use the `inline` keyword, which is not C89, but is C99 and is a common extension in pre-C99 compilers. It is up to the user of these parsers to handle portability issues. For instance, if using Autoconf and the Autoconf macro `AC_C_INLINE`, a mere

```
%{
  #include <config.h>
%}
```

will suffice. Otherwise, we suggest

```
%{
  #if (__STDC_VERSION__ < 199901 && ! defined __GNUC__ \
       && ! defined inline)
  # define inline
  #endif
%}
```

1.6 Locations

Many applications, like interpreters or compilers, have to produce verbose and useful error messages. To achieve this, one must be able to keep track of the *textual location*, or *location*, of each syntactic construct. Bison provides a mechanism for handling these locations.

Each token has a semantic value. In a similar fashion, each token has an associated location, but the type of locations is the same for all tokens and groupings. Moreover, the output parser is equipped with a default data structure for storing locations (see Section 3.5 [Tracking Locations], page 70, for more details).

Like semantic values, locations can be reached in actions using a dedicated set of constructs. In the example above, the location of the whole grouping is @$, while the locations of the subexpressions are @1 and @3.

When a rule is matched, a default action is used to compute the semantic value of its left hand side (see Section 3.4.6 [Actions], page 64). In the same way, another default action is used for locations. However, the action for locations is general enough for most cases, meaning there is usually no need to describe for each rule how @$ should be formed. When building a new location for a given grouping, the default behavior of the output parser is to take the beginning of the first symbol, and the end of the last symbol.

1.7 Bison Output: the Parser Implementation File

When you run Bison, you give it a Bison grammar file as input. The most important output is a C source file that implements a parser for the language described by the grammar. This parser is called a *Bison parser*, and this file is called a *Bison parser implementation file*. Keep in mind that the Bison utility and the Bison parser are two distinct programs: the Bison utility is a program whose output is the Bison parser implementation file that becomes part of your program.

The job of the Bison parser is to group tokens into groupings according to the grammar rules—for example, to build identifiers and operators into expressions. As it does this, it runs the actions for the grammar rules it uses.

The tokens come from a function called the *lexical analyzer* that you must supply in some fashion (such as by writing it in C). The Bison parser calls the lexical analyzer each time it wants a new token. It doesn't know what is "inside" the tokens (though their semantic values may reflect this). Typically the lexical analyzer makes the tokens by parsing characters of text, but Bison does not depend on this. See Section 4.6 [The Lexical Analyzer Function yylex], page 99.

The Bison parser implementation file is C code which defines a function named yyparse which implements that grammar. This function does not make a complete C program: you must supply some additional functions. One is the lexical analyzer. Another is an error-reporting function which the parser calls to report an error. In addition, a complete C program must start with a function called main; you have to provide this, and arrange for it to call yyparse or the parser will never run. See Chapter 4 [Parser C-Language Interface], page 97.

Aside from the token type names and the symbols in the actions you write, all symbols defined in the Bison parser implementation file itself begin with 'yy' or 'YY'. This includes interface functions such as the lexical analyzer function yylex, the error reporting function yyerror and the parser function yyparse itself. This also includes numerous identifiers used for internal purposes. Therefore, you should avoid using C identifiers starting with 'yy' or 'YY' in the Bison grammar file except for the ones defined in this manual. Also, you should avoid using the C identifiers 'malloc' and 'free' for anything other than their usual meanings.

In some cases the Bison parser implementation file includes system headers, and in those cases your code should respect the identifiers reserved by those headers. On some non-GNU hosts, <alloca.h>, <malloc.h>, <stddef.h>, and <stdlib.h> are included as needed to declare memory allocators and related types. <libintl.h> is included if message translation is in use (see Section 4.9 [Internationalization], page 105). Other system headers may be included if you define YYDEBUG to a nonzero value (see Section 8.4 [Tracing Your Parser], page 142).

1.8 Stages in Using Bison

The actual language-design process using Bison, from grammar specification to a working compiler or interpreter, has these parts:

1. Formally specify the grammar in a form recognized by Bison (see Chapter 3 [Bison Grammar Files], page 51). For each grammatical rule in the language, describe the action that is to be taken when an instance of that rule is recognized. The action is described by a sequence of C statements.

2. Write a lexical analyzer to process input and pass tokens to the parser. The lexical analyzer may be written by hand in C (see Section 4.6 [The Lexical Analyzer Function yylex], page 99). It could also be produced using Lex, but the use of Lex is not discussed in this manual.

3. Write a controlling function that calls the Bison-produced parser.

4. Write error-reporting routines.

To turn this source code as written into a runnable program, you must follow these steps:

1. Run Bison on the grammar to produce the parser.

2. Compile the code output by Bison, as well as any other source files.

3. Link the object files to produce the finished product.

1.9 The Overall Layout of a Bison Grammar

The input file for the Bison utility is a *Bison grammar file*. The general form of a Bison grammar file is as follows:

```
%{
Prologue
%}

Bison declarations

%%
Grammar rules
%%
Epilogue
```

The '%%', '%{' and '%}' are punctuation that appears in every Bison grammar file to separate the sections.

The prologue may define types and variables used in the actions. You can also use preprocessor commands to define macros used there, and use #include to include header files that do any of these things. You need to declare the lexical analyzer yylex and the error printer yyerror here, along with any other global identifiers used by the actions in the grammar rules.

The Bison declarations declare the names of the terminal and nonterminal symbols, and may also describe operator precedence and the data types of semantic values of various symbols.

The grammar rules define how to construct each nonterminal symbol from its parts.

The epilogue can contain any code you want to use. Often the definitions of functions declared in the prologue go here. In a simple program, all the rest of the program can go here.

2 Examples

Now we show and explain several sample programs written using Bison: a reverse polish notation calculator, an algebraic (infix) notation calculator — later extended to track "locations" — and a multi-function calculator. All produce usable, though limited, interactive desk-top calculators.

These examples are simple, but Bison grammars for real programming languages are written the same way. You can copy these examples into a source file to try them.

2.1 Reverse Polish Notation Calculator

The first example is that of a simple double-precision *reverse polish notation* calculator (a calculator using postfix operators). This example provides a good starting point, since operator precedence is not an issue. The second example will illustrate how operator precedence is handled.

The source code for this calculator is named `rpcalc.y`. The '.y' extension is a convention used for Bison grammar files.

2.1.1 Declarations for `rpcalc`

Here are the C and Bison declarations for the reverse polish notation calculator. As in C, comments are placed between '/*...*/'.

```
/* Reverse polish notation calculator.  */

%{
  #include <stdio.h>
  #include <math.h>
  int yylex (void);
  void yyerror (char const *);
%}

%define api.value.type {double}
%token NUM

%% /* Grammar rules and actions follow.  */
```

The declarations section (see Section 3.1.1 [The prologue], page 51) contains two preprocessor directives and two forward declarations.

The `#include` directive is used to declare the exponentiation function `pow`.

The forward declarations for `yylex` and `yyerror` are needed because the C language requires that functions be declared before they are used. These functions will be defined in the epilogue, but the parser calls them so they must be declared in the prologue.

The second section, Bison declarations, provides information to Bison about the tokens and their types (see Section 3.1.3 [The Bison Declarations Section], page 56).

The `%define` directive defines the variable `api.value.type`, thus specifying the C data type for semantic values of both tokens and groupings (see Section 3.4.1 [Data Types of Semantic Values], page 61). The Bison parser will use whatever type `api.value.type` is defined as; if you don't define it, `int` is the default. Because we specify '`{double}`', each token and each expression has an associated value, which is a floating point number. C code can use YYSTYPE to refer to the value `api.value.type`.

Each terminal symbol that is not a single-character literal must be declared. (Single-character literals normally don't need to be declared.) In this example, all the arithmetic operators are designated by single-character literals, so the only terminal symbol that needs to be declared is NUM, the token type for numeric constants.

2.1.2 Grammar Rules for `rpcalc`

Here are the grammar rules for the reverse polish notation calculator.

```
input:
  %empty
| input line
;


line:
  '\n'
| exp '\n'        { printf ("%.10g\n", $1); }
;


exp:
  NUM            { $$ = $1;           }
| exp exp '+'    { $$ = $1 + $2;      }
| exp exp '-'    { $$ = $1 - $2;      }
| exp exp '*'    { $$ = $1 * $2;      }
| exp exp '/'    { $$ = $1 / $2;      }
| exp exp '^'    { $$ = pow ($1, $2); }  /* Exponentiation */
| exp 'n'        { $$ = -$1;          }  /* Unary minus    */
;
%%
```

The groupings of the rpcalc "language" defined here are the expression (given the name `exp`), the line of input (`line`), and the complete input transcript (`input`). Each of these nonterminal symbols has several alternate rules, joined by the vertical bar '`|`' which is read as "or". The following sections explain what these rules mean.

The semantics of the language is determined by the actions taken when a grouping is recognized. The actions are the C code that appears inside braces. See Section 3.4.6 [Actions], page 64.

You must specify these actions in C, but Bison provides the means for passing semantic values between the rules. In each action, the pseudo-variable $$ stands for the semantic value for the grouping that the rule is going to construct. Assigning a value to $$ is the main job of most actions. The semantic values of the components of the rule are referred to as $1, $2, and so on.

2.1.2.1 Explanation of `input`

Consider the definition of `input`:

```
input:
  %empty
| input line
;
```

This definition reads as follows: "A complete input is either an empty string, or a complete input followed by an input line". Notice that "complete input" is defined in terms of itself. This definition is said to be *left recursive* since `input` appears always as the leftmost symbol in the sequence. See Section 3.3.3 [Recursive Rules], page 60.

The first alternative is empty because there are no symbols between the colon and the first '|'; this means that `input` can match an empty string of input (no tokens). We write the rules this way because it is legitimate to type *Ctrl-d* right after you start the calculator. It's conventional to put an empty alternative first and to use the (optional) `%empty` directive, or to write the comment '`/* empty */`' in it (see Section 3.3.2 [Empty Rules], page 60).

The second alternate rule (`input line`) handles all nontrivial input. It means, "After reading any number of lines, read one more line if possible." The left recursion makes this rule into a loop. Since the first alternative matches empty input, the loop can be executed zero or more times.

The parser function `yyparse` continues to process input until a grammatical error is seen or the lexical analyzer says there are no more input tokens; we will arrange for the latter to happen at end-of-input.

2.1.2.2 Explanation of `line`

Now consider the definition of `line`:

```
line:
  '\n'
| exp '\n'  { printf ("%.10g\n", $1); }
;
```

The first alternative is a token which is a newline character; this means that rpcalc accepts a blank line (and ignores it, since there is no action). The second alternative is an expression followed by a newline. This is the alternative that makes rpcalc useful. The semantic value of the `exp` grouping is the value of `$1` because the `exp` in question is the first symbol in the alternative. The action prints this value, which is the result of the computation the user asked for.

This action is unusual because it does not assign a value to `$$`. As a consequence, the semantic value associated with the `line` is uninitialized (its value will be unpredictable). This would be a bug if that value were ever used, but we don't use it: once rpcalc has printed the value of the user's input line, that value is no longer needed.

2.1.2.3 Explanation of `expr`

The `exp` grouping has several rules, one for each kind of expression. The first rule handles the simplest expressions: those that are just numbers. The second handles an addition-expression, which looks like two expressions followed by a plus-sign. The third handles subtraction, and so on.

```
exp:
  NUM
```

```
| exp exp '+'    { $$ = $1 + $2;    }
| exp exp '-'    { $$ = $1 - $2;    }
...
;
```

We have used '|' to join all the rules for **exp**, but we could equally well have written them separately:

```
exp: NUM ;
exp: exp exp '+'    { $$ = $1 + $2; };
exp: exp exp '-'    { $$ = $1 - $2; };
...
```

Most of the rules have actions that compute the value of the expression in terms of the value of its parts. For example, in the rule for addition, **$1** refers to the first component **exp** and **$2** refers to the second one. The third component, **'+'**, has no meaningful associated semantic value, but if it had one you could refer to it as **$3**. When **yyparse** recognizes a sum expression using this rule, the sum of the two subexpressions' values is produced as the value of the entire expression. See Section 3.4.6 [Actions], page 64.

You don't have to give an action for every rule. When a rule has no action, Bison by default copies the value of **$1** into **$$**. This is what happens in the first rule (the one that uses **NUM**).

The formatting shown here is the recommended convention, but Bison does not require it. You can add or change white space as much as you wish. For example, this:

```
exp: NUM | exp exp '+' {$$ = $1 + $2; } | ... ;
```

means the same thing as this:

```
exp:
  NUM
| exp exp '+'    { $$ = $1 + $2; }
| ...
;
```

The latter, however, is much more readable.

2.1.3 The `rpcalc` Lexical Analyzer

The lexical analyzer's job is low-level parsing: converting characters or sequences of characters into tokens. The Bison parser gets its tokens by calling the lexical analyzer. See Section 4.6 [The Lexical Analyzer Function yylex], page 99.

Only a simple lexical analyzer is needed for the RPN calculator. This lexical analyzer skips blanks and tabs, then reads in numbers as **double** and returns them as **NUM** tokens. Any other character that isn't part of a number is a separate token. Note that the token-code for such a single-character token is the character itself.

The return value of the lexical analyzer function is a numeric code which represents a token type. The same text used in Bison rules to stand for this token type is also a C expression for the numeric code for the type. This works in two ways. If the token type is a character literal, then its numeric code is that of the character; you can use the same character literal in the lexical analyzer to express the number. If the token type is an identifier, that identifier is defined by Bison as a C macro whose definition is the appropriate number. In this example, therefore, **NUM** becomes a macro for **yylex** to use.

The semantic value of the token (if it has one) is stored into the global variable `yylval`, which is where the Bison parser will look for it. (The C data type of `yylval` is `YYSTYPE`, whose value was defined at the beginning of the grammar via '`%define api.value.type {double}`'; see Section 2.1.1 [Declarations for `rpcalc`], page 31.)

A token type code of zero is returned if the end-of-input is encountered. (Bison recognizes any nonpositive value as indicating end-of-input.)

Here is the code for the lexical analyzer:

```
/* The lexical analyzer returns a double floating point
   number on the stack and the token NUM, or the numeric code
   of the character read if not a number.  It skips all blanks
   and tabs, and returns 0 for end-of-input.  */

#include <ctype.h>

int
yylex (void)
{
  int c;

  /* Skip white space.  */
  while ((c = getchar ()) == ' ' || c == '\t')
    continue;
  /* Process numbers.  */
  if (c == '.' || isdigit (c))
    {
      ungetc (c, stdin);
      scanf ("%lf", &yylval);
      return NUM;
    }
  /* Return end-of-input.  */
  if (c == EOF)
    return 0;
  /* Return a single char.  */
  return c;
}
```

2.1.4 The Controlling Function

In keeping with the spirit of this example, the controlling function is kept to the bare minimum. The only requirement is that it call `yyparse` to start the process of parsing.

```
int
main (void)
{
  return yyparse ();
}
```

2.1.5 The Error Reporting Routine

When **yyparse** detects a syntax error, it calls the error reporting function **yyerror** to print an error message (usually but not always **"syntax error"**). It is up to the programmer to supply **yyerror** (see Chapter 4 [Parser C-Language Interface], page 97), so here is the definition we will use:

```
#include <stdio.h>

/* Called by yyparse on error.  */
void
yyerror (char const *s)
{
  fprintf (stderr, "%s\n", s);
}
```

After **yyerror** returns, the Bison parser may recover from the error and continue parsing if the grammar contains a suitable error rule (see Chapter 6 [Error Recovery], page 127). Otherwise, **yyparse** returns nonzero. We have not written any error rules in this example, so any invalid input will cause the calculator program to exit. This is not clean behavior for a real calculator, but it is adequate for the first example.

2.1.6 Running Bison to Make the Parser

Before running Bison to produce a parser, we need to decide how to arrange all the source code in one or more source files. For such a simple example, the easiest thing is to put everything in one file, the grammar file. The definitions of **yylex**, **yyerror** and **main** go at the end, in the epilogue of the grammar file (see Section 1.9 [The Overall Layout of a Bison Grammar], page 29).

For a large project, you would probably have several source files, and use **make** to arrange to recompile them.

With all the source in the grammar file, you use the following command to convert it into a parser implementation file:

```
bison file.y
```

In this example, the grammar file is called **rpcalc.y** (for "Reverse Polish CALCulator"). Bison produces a parser implementation file named *file.tab.c*, removing the '.y' from the grammar file name. The parser implementation file contains the source code for **yyparse**. The additional functions in the grammar file (**yylex**, **yyerror** and **main**) are copied verbatim to the parser implementation file.

2.1.7 Compiling the Parser Implementation File

Here is how to compile and run the parser implementation file:

```
# List files in current directory.
$ ls
rpcalc.tab.c  rpcalc.y

# Compile the Bison parser.
# '-lm' tells compiler to search math library for pow.
$ cc -lm -o rpcalc rpcalc.tab.c
```

```
# List files again.
$ ls
rpcalc  rpcalc.tab.c  rpcalc.y
```

The file `rpcalc` now contains the executable code. Here is an example session using `rpcalc`.

```
$ rpcalc
4 9 +
⇒ 13
3 7 + 3 4 5 *+-
⇒ -13
3 7 + 3 4 5 * + - n          Note the unary minus, 'n'
⇒ 13
5 6 / 4 n +
⇒ -3.166666667
3 4 ^                        Exponentiation
⇒ 81
^D                           End-of-file indicator
$
```

2.2 Infix Notation Calculator: `calc`

We now modify rpcalc to handle infix operators instead of postfix. Infix notation involves the concept of operator precedence and the need for parentheses nested to arbitrary depth. Here is the Bison code for `calc.y`, an infix desk-top calculator.

```
/* Infix notation calculator.  */

%{
  #include <math.h>
  #include <stdio.h>
  int yylex (void);
  void yyerror (char const *);
%}

/* Bison declarations.  */
%define api.value.type {double}
%token NUM
%left '-' '+'
%left '*' '/'
%precedence NEG   /* negation--unary minus */
%right '^'        /* exponentiation */

%% /* The grammar follows.  */
input:
  %empty
| input line
;
```

```
line:
  '\n'
| exp '\n'  { printf ("\t%.10g\n", $1); }
;

exp:
  NUM                    { $$ = $1;          }
| exp '+' exp            { $$ = $1 + $3;     }
| exp '-' exp            { $$ = $1 - $3;     }
| exp '*' exp            { $$ = $1 * $3;     }
| exp '/' exp            { $$ = $1 / $3;     }
| '-' exp    %prec NEG   { $$ = -$2;         }
| exp '^' exp            { $$ = pow ($1, $3); }
| '(' exp ')'            { $$ = $2;          }
;
%%
```

The functions `yylex`, `yyerror` and `main` can be the same as before.

There are two important new features shown in this code.

In the second section (Bison declarations), `%left` declares token types and says they are left-associative operators. The declarations `%left` and `%right` (right associativity) take the place of `%token` which is used to declare a token type name without associativity/precedence. (These tokens are single-character literals, which ordinarily don't need to be declared. We declare them here to specify the associativity/precedence.)

Operator precedence is determined by the line ordering of the declarations; the higher the line number of the declaration (lower on the page or screen), the higher the precedence. Hence, exponentiation has the highest precedence, unary minus (`NEG`) is next, followed by '*' and '/', and so on. Unary minus is not associative, only precedence matters (`%precedence`. See Section 5.3 [Operator Precedence], page 109.

The other important new feature is the `%prec` in the grammar section for the unary minus operator. The `%prec` simply instructs Bison that the rule '| '-' exp' has the same precedence as `NEG`—in this case the next-to-highest. See Section 5.4 [Context-Dependent Precedence], page 112.

Here is a sample run of `calc.y`:
```
$ calc
4 + 4.5 - (34/(8*3+-3))
6.880952381
-56 + 2
-54
3 ^ 2
9
```

2.3 Simple Error Recovery

Up to this point, this manual has not addressed the issue of *error recovery*—how to continue parsing after the parser detects a syntax error. All we have handled is error reporting with yyerror. Recall that by default yyparse returns after calling yyerror. This means that an erroneous input line causes the calculator program to exit. Now we show how to rectify this deficiency.

The Bison language itself includes the reserved word error, which may be included in the grammar rules. In the example below it has been added to one of the alternatives for line:

```
line:
  '\n'
| exp '\n'   { printf ("\t%.10g\n", $1); }
| error '\n' { yyerrok;                  }
;
```

This addition to the grammar allows for simple error recovery in the event of a syntax error. If an expression that cannot be evaluated is read, the error will be recognized by the third rule for line, and parsing will continue. (The yyerror function is still called upon to print its message as well.) The action executes the statement yyerrok, a macro defined automatically by Bison; its meaning is that error recovery is complete (see Chapter 6 [Error Recovery], page 127). Note the difference between yyerrok and yyerror; neither one is a misprint.

This form of error recovery deals with syntax errors. There are other kinds of errors; for example, division by zero, which raises an exception signal that is normally fatal. A real calculator program must handle this signal and use longjmp to return to main and resume parsing input lines; it would also have to discard the rest of the current line of input. We won't discuss this issue further because it is not specific to Bison programs.

2.4 Location Tracking Calculator: ltcalc

This example extends the infix notation calculator with location tracking. This feature will be used to improve the error messages. For the sake of clarity, this example is a simple integer calculator, since most of the work needed to use locations will be done in the lexical analyzer.

2.4.1 Declarations for ltcalc

The C and Bison declarations for the location tracking calculator are the same as the declarations for the infix notation calculator.

```
/* Location tracking calculator.  */

%{
  #include <math.h>
  int yylex (void);
  void yyerror (char const *);
%}

/* Bison declarations.  */
%define api.value.type {int}
%token NUM
```

```
%left '-' '+'
%left '*' '/'
%precedence NEG
%right '^'
```

```
%% /* The grammar follows.  */
```

Note there are no declarations specific to locations. Defining a data type for storing locations is not needed: we will use the type provided by default (see Section 3.5.1 [Data Types of Locations], page 70), which is a four member structure with the following integer fields: `first_line`, `first_column`, `last_line` and `last_column`. By conventions, and in accordance with the GNU Coding Standards and common practice, the line and column count both start at 1.

2.4.2 Grammar Rules for `ltcalc`

Whether handling locations or not has no effect on the syntax of your language. Therefore, grammar rules for this example will be very close to those of the previous example: we will only modify them to benefit from the new information.

Here, we will use locations to report divisions by zero, and locate the wrong expressions or subexpressions.

```
input:
  %empty
| input line
;

line:
  '\n'
| exp '\n' { printf ("%d\n", $1); }
;

exp:
  NUM        { $$ = $1; }
| exp '+' exp  { $$ = $1 + $3; }
| exp '-' exp  { $$ = $1 - $3; }
| exp '*' exp  { $$ = $1 * $3; }
| exp '/' exp
    {
      if ($3)
        $$ = $1 / $3;
      else
        {
          $$ = 1;
          fprintf (stderr, "%d.%d-%d.%d: division by zero",
                   @3.first_line, @3.first_column,
                   @3.last_line, @3.last_column);
        }
    }
```

```
   | '-' exp %prec NEG      { $$ = -$2; }
   | exp '^' exp            { $$ = pow ($1, $3); }
   | '(' exp ')'            { $$ = $2; }
```

This code shows how to reach locations inside of semantic actions, by using the pseudo-variables @n for rule components, and the pseudo-variable @$ for groupings.

We don't need to assign a value to @$: the output parser does it automatically. By default, before executing the C code of each action, @$ is set to range from the beginning of @1 to the end of @n, for a rule with n components. This behavior can be redefined (see Section 3.5.3 [Default Action for Locations], page 72), and for very specific rules, @$ can be computed by hand.

2.4.3 The ltcalc Lexical Analyzer.

Until now, we relied on Bison's defaults to enable location tracking. The next step is to rewrite the lexical analyzer, and make it able to feed the parser with the token locations, as it already does for semantic values.

To this end, we must take into account every single character of the input text, to avoid the computed locations of being fuzzy or wrong:

```
int
yylex (void)
{
  int c;

  /* Skip white space.  */
  while ((c = getchar ()) == ' ' || c == '\t')
    ++yylloc.last_column;

  /* Step.  */
  yylloc.first_line = yylloc.last_line;
  yylloc.first_column = yylloc.last_column;

  /* Process numbers.  */
  if (isdigit (c))
    {
      yylval = c - '0';
      ++yylloc.last_column;
      while (isdigit (c = getchar ()))
        {
          ++yylloc.last_column;
          yylval = yylval * 10 + c - '0';
        }
      ungetc (c, stdin);
      return NUM;
    }

  /* Return end-of-input.  */
  if (c == EOF)
```

```
      return 0;

   /* Return a single char, and update location.  */
   if (c == '\n')
     {
       ++yylloc.last_line;
       yylloc.last_column = 0;
     }
   else
     ++yylloc.last_column;
   return c;
}
```

Basically, the lexical analyzer performs the same processing as before: it skips blanks and tabs, and reads numbers or single-character tokens. In addition, it updates yylloc, the global variable (of type YYLTYPE) containing the token's location.

Now, each time this function returns a token, the parser has its number as well as its semantic value, and its location in the text. The last needed change is to initialize yylloc, for example in the controlling function:

```
int
main (void)
{
  yylloc.first_line = yylloc.last_line = 1;
  yylloc.first_column = yylloc.last_column = 0;
  return yyparse ();
}
```

Remember that computing locations is not a matter of syntax. Every character must be associated to a location update, whether it is in valid input, in comments, in literal strings, and so on.

2.5 Multi-Function Calculator: mfcalc

Now that the basics of Bison have been discussed, it is time to move on to a more advanced problem. The above calculators provided only five functions, '+', '-', '*', '/' and '^'. It would be nice to have a calculator that provides other mathematical functions such as sin, cos, etc.

It is easy to add new operators to the infix calculator as long as they are only single-character literals. The lexical analyzer yylex passes back all nonnumeric characters as tokens, so new grammar rules suffice for adding a new operator. But we want something more flexible: built-in functions whose syntax has this form:

    function_name (argument)

At the same time, we will add memory to the calculator, by allowing you to create named variables, store values in them, and use them later. Here is a sample session with the multi-function calculator:

```
$ mfcalc
pi = 3.141592653589
⇒ 3.1415926536
```

```
sin(pi)
⇒ 0.0000000000
alpha = beta1 = 2.3
⇒ 2.3000000000
alpha
⇒ 2.3000000000
ln(alpha)
⇒ 0.8329091229
exp(ln(beta1))
⇒ 2.3000000000
$
```

Note that multiple assignment and nested function calls are permitted.

2.5.1 Declarations for `mfcalc`

Here are the C and Bison declarations for the multi-function calculator.

```
%{
  #include <stdio.h>  /* For printf, etc. */
  #include <math.h>   /* For pow, used in the grammar.  */
  #include "calc.h"   /* Contains definition of 'symrec'. */
  int yylex (void);
  void yyerror (char const *);
%}

%define api.value.type union /* Generate YYSTYPE from these types:  */
%token <double>  NUM         /* Simple double precision number.  */
%token <symrec*> VAR FNCT    /* Symbol table pointer: variable and func-
tion.  */
%type  <double>  exp

%precedence '='
%left '-' '+'
%left '*' '/'
%precedence NEG /* negation--unary minus */
%right '^'      /* exponentiation */
```

The above grammar introduces only two new features of the Bison language. These features allow semantic values to have various data types (see Section 3.4.2 [More Than One Value Type], page 62).

The special `union` value assigned to the `%define` variable `api.value.type` specifies that the symbols are defined with their data types. Bison will generate an appropriate definition of `YYSTYPE` to store these values.

Since values can now have various types, it is necessary to associate a type with each grammar symbol whose semantic value is used. These symbols are NUM, VAR, FNCT, and `exp`. Their declarations are augmented with their data type (placed between angle brackets). For instance, values of NUM are stored in `double`.

The Bison construct `%type` is used for declaring nonterminal symbols, just as `%token` is used for declaring token types. Previously we did not use `%type` before because nonterminal symbols are normally declared implicitly by the rules that define them. But `exp` must be declared explicitly so we can specify its value type. See Section 3.7.4 [Nonterminal Symbols], page 76.

2.5.2 Grammar Rules for `mfcalc`

Here are the grammar rules for the multi-function calculator. Most of them are copied directly from `calc`; three rules, those which mention VAR or FNCT, are new.

```
%% /* The grammar follows.  */
input:
  %empty
| input line
;

line:
  '\n'
| exp '\n'   { printf ("%.10g\n", $1); }
| error '\n' { yyerrok;               }
;

exp:
  NUM                { $$ = $1;                        }
| VAR                { $$ = $1->value.var;             }
| VAR '=' exp        { $$ = $3; $1->value.var = $3;    }
| FNCT '(' exp ')'   { $$ = (*($1->value.fnctptr))($3); }
| exp '+' exp        { $$ = $1 + $3;                   }
| exp '-' exp        { $$ = $1 - $3;                   }
| exp '*' exp        { $$ = $1 * $3;                   }
| exp '/' exp        { $$ = $1 / $3;                   }
| '-' exp  %prec NEG { $$ = -$2;                       }
| exp '^' exp        { $$ = pow ($1, $3);              }
| '(' exp ')'        { $$ = $2;                        }
;
/* End of grammar.  */
%%
```

2.5.3 The `mfcalc` Symbol Table

The multi-function calculator requires a symbol table to keep track of the names and meanings of variables and functions. This doesn't affect the grammar rules (except for the actions) or the Bison declarations, but it requires some additional C functions for support.

The symbol table itself consists of a linked list of records. Its definition, which is kept in the header `calc.h`, is as follows. It provides for either functions or variables to be placed in the table.

```
/* Function type.  */
typedef double (*func_t) (double);
```

```
/* Data type for links in the chain of symbols.  */
struct symrec
{
  char *name;  /* name of symbol */
  int type;    /* type of symbol: either VAR or FNCT */
  union
  {
    double var;       /* value of a VAR */
    func_t fnctptr;  /* value of a FNCT */
  } value;
  struct symrec *next;  /* link field */
};

typedef struct symrec symrec;

/* The symbol table: a chain of 'struct symrec'.  */
extern symrec *sym_table;

symrec *putsym (char const *, int);
symrec *getsym (char const *);
```

The new version of main will call init_table to initialize the symbol table:

```
struct init
{
  char const *fname;
  double (*fnct) (double);
};

struct init const arith_fncts[] =
{
  { "atan", atan },
  { "cos",  cos  },
  { "exp",  exp  },
  { "ln",   log  },
  { "sin",  sin  },
  { "sqrt", sqrt },
  { 0, 0 },
};

/* The symbol table: a chain of 'struct symrec'.  */
symrec *sym_table;
```

```
/* Put arithmetic functions in table.  */
static
void
init_table (void)
{
  int i;
  for (i = 0; arith_fncts[i].fname != 0; i++)
    {
      symrec *ptr = putsym (arith_fncts[i].fname, FNCT);
      ptr->value.fnctptr = arith_fncts[i].fnct;
    }
}
```

By simply editing the initialization list and adding the necessary include files, you can add additional functions to the calculator.

Two important functions allow look-up and installation of symbols in the symbol table. The function putsym is passed a name and the type (VAR or FNCT) of the object to be installed. The object is linked to the front of the list, and a pointer to the object is returned. The function getsym is passed the name of the symbol to look up. If found, a pointer to that symbol is returned; otherwise zero is returned.

```
#include <stdlib.h> /* malloc. */
#include <string.h> /* strlen. */

symrec *
putsym (char const *sym_name, int sym_type)
{
  symrec *ptr = (symrec *) malloc (sizeof (symrec));
  ptr->name = (char *) malloc (strlen (sym_name) + 1);
  strcpy (ptr->name,sym_name);
  ptr->type = sym_type;
  ptr->value.var = 0; /* Set value to 0 even if fctn.  */
  ptr->next = (struct symrec *)sym_table;
  sym_table = ptr;
  return ptr;
}

symrec *
getsym (char const *sym_name)
{
  symrec *ptr;
  for (ptr = sym_table; ptr != (symrec *) 0;
       ptr = (symrec *)ptr->next)
    if (strcmp (ptr->name, sym_name) == 0)
      return ptr;
  return 0;
}
```

2.5.4 The mfcalc Lexer

The function yylex must now recognize variables, numeric values, and the single-character arithmetic operators. Strings of alphanumeric characters with a leading letter are recognized as either variables or functions depending on what the symbol table says about them.

The string is passed to getsym for look up in the symbol table. If the name appears in the table, a pointer to its location and its type (VAR or FNCT) is returned to yyparse. If it is not already in the table, then it is installed as a VAR using putsym. Again, a pointer and its type (which must be VAR) is returned to yyparse.

No change is needed in the handling of numeric values and arithmetic operators in yylex.

```
#include <ctype.h>

int
yylex (void)
{
  int c;

  /* Ignore white space, get first nonwhite character.  */
  while ((c = getchar ()) == ' ' || c == '\t')
    continue;

  if (c == EOF)
    return 0;

  /* Char starts a number => parse the number.          */
  if (c == '.' || isdigit (c))
    {
      ungetc (c, stdin);
      scanf ("%lf", &yylval.NUM);
      return NUM;
    }
```

Bison generated a definition of YYSTYPE with a member named NUM to store value of NUM symbols.

```
  /* Char starts an identifier => read the name.        */
  if (isalpha (c))
    {
      /* Initially make the buffer long enough
         for a 40-character symbol name.  */
      static size_t length = 40;
      static char *symbuf = 0;
      symrec *s;
      int i;
      if (!symbuf)
        symbuf = (char *) malloc (length + 1);

      i = 0;
```

```
      do
        {
          /* If buffer is full, make it bigger.         */
          if (i == length)
            {
              length *= 2;
              symbuf = (char *) realloc (symbuf, length + 1);
            }
          /* Add this character to the buffer.           */
          symbuf[i++] = c;
          /* Get another character.                      */
          c = getchar ();
        }
      while (isalnum (c));

      ungetc (c, stdin);
      symbuf[i] = '\0';

      s = getsym (symbuf);
      if (s == 0)
        s = putsym (symbuf, VAR);
      *((symrec**) &yylval) = s;
      return s->type;
    }

  /* Any other character is a token by itself.      */
  return c;
}
```

2.5.5 The mfcalc Main

The error reporting function is unchanged, and the new version of main includes a call to init_table and sets the yydebug on user demand (See Section 8.4 [Tracing Your Parser], page 142, for details):

```
/* Called by yyparse on error.  */
void
yyerror (char const *s)
{
  fprintf (stderr, "%s\n", s);
}
```

```
int
main (int argc, char const* argv[])
{
  int i;
  /* Enable parse traces on option -p.  */
  for (i = 1; i < argc; ++i)
    if (!strcmp(argv[i], "-p"))
      yydebug = 1;
  init_table ();
  return yyparse ();
}
```

This program is both powerful and flexible. You may easily add new functions, and it is a simple job to modify this code to install predefined variables such as pi or e as well.

2.6 Exercises

1. Add some new functions from `math.h` to the initialization list.

2. Add another array that contains constants and their values. Then modify `init_table` to add these constants to the symbol table. It will be easiest to give the constants type VAR.

3. Make the program report an error if the user refers to an uninitialized variable in any way except to store a value in it.

3 Bison Grammar Files

Bison takes as input a context-free grammar specification and produces a C-language function that recognizes correct instances of the grammar.

The Bison grammar file conventionally has a name ending in '.y'. See Chapter 9 [Invoking Bison], page 149.

3.1 Outline of a Bison Grammar

A Bison grammar file has four main sections, shown here with the appropriate delimiters:

```
%{
  Prologue
%}

Bison declarations

%%
Grammar rules
%%

Epilogue
```

Comments enclosed in '/* ... */' may appear in any of the sections. As a GNU extension, '//' introduces a comment that continues until end of line.

3.1.1 The prologue

The *Prologue* section contains macro definitions and declarations of functions and variables that are used in the actions in the grammar rules. These are copied to the beginning of the parser implementation file so that they precede the definition of yyparse. You can use '#include' to get the declarations from a header file. If you don't need any C declarations, you may omit the '%{' and '%}' delimiters that bracket this section.

The *Prologue* section is terminated by the first occurrence of '%}' that is outside a comment, a string literal, or a character constant.

You may have more than one *Prologue* section, intermixed with the *Bison declarations*. This allows you to have C and Bison declarations that refer to each other. For example, the %union declaration may use types defined in a header file, and you may wish to prototype functions that take arguments of type YYSTYPE. This can be done with two *Prologue* blocks, one before and one after the %union declaration.

```
%{
  #define _GNU_SOURCE
  #include <stdio.h>
  #include "ptypes.h"
%}

%union {
  long int n;
  tree t;  /* tree is defined in ptypes.h. */
}
```

```
%{
  static void print_token_value (FILE *, int, YYSTYPE);
  #define YYPRINT(F, N, L) print_token_value (F, N, L)
%}
```

  . . .

When in doubt, it is usually safer to put prologue code before all Bison declarations, rather than after. For example, any definitions of feature test macros like `_GNU_SOURCE` or `_POSIX_C_SOURCE` should appear before all Bison declarations, as feature test macros can affect the behavior of Bison-generated `#include` directives.

3.1.2 Prologue Alternatives

The functionality of *Prologue* sections can often be subtle and inflexible. As an alternative, Bison provides a `%code` directive with an explicit qualifier field, which identifies the purpose of the code and thus the location(s) where Bison should generate it. For C/C++, the qualifier can be omitted for the default location, or it can be one of `requires`, `provides`, `top`. See Section 3.7.14 [%code Summary], page 92.

Look again at the example of the previous section:

```
%{
  #define _GNU_SOURCE
  #include <stdio.h>
  #include "ptypes.h"
%}

%union {
  long int n;
  tree t;  /* tree is defined in ptypes.h. */
}

%{
  static void print_token_value (FILE *, int, YYSTYPE);
  #define YYPRINT(F, N, L) print_token_value (F, N, L)
%}
```

  . . .

Notice that there are two *Prologue* sections here, but there's a subtle distinction between their functionality. For example, if you decide to override Bison's default definition for YYLTYPE, in which *Prologue* section should you write your new definition? You should write it in the first since Bison will insert that code into the parser implementation file *before* the default YYLTYPE definition. In which *Prologue* section should you prototype an internal function, `trace_token`, that accepts YYLTYPE and yytokentype as arguments? You should prototype it in the second since Bison will insert that code *after* the YYLTYPE and yytokentype definitions.

This distinction in functionality between the two *Prologue* sections is established by the appearance of the `%union` between them. This behavior raises a few questions. First, why should the position of a %union affect definitions related to YYLTYPE and yytokentype? Second, what if there is no %union? In that case, the second kind of *Prologue* section is not available. This behavior is not intuitive.

To avoid this subtle %union dependency, rewrite the example using a %code top and an unqualified %code. Let's go ahead and add the new YYLTYPE definition and the trace_token prototype at the same time:

```
%code top {
  #define _GNU_SOURCE
  #include <stdio.h>

  /* WARNING: The following code really belongs
   * in a '%code requires'; see below.  */

  #include "ptypes.h"
  #define YYLTYPE YYLTYPE
  typedef struct YYLTYPE
  {
    int first_line;
    int first_column;
    int last_line;
    int last_column;
    char *filename;
  } YYLTYPE;
}

%union {
  long int n;
  tree t;  /* tree is defined in ptypes.h. */
}

%code {
  static void print_token_value (FILE *, int, YYSTYPE);
  #define YYPRINT(F, N, L) print_token_value (F, N, L)
  static void trace_token (enum yytokentype token, YYLTYPE loc);
}

  ...
```

In this way, %code top and the unqualified %code achieve the same functionality as the two kinds of *Prologue* sections, but it's always explicit which kind you intend. Moreover, both kinds are always available even in the absence of %union.

The %code top block above logically contains two parts. The first two lines before the warning need to appear near the top of the parser implementation file. The first line after the warning is required by YYSTYPE and thus also needs to appear in the parser implementation file. However, if you've instructed Bison to generate a parser header file (see Section 3.7.12 [%defines], page 82), you probably want that line to appear before the YYSTYPE definition

in that header file as well. The YYLTYPE definition should also appear in the parser header
file to override the default YYLTYPE definition there.

In other words, in the %code top block above, all but the first two lines are dependency
code required by the YYSTYPE and YYLTYPE definitions. Thus, they belong in one or more
%code requires:

```
%code top {
  #define _GNU_SOURCE
  #include <stdio.h>
}

%code requires {
  #include "ptypes.h"
}
%union {
  long int n;
  tree t;  /* tree is defined in ptypes.h. */
}

%code requires {
  #define YYLTYPE YYLTYPE
  typedef struct YYLTYPE
  {
    int first_line;
    int first_column;
    int last_line;
    int last_column;
    char *filename;
  } YYLTYPE;
}

%code {
  static void print_token_value (FILE *, int, YYSTYPE);
  #define YYPRINT(F, N, L) print_token_value (F, N, L)
  static void trace_token (enum yytokentype token, YYLTYPE loc);
}

  ...
```

Now Bison will insert #include "ptypes.h" and the new YYLTYPE definition before the
Bison-generated YYSTYPE and YYLTYPE definitions in both the parser implementation file
and the parser header file. (By the same reasoning, %code requires would also be the
appropriate place to write your own definition for YYSTYPE.)

When you are writing dependency code for YYSTYPE and YYLTYPE, you should prefer
%code requires over %code top regardless of whether you instruct Bison to generate a
parser header file. When you are writing code that you need Bison to insert only into the
parser implementation file and that has no special need to appear at the top of that file, you
should prefer the unqualified %code over %code top. These practices will make the purpose

of each block of your code explicit to Bison and to other developers reading your grammar file. Following these practices, we expect the unqualified %code and %code requires to be the most important of the four *Prologue* alternatives.

At some point while developing your parser, you might decide to provide trace_token to modules that are external to your parser. Thus, you might wish for Bison to insert the prototype into both the parser header file and the parser implementation file. Since this function is not a dependency required by YYSTYPE or YYLTYPE, it doesn't make sense to move its prototype to a %code requires. More importantly, since it depends upon YYLTYPE and yytokentype, %code requires is not sufficient. Instead, move its prototype from the unqualified %code to a %code provides:

```
%code top {
  #define _GNU_SOURCE
  #include <stdio.h>
}

%code requires {
  #include "ptypes.h"
}
%union {
  long int n;
  tree t;  /* tree is defined in ptypes.h. */
}

%code requires {
  #define YYLTYPE YYLTYPE
  typedef struct YYLTYPE
  {
    int first_line;
    int first_column;
    int last_line;
    int last_column;
    char *filename;
  } YYLTYPE;
}

%code provides {
  void trace_token (enum yytokentype token, YYLTYPE loc);
}

%code {
  static void print_token_value (FILE *, int, YYSTYPE);
  #define YYPRINT(F, N, L) print_token_value (F, N, L)
}

  ...
```

Bison will insert the `trace_token` prototype into both the parser header file and the parser implementation file after the definitions for `yytokentype`, `YYLTYPE`, and `YYSTYPE`.

The above examples are careful to write directives in an order that reflects the layout of the generated parser implementation and header files: `%code top`, `%code requires`, `%code provides`, and then `%code`. While your grammar files may generally be easier to read if you also follow this order, Bison does not require it. Instead, Bison lets you choose an organization that makes sense to you.

You may declare any of these directives multiple times in the grammar file. In that case, Bison concatenates the contained code in declaration order. This is the only way in which the position of one of these directives within the grammar file affects its functionality.

The result of the previous two properties is greater flexibility in how you may organize your grammar file. For example, you may organize semantic-type-related directives by semantic type:

```
%code requires { #include "type1.h" }
%union { type1 field1; }
%destructor { type1_free ($$); } <field1>
%printer { type1_print (yyoutput, $$); } <field1>

%code requires { #include "type2.h" }
%union { type2 field2; }
%destructor { type2_free ($$); } <field2>
%printer { type2_print (yyoutput, $$); } <field2>
```

You could even place each of the above directive groups in the rules section of the grammar file next to the set of rules that uses the associated semantic type. (In the rules section, you must terminate each of those directives with a semicolon.) And you don't have to worry that some directive (like a `%union`) in the definitions section is going to adversely affect their functionality in some counter-intuitive manner just because it comes first. Such an organization is not possible using *Prologue* sections.

This section has been concerned with explaining the advantages of the four *Prologue* alternatives over the original Yacc *Prologue*. However, in most cases when using these directives, you shouldn't need to think about all the low-level ordering issues discussed here. Instead, you should simply use these directives to label each block of your code according to its purpose and let Bison handle the ordering. `%code` is the most generic label. Move code to `%code requires`, `%code provides`, or `%code top` as needed.

3.1.3 The Bison Declarations Section

The *Bison declarations* section contains declarations that define terminal and nonterminal symbols, specify precedence, and so on. In some simple grammars you may not need any declarations. See Section 3.7 [Bison Declarations], page 74.

3.1.4 The Grammar Rules Section

The *grammar rules* section contains one or more Bison grammar rules, and nothing else. See Section 3.3 [Syntax of Grammar Rules], page 59.

There must always be at least one grammar rule, and the first '%%' (which precedes the grammar rules) may never be omitted even if it is the first thing in the file.

3.1.5 The epilogue

The *Epilogue* is copied verbatim to the end of the parser implementation file, just as the *Prologue* is copied to the beginning. This is the most convenient place to put anything that you want to have in the parser implementation file but which need not come before the definition of yyparse. For example, the definitions of yylex and yyerror often go here. Because C requires functions to be declared before being used, you often need to declare functions like yylex and yyerror in the Prologue, even if you define them in the Epilogue. See Chapter 4 [Parser C-Language Interface], page 97.

If the last section is empty, you may omit the '%%' that separates it from the grammar rules.

The Bison parser itself contains many macros and identifiers whose names start with 'yy' or 'YY', so it is a good idea to avoid using any such names (except those documented in this manual) in the epilogue of the grammar file.

3.2 Symbols, Terminal and Nonterminal

Symbols in Bison grammars represent the grammatical classifications of the language.

A *terminal symbol* (also known as a *token type*) represents a class of syntactically equivalent tokens. You use the symbol in grammar rules to mean that a token in that class is allowed. The symbol is represented in the Bison parser by a numeric code, and the yylex function returns a token type code to indicate what kind of token has been read. You don't need to know what the code value is; you can use the symbol to stand for it.

A *nonterminal symbol* stands for a class of syntactically equivalent groupings. The symbol name is used in writing grammar rules. By convention, it should be all lower case.

Symbol names can contain letters, underscores, periods, and non-initial digits and dashes. Dashes in symbol names are a GNU extension, incompatible with POSIX Yacc. Periods and dashes make symbol names less convenient to use with named references, which require brackets around such names (see Section 3.6 [Named References], page 73). Terminal symbols that contain periods or dashes make little sense: since they are not valid symbols (in most programming languages) they are not exported as token names.

There are three ways of writing terminal symbols in the grammar:

- A *named token type* is written with an identifier, like an identifier in C. By convention, it should be all upper case. Each such name must be defined with a Bison declaration such as %token. See Section 3.7.2 [Token Type Names], page 75.

- A *character token type* (or *literal character token*) is written in the grammar using the same syntax used in C for character constants; for example, '+' is a character token type. A character token type doesn't need to be declared unless you need to specify its semantic value data type (see Section 3.4.1 [Data Types of Semantic Values], page 61), associativity, or precedence (see Section 5.3 [Operator Precedence], page 109).

  By convention, a character token type is used only to represent a token that consists of that particular character. Thus, the token type '+' is used to represent the character '+' as a token. Nothing enforces this convention, but if you depart from it, your program will confuse other readers.

  All the usual escape sequences used in character literals in C can be used in Bison as well, but you must not use the null character as a character literal because its numeric code, zero, signifies end-of-input (see Section 4.6.1 [Calling Convention for yylex], page 99). Also, unlike standard C, trigraphs have no special meaning in Bison character literals, nor is backslash-newline allowed.

- A *literal string token* is written like a C string constant; for example, "<=" is a literal string token. A literal string token doesn't need to be declared unless you need to specify its semantic value data type (see Section 3.4.1 [Value Type], page 61), associativity, or precedence (see Section 5.3 [Precedence], page 109).

  You can associate the literal string token with a symbolic name as an alias, using the **%token** declaration (see Section 3.7.2 [Token Declarations], page 75). If you don't do that, the lexical analyzer has to retrieve the token number for the literal string token from the **yytname** table (see Section 4.6.1 [Calling Convention], page 99).

  Warning: literal string tokens do not work in Yacc.

  By convention, a literal string token is used only to represent a token that consists of that particular string. Thus, you should use the token type "<=" to represent the string '<=' as a token. Bison does not enforce this convention, but if you depart from it, people who read your program will be confused.

  All the escape sequences used in string literals in C can be used in Bison as well, except that you must not use a null character within a string literal. Also, unlike Standard C, trigraphs have no special meaning in Bison string literals, nor is backslash-newline allowed. A literal string token must contain two or more characters; for a token containing just one character, use a character token (see above).

How you choose to write a terminal symbol has no effect on its grammatical meaning. That depends only on where it appears in rules and on when the parser function returns that symbol.

The value returned by **yylex** is always one of the terminal symbols, except that a zero or negative value signifies end-of-input. Whichever way you write the token type in the grammar rules, you write it the same way in the definition of **yylex**. The numeric code for a character token type is simply the positive numeric code of the character, so **yylex** can use the identical value to generate the requisite code, though you may need to convert it to **unsigned char** to avoid sign-extension on hosts where **char** is signed. Each named token type becomes a C macro in the parser implementation file, so **yylex** can use the name to stand for the code. (This is why periods don't make sense in terminal symbols.) See Section 4.6.1 [Calling Convention for **yylex**], page 99.

If **yylex** is defined in a separate file, you need to arrange for the token-type macro definitions to be available there. Use the '-d' option when you run Bison, so that it will write these macro definitions into a separate header file *name.tab.h* which you can include in the other source files that need it. See Chapter 9 [Invoking Bison], page 149.

If you want to write a grammar that is portable to any Standard C host, you must use only nonnull character tokens taken from the basic execution character set of Standard C. This set consists of the ten digits, the 52 lower- and upper-case English letters, and the characters in the following C-language string:

```
"\a\b\t\n\v\f\r !\"#%&'()*+,-./:;<=>?[\\]^_{|}~"
```

The **yylex** function and Bison must use a consistent character set and encoding for character tokens. For example, if you run Bison in an ASCII environment, but then compile and run the resulting program in an environment that uses an incompatible character set like EBCDIC, the resulting program may not work because the tables generated by Bison will assume ASCII numeric values for character tokens. It is standard practice for software distributions to contain C source files that were generated by Bison in an ASCII environment, so installers on platforms that are incompatible with ASCII must rebuild those files before compiling them.

The symbol `error` is a terminal symbol reserved for error recovery (see Chapter 6 [Error Recovery], page 127); you shouldn't use it for any other purpose. In particular, `yylex` should never return this value. The default value of the error token is 256, unless you explicitly assigned 256 to one of your tokens with a `%token` declaration.

3.3 Grammar Rules

A Bison grammar is a list of rules.

3.3.1 Syntax of Grammar Rules

A Bison grammar rule has the following general form:

```
result: components...;
```

where *result* is the nonterminal symbol that this rule describes, and *components* are various terminal and nonterminal symbols that are put together by this rule (see Section 3.2 [Symbols], page 57).

For example,

```
exp: exp '+' exp;
```

says that two groupings of type `exp`, with a '+' token in between, can be combined into a larger grouping of type `exp`.

White space in rules is significant only to separate symbols. You can add extra white space as you wish.

Scattered among the components can be *actions* that determine the semantics of the rule. An action looks like this:

```
{C statements}
```

This is an example of *braced code*, that is, C code surrounded by braces, much like a compound statement in C. Braced code can contain any sequence of C tokens, so long as its braces are balanced. Bison does not check the braced code for correctness directly; it merely copies the code to the parser implementation file, where the C compiler can check it.

Within braced code, the balanced-brace count is not affected by braces within comments, string literals, or character constants, but it is affected by the C digraphs '<%' and '%>' that represent braces. At the top level braced code must be terminated by '}' and not by a digraph. Bison does not look for trigraphs, so if braced code uses trigraphs you should ensure that they do not affect the nesting of braces or the boundaries of comments, string literals, or character constants.

Usually there is only one action and it follows the components. See Section 3.4.6 [Actions], page 64.

Multiple rules for the same *result* can be written separately or can be joined with the vertical-bar character '|' as follows:

```
result:
  rule1-components...
| rule2-components...
...
;
```

They are still considered distinct rules even when joined in this way.

3.3.2 Empty Rules

A rule is said to be *empty* if its right-hand side (*components*) is empty. It means that *result* can match the empty string. For example, here is how to define an optional semicolon:

```
semicolon.opt: | ";";
```

It is easy not to see an empty rule, especially when | is used. The `%empty` directive allows to make explicit that a rule is empty on purpose:

```
semicolon.opt:
  %empty
| ";"
;
```

Flagging a non-empty rule with `%empty` is an error. If run with `-Wempty-rule`, `bison` will report empty rules without `%empty`. Using `%empty` enables this warning, unless `-Wno-empty-rule` was specified.

The `%empty` directive is a Bison extension, it does not work with Yacc. To remain compatible with POSIX Yacc, it is customary to write a comment '/* empty */' in each rule with no components:

```
semicolon.opt:
  /* empty */
| ";"
;
```

3.3.3 Recursive Rules

A rule is called *recursive* when its *result* nonterminal appears also on its right hand side. Nearly all Bison grammars need to use recursion, because that is the only way to define a sequence of any number of a particular thing. Consider this recursive definition of a comma-separated sequence of one or more expressions:

```
expseq1:
  exp
| expseq1 ',' exp
;
```

Since the recursive use of `expseq1` is the leftmost symbol in the right hand side, we call this *left recursion*. By contrast, here the same construct is defined using *right recursion*:

```
expseq1:
  exp
| exp ',' expseq1
;
```

Any kind of sequence can be defined using either left recursion or right recursion, but you should always use left recursion, because it can parse a sequence of any number of elements with bounded stack space. Right recursion uses up space on the Bison stack in proportion to the number of elements in the sequence, because all the elements must be shifted onto the stack before the rule can be applied even once. See Chapter 5 [The Bison Parser Algorithm], page 107, for further explanation of this.

Indirect or *mutual* recursion occurs when the result of the rule does not appear directly on its right hand side, but does appear in rules for other nonterminals which do appear on its right hand side.

For example:

```
expr:
  primary
| primary '+' primary
;

primary:
  constant
| '(' expr ')'
;
```

defines two mutually-recursive nonterminals, since each refers to the other.

3.4 Defining Language Semantics

The grammar rules for a language determine only the syntax. The semantics are determined by the semantic values associated with various tokens and groupings, and by the actions taken when various groupings are recognized.

For example, the calculator calculates properly because the value associated with each expression is the proper number; it adds properly because the action for the grouping 'x + y' is to add the numbers associated with x and y.

3.4.1 Data Types of Semantic Values

In a simple program it may be sufficient to use the same data type for the semantic values of all language constructs. This was true in the RPN and infix calculator examples (see Section 2.1 [Reverse Polish Notation Calculator], page 31).

Bison normally uses the type `int` for semantic values if your program uses the same data type for all language constructs. To specify some other type, define the `%define` variable `api.value.type` like this:

```
%define api.value.type {double}
```
or
```
%define api.value.type {struct semantic_type}
```

The value of `api.value.type` should be a type name that does not contain parentheses or square brackets.

Alternatively, instead of relying of Bison's `%define` support, you may rely on the C/C++ preprocessor and define `YYSTYPE` as a macro, like this:

```
#define YYSTYPE double
```

This macro definition must go in the prologue of the grammar file (see Section 3.1 [Outline of a Bison Grammar], page 51). If compatibility with POSIX Yacc matters to you, use this. Note however that Bison cannot know YYSTYPE's value, not even whether it is defined, so there are services it cannot provide. Besides this works only for languages that have a preprocessor.

3.4.2 More Than One Value Type

In most programs, you will need different data types for different kinds of tokens and groupings. For example, a numeric constant may need type int or long int, while a string constant needs type char *, and an identifier might need a pointer to an entry in the symbol table.

To use more than one data type for semantic values in one parser, Bison requires you to do two things:

- Specify the entire collection of possible data types. There are several options:
  - let Bison compute the union type from the tags you assign to symbols;
  - use the %union Bison declaration (see Section 3.4.4 [The Union Declaration], page 63);
  - define the %define variable api.value.type to be a union type whose members are the type tags (see Section 3.4.5 [Providing a Structured Semantic Value Type], page 64);
  - use a typedef or a #define to define YYSTYPE to be a union type whose member names are the type tags.
- Choose one of those types for each symbol (terminal or nonterminal) for which semantic values are used. This is done for tokens with the %token Bison declaration (see Section 3.7.2 [Token Type Names], page 75) and for groupings with the %type Bison declaration (see Section 3.7.4 [Nonterminal Symbols], page 76).

3.4.3 Generating the Semantic Value Type

The special value union of the %define variable api.value.type instructs Bison that the tags used with the %token and %type directives are genuine types, not names of members of YYSTYPE.

For example:

```
%define api.value.type union
%token <int> INT "integer"
%token <int> 'n'
%type <int> expr
%token <char const *> ID "identifier"
```

generates an appropriate value of YYSTYPE to support each symbol type. The name of the member of YYSTYPE for tokens than have a declared identifier *id* (such as INT and ID above, but not 'n') is *id*. The other symbols have unspecified names on which you should not depend; instead, relying on C casts to access the semantic value with the appropriate type:

```
/* For an "integer".  */
yylval.INT = 42;
return INT;

/* For an 'n', also declared as int.  */
```

```
    *((int*)&yylval) = 42;
    return 'n';

    /* For an "identifier".  */
    yylval.ID = "42";
    return ID;
```

If the %define variable api.token.prefix is defined (see Section 3.7.13 [api.token.prefix], page 86), then it is also used to prefix the union member names. For instance, with '%define api.token.prefix {TOK_}':

```
    /* For an "integer".  */
    yylval.TOK_INT = 42;
    return TOK_INT;
```

This Bison extension cannot work if %yacc (or -y/--yacc) is enabled, as POSIX mandates that Yacc generate tokens as macros (e.g., '#define INT 258', or '#define TOK_INT 258').

This feature is new, and user feedback would be most welcome.

A similar feature is provided for C++ that in addition overcomes C++ limitations (that forbid non-trivial objects to be part of a union): '%define api.value.type variant', see Section 10.1.2.2 [C++ Variants], page 158.

3.4.4 The Union Declaration

The %union declaration specifies the entire collection of possible data types for semantic values. The keyword %union is followed by braced code containing the same thing that goes inside a union in C.

For example:

```
    %union {
      double val;
      symrec *tptr;
    }
```

This says that the two alternative types are double and symrec *. They are given names val and tptr; these names are used in the %token and %type declarations to pick one of the types for a terminal or nonterminal symbol (see Section 3.7.4 [Nonterminal Symbols], page 76).

As an extension to POSIX, a tag is allowed after the %union. For example:

```
    %union value {
      double val;
      symrec *tptr;
    }
```

specifies the union tag value, so the corresponding C type is union value. If you do not specify a tag, it defaults to YYSTYPE (see Section 3.7.13 [api.value.union.name], page 86).

As another extension to POSIX, you may specify multiple %union declarations; their contents are concatenated. However, only the first %union declaration can specify a tag.

Note that, unlike making a union declaration in C, you need not write a semicolon after the closing brace.

3.4.5 Providing a Structured Semantic Value Type

Instead of %union, you can define and use your own union type YYSTYPE if your grammar contains at least one '<type>' tag. For example, you can put the following into a header file parser.h:

```
union YYSTYPE {
  double val;
  symrec *tptr;
};
```

and then your grammar can use the following instead of %union:

```
%{
#include "parser.h"
%}
%define api.value.type {union YYSTYPE}
%type <val> expr
%token <tptr> ID
```

Actually, you may also provide a **struct** rather that a **union**, which may be handy if you want to track information for every symbol (such as preceding comments).

The type you provide may even be structured and include pointers, in which case the type tags you provide may be composite, with '.' and '->' operators.

3.4.6 Actions

An action accompanies a syntactic rule and contains C code to be executed each time an instance of that rule is recognized. The task of most actions is to compute a semantic value for the grouping built by the rule from the semantic values associated with tokens or smaller groupings.

An action consists of braced code containing C statements, and can be placed at any position in the rule; it is executed at that position. Most rules have just one action at the end of the rule, following all the components. Actions in the middle of a rule are tricky and used only for special purposes (see Section 3.4.8 [Actions in Mid-Rule], page 66).

The C code in an action can refer to the semantic values of the components matched by the rule with the construct $n, which stands for the value of the *n*th component. The semantic value for the grouping being constructed is $$. In addition, the semantic values of symbols can be accessed with the named references construct $*name* or $[*name*]. Bison translates both of these constructs into expressions of the appropriate type when it copies the actions into the parser implementation file. $$ (or $*name*, when it stands for the current grouping) is translated to a modifiable lvalue, so it can be assigned to.

Here is a typical example:

```
exp:
  ...
| exp '+' exp      { $$ = $1 + $3; }
```

Or, in terms of named references:

```
exp[result]:
  ...
| exp[left] '+' exp[right]   { $result = $left + $right; }
```

This rule constructs an **exp** from two smaller **exp** groupings connected by a plus-sign token. In the action, **$1** and **$3** (**$left** and **$right**) refer to the semantic values of the two component **exp** groupings, which are the first and third symbols on the right hand side of the rule. The sum is stored into **$$** (**$result**) so that it becomes the semantic value of the addition-expression just recognized by the rule. If there were a useful semantic value associated with the '**+**' token, it could be referred to as **$2**.

See Section 3.6 [Named References], page 73, for more information about using the named references construct.

Note that the vertical-bar character '**|**' is really a rule separator, and actions are attached to a single rule. This is a difference with tools like Flex, for which '**|**' stands for either "or", or "the same action as that of the next rule". In the following example, the action is triggered only when 'b' is found:

```
a-or-b: 'a' | 'b'    { a_or_b_found = 1; };
```

If you don't specify an action for a rule, Bison supplies a default: **$$** = **$1**. Thus, the value of the first symbol in the rule becomes the value of the whole rule. Of course, the default action is valid only if the two data types match. There is no meaningful default action for an empty rule; every empty rule must have an explicit action unless the rule's value does not matter.

$n with *n* zero or negative is allowed for reference to tokens and groupings on the stack *before* those that match the current rule. This is a very risky practice, and to use it reliably you must be certain of the context in which the rule is applied. Here is a case in which you can use this reliably:

```
foo:
  expr bar '+' expr  { ... }
| expr bar '-' expr  { ... }
;

bar:
  %empty   { previous_expr = $0; }
;
```

As long as **bar** is used only in the fashion shown here, **$0** always refers to the **expr** which precedes **bar** in the definition of **foo**.

It is also possible to access the semantic value of the lookahead token, if any, from a semantic action. This semantic value is stored in **yylval**. See Section 4.8 [Special Features for Use in Actions], page 103.

3.4.7 Data Types of Values in Actions

If you have chosen a single data type for semantic values, the **$$** and **$n** constructs always have that data type.

If you have used **%union** to specify a variety of data types, then you must declare a choice among these types for each terminal or nonterminal symbol that can have a semantic value. Then each time you use **$$** or **$n**, its data type is determined by which symbol it refers to in the rule. In this example,

```
exp:
  ...
| exp '+' exp    { $$ = $1 + $3; }
```

$1 and $3 refer to instances of exp, so they all have the data type declared for the nonterminal symbol exp. If $2 were used, it would have the data type declared for the terminal symbol '+', whatever that might be.

Alternatively, you can specify the data type when you refer to the value, by inserting '<type>' after the '$' at the beginning of the reference. For example, if you have defined types as shown here:

```
%union {
  int itype;
  double dtype;
}
```

then you can write $<itype>1 to refer to the first subunit of the rule as an integer, or $<dtype>1 to refer to it as a double.

3.4.8 Actions in Mid-Rule

Occasionally it is useful to put an action in the middle of a rule. These actions are written just like usual end-of-rule actions, but they are executed before the parser even recognizes the following components.

3.4.8.1 Using Mid-Rule Actions

A mid-rule action may refer to the components preceding it using $n, but it may not refer to subsequent components because it is run before they are parsed.

The mid-rule action itself counts as one of the components of the rule. This makes a difference when there is another action later in the same rule (and usually there is another at the end): you have to count the actions along with the symbols when working out which number n to use in $n.

The mid-rule action can also have a semantic value. The action can set its value with an assignment to $$, and actions later in the rule can refer to the value using $n. Since there is no symbol to name the action, there is no way to declare a data type for the value in advance, so you must use the '$<...>n' construct to specify a data type each time you refer to this value.

There is no way to set the value of the entire rule with a mid-rule action, because assignments to $$ do not have that effect. The only way to set the value for the entire rule is with an ordinary action at the end of the rule.

Here is an example from a hypothetical compiler, handling a let statement that looks like 'let (variable) statement' and serves to create a variable named variable temporarily for the duration of statement. To parse this construct, we must put variable into the symbol table while statement is parsed, then remove it afterward. Here is how it is done:

```
stmt:
  "let" '(' var ')'
    {
      $<context>$ = push_context ();
      declare_variable ($3);
    }
  stmt
    {
      $$ = $6;
      pop_context ($<context>5);
    }
```

As soon as 'let (*variable*)' has been recognized, the first action is run. It saves a copy of the current semantic context (the list of accessible variables) as its semantic value, using alternative **context** in the data-type union. Then it calls **declare_variable** to add the new variable to that list. Once the first action is finished, the embedded statement **stmt** can be parsed.

Note that the mid-rule action is component number 5, so the 'stmt' is component number 6. Named references can be used to improve the readability and maintainability (see Section 3.6 [Named References], page 73):

```
stmt:
  "let" '(' var ')'
    {
      $<context>let = push_context ();
      declare_variable ($3);
    }[let]
  stmt
    {
      $$ = $6;
      pop_context ($<context>let);
    }
```

After the embedded statement is parsed, its semantic value becomes the value of the entire **let**-statement. Then the semantic value from the earlier action is used to restore the prior list of variables. This removes the temporary **let**-variable from the list so that it won't appear to exist while the rest of the program is parsed.

In the above example, if the parser initiates error recovery (see Chapter 6 [Error Recovery], page 127) while parsing the tokens in the embedded statement **stmt**, it might discard the previous semantic context $<context>5 without restoring it. Thus, $<context>5 needs a destructor (see Section 3.7.6 [Freeing Discarded Symbols], page 77). However, Bison currently provides no means to declare a destructor specific to a particular mid-rule action's semantic value.

One solution is to bury the mid-rule action inside a nonterminal symbol and to declare a destructor for that symbol:

```
%type <context> let
%destructor { pop_context ($$); } let
```

```
%%

stmt:
  let stmt
    {
      $$ = $2;
      pop_context ($let);
    };

let:
  "let" '(' var ')'
    {
      $let = push_context ();
      declare_variable ($3);
    };
```

Note that the action is now at the end of its rule. Any mid-rule action can be converted to an end-of-rule action in this way, and this is what Bison actually does to implement mid-rule actions.

3.4.8.2 Mid-Rule Action Translation

As hinted earlier, mid-rule actions are actually transformed into regular rules and actions. The various reports generated by Bison (textual, graphical, etc., see Section 8.1 [Understanding Your Parser], page 133) reveal this translation, best explained by means of an example. The following rule:

```
exp: { a(); } "b" { c(); } { d(); } "e" { f(); };
```

is translated into:

```
$@1: %empty { a(); };
$@2: %empty { c(); };
$@3: %empty { d(); };
exp: $@1 "b" $@2 $@3 "e" { f(); };
```

with new nonterminal symbols $@n, where n is a number.

A mid-rule action is expected to generate a value if it uses $$, or the (final) action uses $n where n denote the mid-rule action. In that case its nonterminal is rather named @n:

```
exp: { a(); } "b" { $$ = c(); } { d(); } "e" { f = $1; };
```

is translated into

```
@1: %empty { a(); };
@2: %empty { $$ = c(); };
$@3: %empty { d(); };
exp: @1 "b" @2 $@3 "e" { f = $1; }
```

There are probably two errors in the above example: the first mid-rule action does not generate a value (it does not use $$ although the final action uses it), and the value of the second one is not used (the final action does not use $3). Bison reports these errors when the `midrule-value` warnings are enabled (see Chapter 9 [Invoking Bison], page 149):

```
$ bison -fcaret -Wmidrule-value mid.y
mid.y:2.6-13: warning: unset value: $$
  exp: { a(); } "b" { $$ = c(); } { d(); } "e" { f = $1; };
            ~~~~~~~~~
mid.y:2.19-31: warning: unused value: $3
  exp: { a(); } "b" { $$ = c(); } { d(); } "e" { f = $1; };
                    ~~~~~~~~~~~~~~
```

3.4.8.3 Conflicts due to Mid-Rule Actions

Taking action before a rule is completely recognized often leads to conflicts since the parser must commit to a parse in order to execute the action. For example, the following two rules, without mid-rule actions, can coexist in a working parser because the parser can shift the open-brace token and look at what follows before deciding whether there is a declaration or not:

```
compound:
  '{' declarations statements '}'
| '{' statements '}'
;
```

But when we add a mid-rule action as follows, the rules become nonfunctional:

```
compound:
  { prepare_for_local_variables (); }
    '{' declarations statements '}'
|   '{' statements '}'
;
```

Now the parser is forced to decide whether to run the mid-rule action when it has read no farther than the open-brace. In other words, it must commit to using one rule or the other, without sufficient information to do it correctly. (The open-brace token is what is called the *lookahead* token at this time, since the parser is still deciding what to do about it. See Section 5.1 [Lookahead Tokens], page 107.)

You might think that you could correct the problem by putting identical actions into the two rules, like this:

```
compound:
  { prepare_for_local_variables (); }
    '{' declarations statements '}'
| { prepare_for_local_variables (); }
    '{' statements '}'
;
```

But this does not help, because Bison does not realize that the two actions are identical. (Bison never tries to understand the C code in an action.)

If the grammar is such that a declaration can be distinguished from a statement by the first token (which is true in C), then one solution which does work is to put the action after the open-brace, like this:

```
compound:
  '{' { prepare_for_local_variables (); }
    declarations statements '}'
| '{' statements '}'
;
```

Now the first token of the following declaration or statement, which would in any case tell Bison which rule to use, can still do so.

Another solution is to bury the action inside a nonterminal symbol which serves as a subroutine:

```
subroutine:
  %empty  { prepare_for_local_variables (); }
;


compound:
  subroutine '{' declarations statements '}'
| subroutine '{' statements '}'
;
```

Now Bison can execute the action in the rule for subroutine without deciding which rule for compound it will eventually use.

3.5 Tracking Locations

Though grammar rules and semantic actions are enough to write a fully functional parser, it can be useful to process some additional information, especially symbol locations.

The way locations are handled is defined by providing a data type, and actions to take when rules are matched.

3.5.1 Data Type of Locations

Defining a data type for locations is much simpler than for semantic values, since all tokens and groupings always use the same type.

You can specify the type of locations by defining a macro called YYLTYPE, just as you can specify the semantic value type by defining a YYSTYPE macro (see Section 3.4.1 [Value Type], page 61). When YYLTYPE is not defined, Bison uses a default structure type with four members:

```
typedef struct YYLTYPE
{
  int first_line;
  int first_column;
  int last_line;
  int last_column;
} YYLTYPE;
```

When YYLTYPE is not defined, at the beginning of the parsing, Bison initializes all these fields to 1 for yylloc. To initialize yylloc with a custom location type (or to chose a different initialization), use the %initial-action directive. See Section 3.7.5 [Performing Actions before Parsing], page 77.

3.5.2 Actions and Locations

Actions are not only useful for defining language semantics, but also for describing the behavior of the output parser with locations.

The most obvious way for building locations of syntactic groupings is very similar to the way semantic values are computed. In a given rule, several constructs can be used to access the locations of the elements being matched. The location of the nth component of the right hand side is @n, while the location of the left hand side grouping is @$.

In addition, the named references construct @name and @[name] may also be used to address the symbol locations. See Section 3.6 [Named References], page 73, for more information about using the named references construct.

Here is a basic example using the default data type for locations:

```
exp:
  ...
| exp '/' exp
    {
      @$.first_column = @1.first_column;
      @$.first_line = @1.first_line;
      @$.last_column = @3.last_column;
      @$.last_line = @3.last_line;
      if ($3)
        $$ = $1 / $3;
      else
        {
          $$ = 1;
          fprintf (stderr, "%d.%d-%d.%d: division by zero",
                   @3.first_line, @3.first_column,
                   @3.last_line, @3.last_column);
        }
    }
```

As for semantic values, there is a default action for locations that is run each time a rule is matched. It sets the beginning of @$ to the beginning of the first symbol, and the end of @$ to the end of the last symbol.

With this default action, the location tracking can be fully automatic. The example above simply rewrites this way:

```
exp:
  ...
| exp '/' exp
    {
      if ($3)
        $$ = $1 / $3;
      else
        {
          $$ = 1;
          fprintf (stderr, "%d.%d-%d.%d: division by zero",
                   @3.first_line, @3.first_column,
                   @3.last_line, @3.last_column);
        }
    }
```

It is also possible to access the location of the lookahead token, if any, from a semantic action. This location is stored in `yylloc`. See Section 4.8 [Special Features for Use in Actions], page 103.

3.5.3 Default Action for Locations

Actually, actions are not the best place to compute locations. Since locations are much more general than semantic values, there is room in the output parser to redefine the default action to take for each rule. The `YYLLOC_DEFAULT` macro is invoked each time a rule is matched, before the associated action is run. It is also invoked while processing a syntax error, to compute the error's location. Before reporting an unresolvable syntactic ambiguity, a GLR parser invokes `YYLLOC_DEFAULT` recursively to compute the location of that ambiguity.

Most of the time, this macro is general enough to suppress location dedicated code from semantic actions.

The `YYLLOC_DEFAULT` macro takes three parameters. The first one is the location of the grouping (the result of the computation). When a rule is matched, the second parameter identifies locations of all right hand side elements of the rule being matched, and the third parameter is the size of the rule's right hand side. When a GLR parser reports an ambiguity, which of multiple candidate right hand sides it passes to `YYLLOC_DEFAULT` is undefined. When processing a syntax error, the second parameter identifies locations of the symbols that were discarded during error processing, and the third parameter is the number of discarded symbols.

By default, `YYLLOC_DEFAULT` is defined this way:

```
# define YYLLOC_DEFAULT(Cur, Rhs, N)                        \
do                                                          \
  if (N)                                                    \
    {                                                       \
      (Cur).first_line   = YYRHSLOC(Rhs, 1).first_line;   \
      (Cur).first_column = YYRHSLOC(Rhs, 1).first_column; \
      (Cur).last_line    = YYRHSLOC(Rhs, N).last_line;    \
      (Cur).last_column  = YYRHSLOC(Rhs, N).last_column;  \
    }                                                       \
  else                                                      \
    {                                                       \
      (Cur).first_line   = (Cur).last_line   =            \
        YYRHSLOC(Rhs, 0).last_line;                       \
      (Cur).first_column = (Cur).last_column =            \
        YYRHSLOC(Rhs, 0).last_column;                     \
    }                                                       \
while (0)
```

where `YYRHSLOC (rhs, k)` is the location of the *k*th symbol in *rhs* when *k* is positive, and the location of the symbol just before the reduction when *k* and *n* are both zero.

When defining `YYLLOC_DEFAULT`, you should consider that:

- All arguments are free of side-effects. However, only the first one (the result) should be modified by `YYLLOC_DEFAULT`.

- For consistency with semantic actions, valid indexes within the right hand side range from 1 to *n*. When *n* is zero, only 0 is a valid index, and it refers to the symbol just before the reduction. During error processing *n* is always positive.

- Your macro should parenthesize its arguments, if need be, since the actual arguments may not be surrounded by parentheses. Also, your macro should expand to something that can be used as a single statement when it is followed by a semicolon.

3.6 Named References

As described in the preceding sections, the traditional way to refer to any semantic value or location is a *positional reference*, which takes the form $n, $$, @n, and @$. However, such a reference is not very descriptive. Moreover, if you later decide to insert or remove symbols in the right-hand side of a grammar rule, the need to renumber such references can be tedious and error-prone.

To avoid these issues, you can also refer to a semantic value or location using a *named reference*. First of all, original symbol names may be used as named references. For example:

```
invocation: op '(' args ')'
  { $invocation = new_invocation ($op, $args, @invocation); }
```

Positional and named references can be mixed arbitrarily. For example:

```
invocation: op '(' args ')'
  { $$ = new_invocation ($op, $args, @$); }
```

However, sometimes regular symbol names are not sufficient due to ambiguities:

```
exp: exp '/' exp
  { $exp = $exp / $exp; } // $exp is ambiguous.

exp: exp '/' exp
  { $$ = $1 / $exp; } // One usage is ambiguous.

exp: exp '/' exp
  { $$ = $1 / $3; } // No error.
```

When ambiguity occurs, explicitly declared names may be used for values and locations. Explicit names are declared as a bracketed name after a symbol appearance in rule definitions. For example:

```
exp[result]: exp[left] '/' exp[right]
  { $result = $left / $right; }
```

In order to access a semantic value generated by a mid-rule action, an explicit name may also be declared by putting a bracketed name after the closing brace of the mid-rule action code:

```
exp[res]: exp[x] '+' {$left = $x;}[left] exp[right]
  { $res = $left + $right; }
```

In references, in order to specify names containing dots and dashes, an explicit bracketed syntax $[name] and @[name] must be used:

```
if-stmt: "if" '(' expr ')' "then" then.stmt ';'
  { $[if-stmt] = new_if_stmt ($expr, $[then.stmt]); }
```

It often happens that named references are followed by a dot, dash or other C punctuation marks and operators. By default, Bison will read '$name.suffix' as a reference to symbol value $name followed by '.suffix', i.e., an access to the suffix field of the semantic value. In order to force Bison to recognize 'name.suffix' in its entirety as the name of a semantic value, the bracketed syntax '$[name.suffix]' must be used.

The named references feature is experimental. More user feedback will help to stabilize it.

3.7 Bison Declarations

The *Bison declarations* section of a Bison grammar defines the symbols used in formulating the grammar and the data types of semantic values. See Section 3.2 [Symbols], page 57.

All token type names (but not single-character literal tokens such as '+' and '*') must be declared. Nonterminal symbols must be declared if you need to specify which data type to use for the semantic value (see Section 3.4.2 [More Than One Value Type], page 62).

The first rule in the grammar file also specifies the start symbol, by default. If you want some other symbol to be the start symbol, you must declare it explicitly (see Section 1.1 [Languages and Context-Free Grammars], page 17).

3.7.1 Require a Version of Bison

You may require the minimum version of Bison to process the grammar. If the requirement is not met, **bison** exits with an error (exit status 63).

```
%require "version"
```

3.7.2 Token Type Names

The basic way to declare a token type name (terminal symbol) is as follows:

```
%token name
```

Bison will convert this into a **#define** directive in the parser, so that the function **yylex** (if it is in this file) can use the name *name* to stand for this token type's code.

Alternatively, you can use **%left**, **%right**, **%precedence**, or **%nonassoc** instead of **%token**, if you wish to specify associativity and precedence. See Section 3.7.3 [Operator Precedence], page 76.

You can explicitly specify the numeric code for a token type by appending a nonnegative decimal or hexadecimal integer value in the field immediately following the token name:

```
%token NUM 300
%token XNUM 0x12d // a GNU extension
```

It is generally best, however, to let Bison choose the numeric codes for all token types. Bison will automatically select codes that don't conflict with each other or with normal characters.

In the event that the stack type is a union, you must augment the **%token** or other token declaration to include the data type alternative delimited by angle-brackets (see Section 3.4.2 [More Than One Value Type], page 62).

For example:

```
%union {                /* define stack type */
  double val;
  symrec *tptr;
}
%token <val> NUM        /* define token NUM and its type */
```

You can associate a literal string token with a token type name by writing the literal string at the end of a **%token** declaration which declares the name. For example:

```
%token arrow "=>"
```

For example, a grammar for the C language might specify these names with equivalent literal string tokens:

```
%token  <operator>  OR      "||"
%token  <operator>  LE 134  "<="
%left   OR  "<="
```

Once you equate the literal string and the token name, you can use them interchangeably in further declarations or the grammar rules. The **yylex** function can use the token name or the literal string to obtain the token type code number (see Section 4.6.1 [Calling Convention], page 99). Syntax error messages passed to **yyerror** from the parser will reference the literal string instead of the token name.

The token numbered as 0 corresponds to end of file; the following line allows for nicer error messages referring to "end of file" instead of "$end":

```
%token END 0 "end of file"
```

3.7.3 Operator Precedence

Use the `%left`, `%right`, `%nonassoc`, or `%precedence` declaration to declare a token and specify its precedence and associativity, all at once. These are called *precedence declarations*. See Section 5.3 [Operator Precedence], page 109, for general information on operator precedence.

The syntax of a precedence declaration is nearly the same as that of `%token`: either

```
%left symbols...
```

or

```
%left <type> symbols...
```

And indeed any of these declarations serves the purposes of `%token`. But in addition, they specify the associativity and relative precedence for all the *symbols*:

- The associativity of an operator *op* determines how repeated uses of the operator nest: whether '*x op y op z*' is parsed by grouping *x* with *y* first or by grouping *y* with *z* first. `%left` specifies left-associativity (grouping *x* with *y* first) and `%right` specifies right-associativity (grouping *y* with *z* first). `%nonassoc` specifies no associativity, which means that '*x op y op z*' is considered a syntax error.

  `%precedence` gives only precedence to the *symbols*, and defines no associativity at all. Use this to define precedence only, and leave any potential conflict due to associativity enabled.

- The precedence of an operator determines how it nests with other operators. All the tokens declared in a single precedence declaration have equal precedence and nest together according to their associativity. When two tokens declared in different precedence declarations associate, the one declared later has the higher precedence and is grouped first.

For backward compatibility, there is a confusing difference between the argument lists of `%token` and precedence declarations. Only a `%token` can associate a literal string with a token type name. A precedence declaration always interprets a literal string as a reference to a separate token. For example:

```
%left  OR "<="          // Does not declare an alias.
%left  OR 134 "<=" 135 // Declares 134 for OR and 135 for "<=".
```

3.7.4 Nonterminal Symbols

When you use `%union` to specify multiple value types, you must declare the value type of each nonterminal symbol for which values are used. This is done with a `%type` declaration, like this:

```
%type <type> nonterminal...
```

Here *nonterminal* is the name of a nonterminal symbol, and *type* is the name given in the `%union` to the alternative that you want (see Section 3.4.4 [The Union Declaration], page 63). You can give any number of nonterminal symbols in the same `%type` declaration, if they have the same value type. Use spaces to separate the symbol names.

You can also declare the value type of a terminal symbol. To do this, use the same `<type>` construction in a declaration for the terminal symbol. All kinds of token declarations allow `<type>`.

3.7.5 Performing Actions before Parsing

Sometimes your parser needs to perform some initializations before parsing. The `%initial-action` directive allows for such arbitrary code.

`%initial-action { code }`   [Directive]

> Declare that the braced *code* must be invoked before parsing each time `yyparse` is called. The *code* may use `$$` (or `$<tag>$`) and `@$` — initial value and location of the lookahead — and the `%parse-param`.

For instance, if your locations use a file name, you may use

```
%parse-param { char const *file_name };
%initial-action
{
  @$.initialize (file_name);
};
```

3.7.6 Freeing Discarded Symbols

During error recovery (see Chapter 6 [Error Recovery], page 127), symbols already pushed on the stack and tokens coming from the rest of the file are discarded until the parser falls on its feet. If the parser runs out of memory, or if it returns via `YYABORT` or `YYACCEPT`, all the symbols on the stack must be discarded. Even if the parser succeeds, it must discard the start symbol.

When discarded symbols convey heap based information, this memory is lost. While this behavior can be tolerable for batch parsers, such as in traditional compilers, it is unacceptable for programs like shells or protocol implementations that may parse and execute indefinitely.

The `%destructor` directive defines code that is called when a symbol is automatically discarded.

`%destructor { code } symbols`   [Directive]

> Invoke the braced *code* whenever the parser discards one of the *symbols*. Within *code*, `$$` (or `$<tag>$`) designates the semantic value associated with the discarded symbol, and `@$` designates its location. The additional parser parameters are also available (see Section 4.1 [The Parser Function yyparse], page 97).

> When a symbol is listed among *symbols*, its `%destructor` is called a per-symbol `%destructor`. You may also define a per-type `%destructor` by listing a semantic type tag among *symbols*. In that case, the parser will invoke this *code* whenever it discards any grammar symbol that has that semantic type tag unless that symbol has its own per-symbol `%destructor`.

> Finally, you can define two different kinds of default `%destructor`s. (These default forms are experimental. More user feedback will help to determine whether they should become permanent features.) You can place each of `<*>` and `<>` in the *symbols* list of exactly one `%destructor` declaration in your grammar file. The parser will invoke the *code* associated with one of these whenever it discards any user-defined grammar symbol that has no per-symbol and no per-type `%destructor`. The parser uses the *code* for `<*>` in the case of such a grammar symbol for which you have formally

declared a semantic type tag (`%type` counts as such a declaration, but `$<tag>$` does not). The parser uses the *code* for `<>` in the case of such a grammar symbol that has no declared semantic type tag.

For example:

```
%union { char *string; }
%token <string> STRING1 STRING2
%type  <string> string1 string2
%union { char character; }
%token <character> CHR
%type  <character> chr
%token TAGLESS

%destructor { } <character>
%destructor { free ($$); } <*>
%destructor { free ($$); printf ("%d", @$.first_line); } STRING1 string1
%destructor { printf ("Discarding tagless symbol.\n"); } <>
```

guarantees that, when the parser discards any user-defined symbol that has a semantic type tag other than `<character>`, it passes its semantic value to `free` by default. However, when the parser discards a `STRING1` or a `string1`, it also prints its line number to `stdout`. It performs only the second `%destructor` in this case, so it invokes `free` only once. Finally, the parser merely prints a message whenever it discards any symbol, such as `TAGLESS`, that has no semantic type tag.

A Bison-generated parser invokes the default `%destructor`s only for user-defined as opposed to Bison-defined symbols. For example, the parser will not invoke either kind of default `%destructor` for the special Bison-defined symbols `$accept`, `$undefined`, or `$end` (see Appendix A [Bison Symbols], page 189), none of which you can reference in your grammar. It also will not invoke either for the **error** token (see Appendix A [error], page 189), which is always defined by Bison regardless of whether you reference it in your grammar. However, it may invoke one of them for the end token (token 0) if you redefine it from `$end` to, for example, END:

```
%token END 0
```

Finally, Bison will never invoke a `%destructor` for an unreferenced mid-rule semantic value (see Section 3.4.8 [Actions in Mid-Rule], page 66). That is, Bison does not consider a mid-rule to have a semantic value if you do not reference `$$` in the mid-rule's action or `$n` (where *n* is the right-hand side symbol position of the mid-rule) in any later action in that rule. However, if you do reference either, the Bison-generated parser will invoke the `<>` `%destructor` whenever it discards the mid-rule symbol.

Discarded symbols are the following:

- stacked symbols popped during the first phase of error recovery,
- incoming terminals during the second phase of error recovery,
- the current lookahead and the entire stack (except the current right-hand side symbols) when the parser returns immediately, and

- the current lookahead and the entire stack (including the current right-hand side symbols) when the C++ parser (`lalr1.cc`) catches an exception in `parse`,
- the start symbol, when the parser succeeds.

The parser can *return immediately* because of an explicit call to `YYABORT` or `YYACCEPT`, or failed error recovery, or memory exhaustion.

Right-hand side symbols of a rule that explicitly triggers a syntax error via `YYERROR` are not discarded automatically. As a rule of thumb, destructors are invoked only when user actions cannot manage the memory.

3.7.7 Printing Semantic Values

When run-time traces are enabled (see Section 8.4 [Tracing Your Parser], page 142), the parser reports its actions, such as reductions. When a symbol involved in an action is reported, only its kind is displayed, as the parser cannot know how semantic values should be formatted.

The `%printer` directive defines code that is called when a symbol is reported. Its syntax is the same as `%destructor` (see Section 3.7.6 [Freeing Discarded Symbols], page 77).

`%printer { code } symbols`   [Directive]

Invoke the braced *code* whenever the parser displays one of the *symbols*. Within *code*, `yyoutput` denotes the output stream (a `FILE*` in C, and an `std::ostream&` in C++), `$$` (or `$<tag>$`) designates the semantic value associated with the symbol, and `@$` its location. The additional parser parameters are also available (see Section 4.1 [The Parser Function `yyparse`], page 97).

The *symbols* are defined as for `%destructor` (see Section 3.7.6 [Freeing Discarded Symbols], page 77.): they can be per-type (e.g., `<ival>`), per-symbol (e.g., `exp`, `NUM`, `"float"`), typed per-default (i.e., `<*>`, or untyped per-default (i.e., `<>`).

For example:

```
%union { char *string; }
%token <string> STRING1 STRING2
%type  <string> string1 string2
%union { char character; }
%token <character> CHR
%type  <character> chr
%token TAGLESS

%printer { fprintf (yyoutput, "'%c'", $$); } <character>
%printer { fprintf (yyoutput, "&%p", $$); } <*>
%printer { fprintf (yyoutput, "\"%s\"", $$); } STRING1 string1
%printer { fprintf (yyoutput, "<>"); } <>
```

guarantees that, when the parser print any symbol that has a semantic type tag other than `<character>`, it display the address of the semantic value by default. However, when the parser displays a `STRING1` or a `string1`, it formats it as a string in double quotes. It performs only the second `%printer` in this case, so it prints only once. Finally, the parser print '`<>`' for any symbol, such as `TAGLESS`, that has no semantic type tag. See Section 8.4.2 [Enabling Debug Traces for `mfcalc`], page 144, for a complete example.

3.7.8 Suppressing Conflict Warnings

Bison normally warns if there are any conflicts in the grammar (see Section 5.2 [Shift/Reduce Conflicts], page 108), but most real grammars have harmless shift/reduce conflicts which are resolved in a predictable way and would be difficult to eliminate. It is desirable to suppress the warning about these conflicts unless the number of conflicts changes. You can do this with the `%expect` declaration.

The declaration looks like this:

```
%expect n
```

Here n is a decimal integer. The declaration says there should be n shift/reduce conflicts and no reduce/reduce conflicts. Bison reports an error if the number of shift/reduce conflicts differs from n, or if there are any reduce/reduce conflicts.

For deterministic parsers, reduce/reduce conflicts are more serious, and should be eliminated entirely. Bison will always report reduce/reduce conflicts for these parsers. With GLR parsers, however, both kinds of conflicts are routine; otherwise, there would be no need to use GLR parsing. Therefore, it is also possible to specify an expected number of reduce/reduce conflicts in GLR parsers, using the declaration:

```
%expect-rr n
```

In general, using `%expect` involves these steps:

- Compile your grammar without `%expect`. Use the '-v' option to get a verbose list of where the conflicts occur. Bison will also print the number of conflicts.

- Check each of the conflicts to make sure that Bison's default resolution is what you really want. If not, rewrite the grammar and go back to the beginning.

- Add an `%expect` declaration, copying the number n from the number which Bison printed. With GLR parsers, add an `%expect-rr` declaration as well.

Now Bison will report an error if you introduce an unexpected conflict, but will keep silent otherwise.

3.7.9 The Start-Symbol

Bison assumes by default that the start symbol for the grammar is the first nonterminal specified in the grammar specification section. The programmer may override this restriction with the `%start` declaration as follows:

```
%start symbol
```

3.7.10 A Pure (Reentrant) Parser

A *reentrant* program is one which does not alter in the course of execution; in other words, it consists entirely of *pure* (read-only) code. Reentrancy is important whenever asynchronous execution is possible; for example, a nonreentrant program may not be safe to call from a signal handler. In systems with multiple threads of control, a nonreentrant program must be called only within interlocks.

Normally, Bison generates a parser which is not reentrant. This is suitable for most uses, and it permits compatibility with Yacc. (The standard Yacc interfaces are inherently nonreentrant, because they use statically allocated variables for communication with `yylex`, including `yylval` and `yylloc`.)

Alternatively, you can generate a pure, reentrant parser. The Bison declaration '%define api.pure' says that you want the parser to be reentrant. It looks like this:

```
%define api.pure full
```

The result is that the communication variables yylval and yylloc become local variables in yyparse, and a different calling convention is used for the lexical analyzer function yylex. See Section 4.6.4 [Calling Conventions for Pure Parsers], page 101, for the details of this. The variable yynerrs becomes local in yyparse in pull mode but it becomes a member of yypstate in push mode. (see Section 4.7 [The Error Reporting Function yyerror], page 102). The convention for calling yyparse itself is unchanged.

Whether the parser is pure has nothing to do with the grammar rules. You can generate either a pure parser or a nonreentrant parser from any valid grammar.

3.7.11 A Push Parser

(The current push parsing interface is experimental and may evolve. More user feedback will help to stabilize it.)

A pull parser is called once and it takes control until all its input is completely parsed. A push parser, on the other hand, is called each time a new token is made available.

A push parser is typically useful when the parser is part of a main event loop in the client's application. This is typically a requirement of a GUI, when the main event loop needs to be triggered within a certain time period.

Normally, Bison generates a pull parser. The following Bison declaration says that you want the parser to be a push parser (see Section 3.7.13 [api.push-pull], page 86):

```
%define api.push-pull push
```

In almost all cases, you want to ensure that your push parser is also a pure parser (see Section 3.7.10 [A Pure (Reentrant) Parser], page 80). The only time you should create an impure push parser is to have backwards compatibility with the impure Yacc pull mode interface. Unless you know what you are doing, your declarations should look like this:

```
%define api.pure full
%define api.push-pull push
```

There is a major notable functional difference between the pure push parser and the impure push parser. It is acceptable for a pure push parser to have many parser instances, of the same type of parser, in memory at the same time. An impure push parser should only use one parser at a time.

When a push parser is selected, Bison will generate some new symbols in the generated parser. yypstate is a structure that the generated parser uses to store the parser's state. yypstate_new is the function that will create a new parser instance. yypstate_delete will free the resources associated with the corresponding parser instance. Finally, yypush_parse is the function that should be called whenever a token is available to provide the parser. A trivial example of using a pure push parser would look like this:

```
int status;
yypstate *ps = yypstate_new ();
do {
  status = yypush_parse (ps, yylex (), NULL);
} while (status == YYPUSH_MORE);
```

```
yypstate_delete (ps);
```

If the user decided to use an impure push parser, a few things about the generated parser will change. The `yychar` variable becomes a global variable instead of a variable in the `yypush_parse` function. For this reason, the signature of the `yypush_parse` function is changed to remove the token as a parameter. A nonreentrant push parser example would thus look like this:

```
extern int yychar;
int status;
yypstate *ps = yypstate_new ();
do {
  yychar = yylex ();
  status = yypush_parse (ps);
} while (status == YYPUSH_MORE);
yypstate_delete (ps);
```

That's it. Notice the next token is put into the global variable `yychar` for use by the next invocation of the `yypush_parse` function.

Bison also supports both the push parser interface along with the pull parser interface in the same generated parser. In order to get this functionality, you should replace the '`%define api.push-pull push`' declaration with the '`%define api.push-pull both`' declaration. Doing this will create all of the symbols mentioned earlier along with the two extra symbols, `yyparse` and `yypull_parse`. `yyparse` can be used exactly as it normally would be used. However, the user should note that it is implemented in the generated parser by calling `yypull_parse`. This makes the `yyparse` function that is generated with the '`%define api.push-pull both`' declaration slower than the normal `yyparse` function. If the user calls the `yypull_parse` function it will parse the rest of the input stream. It is possible to `yypush_parse` tokens to select a subgrammar and then `yypull_parse` the rest of the input stream. If you would like to switch back and forth between between parsing styles, you would have to write your own `yypull_parse` function that knows when to quit looking for input. An example of using the `yypull_parse` function would look like this:

```
yypstate *ps = yypstate_new ();
yypull_parse (ps); /* Will call the lexer */
yypstate_delete (ps);
```

Adding the '`%define api.pure`' declaration does exactly the same thing to the generated parser with '`%define api.push-pull both`' as it did for '`%define api.push-pull push`'.

3.7.12 Bison Declaration Summary

Here is a summary of the declarations used to define a grammar:

`%union`   [Directive]
> Declare the collection of data types that semantic values may have (see Section 3.4.4 [The Union Declaration], page 63).

`%token`   [Directive]
> Declare a terminal symbol (token type name) with no precedence or associativity specified (see Section 3.7.2 [Token Type Names], page 75).

`%right`   [Directive]

> Declare a terminal symbol (token type name) that is right-associative (see Section 3.7.3 [Operator Precedence], page 76).

`%left`   [Directive]

> Declare a terminal symbol (token type name) that is left-associative (see Section 3.7.3 [Operator Precedence], page 76).

`%nonassoc`   [Directive]

> Declare a terminal symbol (token type name) that is nonassociative (see Section 3.7.3 [Operator Precedence], page 76). Using it in a way that would be associative is a syntax error.

`%type`   [Directive]

> Declare the type of semantic values for a nonterminal symbol (see Section 3.7.4 [Non-terminal Symbols], page 76).

`%start`   [Directive]

> Specify the grammar's start symbol (see Section 3.7.9 [The Start-Symbol], page 80).

`%expect`   [Directive]

> Declare the expected number of shift-reduce conflicts (see Section 3.7.8 [Suppressing Conflict Warnings], page 80).

In order to change the behavior of `bison`, use the following directives:

`%code {code}`   [Directive]
`%code qualifier {code}`   [Directive]

> Insert *code* verbatim into the output parser source at the default location or at the location specified by *qualifier*. See Section 3.7.14 [%code Summary], page 92.

`%debug`   [Directive]

> Instrument the parser for traces. Obsoleted by '`%define parse.trace`'. See Section 8.4 [Tracing Your Parser], page 142.

`%define variable`   [Directive]
`%define variable value`   [Directive]
`%define variable {value}`   [Directive]
`%define variable "value"`   [Directive]

> Define a variable to adjust Bison's behavior. See Section 3.7.13 [%define Summary], page 86.

`%defines`   [Directive]

> Write a parser header file containing macro definitions for the token type names defined in the grammar as well as a few other declarations. If the parser implementation file is named `name.c` then the parser header file is named `name.h`.
>
> For C parsers, the parser header file declares `YYSTYPE` unless `YYSTYPE` is already defined as a macro or you have used a `<type>` tag without using `%union`. Therefore, if you are using a `%union` (see Section 3.4.2 [More Than One Value Type], page 62)

with components that require other definitions, or if you have defined a `YYSTYPE` macro or type definition (see Section 3.4.1 [Data Types of Semantic Values], page 61), you need to arrange for these definitions to be propagated to all modules, e.g., by putting them in a prerequisite header that is included both by your parser and by any other module that needs `YYSTYPE`.

Unless your parser is pure, the parser header file declares `yylval` as an external variable. See Section 3.7.10 [A Pure (Reentrant) Parser], page 80.

If you have also used locations, the parser header file declares `YYLTYPE` and `yylloc` using a protocol similar to that of the `YYSTYPE` macro and `yylval`. See Section 3.5 [Tracking Locations], page 70.

This parser header file is normally essential if you wish to put the definition of `yylex` in a separate source file, because `yylex` typically needs to be able to refer to the above-mentioned declarations and to the token type codes. See Section 4.6.2 [Semantic Values of Tokens], page 100.

If you have declared `%code requires` or `%code provides`, the output header also contains their code. See Section 3.7.14 [%code Summary], page 92.

The generated header is protected against multiple inclusions with a C preprocessor guard: '`YY_PREFIX_FILE_INCLUDED`', where *PREFIX* and *FILE* are the prefix (see Section 3.8 [Multiple Parsers in the Same Program], page 94) and generated file name turned uppercase, with each series of non alphanumerical characters converted to a single underscore.

For instance with '`%define api.prefix {calc}`' and '`%defines "lib/parse.h"`', the header will be guarded as follows.

```
#ifndef YY_CALC_LIB_PARSE_H_INCLUDED
# define YY_CALC_LIB_PARSE_H_INCLUDED
...
#endif /* ! YY_CALC_LIB_PARSE_H_INCLUDED */
```

`%defines` *defines-file*   [Directive]
    Same as above, but save in the file *defines-file*.

`%destructor`   [Directive]
    Specify how the parser should reclaim the memory associated to discarded symbols. See Section 3.7.6 [Freeing Discarded Symbols], page 77.

`%file-prefix "prefix"`   [Directive]
    Specify a prefix to use for all Bison output file names. The names are chosen as if the grammar file were named *prefix*.y.

`%language "language"`   [Directive]
    Specify the programming language for the generated parser. Currently supported languages include C, C++, and Java. *language* is case-insensitive.

`%locations`   [Directive]
    Generate the code processing the locations (see Section 4.8 [Special Features for Use in Actions], page 103). This mode is enabled as soon as the grammar uses the special '`@n`' tokens, but if your grammar does not use it, using '`%locations`' allows for more accurate syntax error messages.

`%name-prefix "prefix"`   [Directive]

> Rename the external symbols used in the parser so that they start with *prefix* in-
> stead of 'yy'. The precise list of symbols renamed in C parsers is `yyparse`, `yylex`,
> `yyerror`, `yynerrs`, `yylval`, `yychar`, `yydebug`, and (if locations are used) `yylloc`.
> If you use a push parser, `yypush_parse`, `yypull_parse`, `yypstate`, `yypstate_new`
> and `yypstate_delete` will also be renamed. For example, if you use '`%name-prefix`
> `"c_"`', the names become `c_parse`, `c_lex`, and so on. For C++ parsers, see the
> '`%define api.namespace`' documentation in this section. See Section 3.8 [Multiple
> Parsers in the Same Program], page 94.

`%no-lines`   [Directive]

> Don't generate any `#line` preprocessor commands in the parser implementation file.
> Ordinarily Bison writes these commands in the parser implementation file so that the
> C compiler and debuggers will associate errors and object code with your source file
> (the grammar file). This directive causes them to associate errors with the parser
> implementation file, treating it as an independent source file in its own right.

`%output "file"`   [Directive]

> Generate the parser implementation in *file*.

`%pure-parser`   [Directive]

> Deprecated version of '`%define api.pure`' (see Section 3.7.13 [api.pure], page 86), for
> which Bison is more careful to warn about unreasonable usage.

`%require "version"`   [Directive]

> Require version *version* or higher of Bison. See Section 3.7.1 [Require a Version of
> Bison], page 74.

`%skeleton "file"`   [Directive]

> Specify the skeleton to use.
>
> If *file* does not contain a /, *file* is the name of a skeleton file in the Bison installation
> directory. If it does, *file* is an absolute file name or a file name relative to the directory
> of the grammar file. This is similar to how most shells resolve commands.

`%token-table`   [Directive]

> Generate an array of token names in the parser implementation file. The name of the
> array is `yytname`; `yytname[i]` is the name of the token whose internal Bison token
> code number is *i*. The first three elements of `yytname` correspond to the predefined
> tokens `"$end"`, `"error"`, and `"$undefined"`; after these come the symbols defined in
> the grammar file.
>
> The name in the table includes all the characters needed to represent the token in
> Bison. For single-character literals and literal strings, this includes the surrounding
> quoting characters and any escape sequences. For example, the Bison single-character
> literal `'+'` corresponds to a three-character name, represented in C as `"'+'"`; and
> the Bison two-character literal string `"\\/"` corresponds to a five-character name,
> represented in C as `"\"\\\\/\""`.
>
> When you specify `%token-table`, Bison also generates macro definitions for macros
> `YYNTOKENS`, `YYNNTS`, and `YYNRULES`, and `YYNSTATES`:

YYNTOKENS
> The highest token number, plus one.

YYNNTS   The number of nonterminal symbols.

YYNRULES   The number of grammar rules,

YYNSTATES
> The number of parser states (see Section 5.5 [Parser States], page 113).

%verbose   [Directive]
> Write an extra output file containing verbose descriptions of the parser states and what is done for each type of lookahead token in that state. See Section 8.1 [Understanding Your Parser], page 133, for more information.

%yacc   [Directive]
> Pretend the option --yacc was given, i.e., imitate Yacc, including its naming conventions. See Section 9.1 [Bison Options], page 149, for more.

3.7.13 %define Summary

There are many features of Bison's behavior that can be controlled by assigning the feature a single value. For historical reasons, some such features are assigned values by dedicated directives, such as %start, which assigns the start symbol. However, newer such features are associated with variables, which are assigned by the %define directive:

%define *variable*   [Directive]
%define *variable value*   [Directive]
%define *variable {value}*   [Directive]
%define *variable* "value"   [Directive]
> Define *variable* to *value*.

> The type of the values depend on the syntax. Braces denote value in the target language (e.g., a namespace, a type, etc.). Keyword values (no delimiters) denote finite choice (e.g., a variation of a feature). String values denote remaining cases (e.g., a file name).

> It is an error if a *variable* is defined by %define multiple times, but see Section 9.1 [-D *name*[=*value*]], page 149.

The rest of this section summarizes variables and values that %define accepts.

Some *variable*s take Boolean values. In this case, Bison will complain if the variable definition does not meet one of the following four conditions:

1. *value* is **true**

2. *value* is omitted (or "" is specified). This is equivalent to **true**.

3. *value* is **false**.

4. *variable* is never defined. In this case, Bison selects a default value.

What *variable*s are accepted, as well as their meanings and default values, depend on the selected target language and/or the parser skeleton (see Section 3.7.12 [%language], page 82, see Section 3.7.12 [%skeleton], page 82). Unaccepted *variable*s produce an error. Some of the accepted *variable*s are described below.

%define api.namespace *{namespace}* [Directive]
- Languages(s): C++
- Purpose: Specify the namespace for the parser class. For example, if you specify:

      %define api.namespace {foo::bar}

  Bison uses `foo::bar` verbatim in references such as:

      foo::bar::parser::semantic_type

  However, to open a namespace, Bison removes any leading `::` and then splits on any remaining occurrences:

      namespace foo { namespace bar {
        class position;
        class location;
      } }

- Accepted Values: Any absolute or relative C++ namespace reference without a trailing "`::`". For example, "`foo`" or "`::foo::bar`".
- Default Value: The value specified by **%name-prefix**, which defaults to **yy**. This usage of **%name-prefix** is for backward compatibility and can be confusing since **%name-prefix** also specifies the textual prefix for the lexical analyzer function. Thus, if you specify **%name-prefix**, it is best to also specify '**%define api.namespace**' so that **%name-prefix** *only* affects the lexical analyzer function. For example, if you specify:

      %define api.namespace {foo}
      %name-prefix "bar::"

  The parser namespace is **foo** and **yylex** is referenced as **bar::lex**.

%define api.location.type *{type}* [Directive]
- Language(s): C++, Java
- Purpose: Define the location type. See Section 10.1.3.3 [User Defined Location Type], page 161.
- Accepted Values: String
- Default Value: none
- History: Introduced in Bison 2.7 for C, C++ and Java. Introduced under the name **location_type** for C++ in Bison 2.5 and for Java in Bison 2.4.

%define api.prefix *{prefix}* [Directive]
- Language(s): All
- Purpose: Rename exported symbols. See Section 3.8 [Multiple Parsers in the Same Program], page 94.
- Accepted Values: String
- Default Value: yy
- History: introduced in Bison 2.6

%define api.pure *purity* [Directive]
- Language(s): C

- Purpose: Request a pure (reentrant) parser program. See Section 3.7.10 [A Pure (Reentrant) Parser], page 80.
- Accepted Values: `true`, `false`, `full`

  The value may be omitted: this is equivalent to specifying `true`, as is the case for Boolean values.

  When `%define api.pure full` is used, the parser is made reentrant. This changes the signature for `yylex` (see Section 4.6.4 [Pure Calling], page 101), and also that of `yyerror` when the tracking of locations has been activated, as shown below.

  The `true` value is very similar to the `full` value, the only difference is in the signature of `yyerror` on Yacc parsers without `%parse-param`, for historical reasons. I.e., if '`%locations %define api.pure`' is passed then the prototypes for `yyerror` are:

  ```
  void yyerror (char const *msg);                    // Yacc parsers.
  void yyerror (YYLTYPE *locp, char const *msg);  // GLR parsers.
  ```

  But if '`%locations %define api.pure %parse-param {int *nastiness}`' is used, then both parsers have the same signature:

  ```
  void yyerror (YYLTYPE *llocp, int *nastiness, char const *msg);
  ```

  (see Section 4.7 [The Error Reporting Function yyerror], page 102)
- Default Value: `false`
- History: the `full` value was introduced in Bison 2.7

`%define api.push-pull` *kind*   [Directive]
- Language(s): C (deterministic parsers only)
- Purpose: Request a pull parser, a push parser, or both. See Section 3.7.11 [A Push Parser], page 81. (The current push parsing interface is experimental and may evolve. More user feedback will help to stabilize it.)
- Accepted Values: `pull`, `push`, `both`
- Default Value: `pull`

`%define api.token.constructor`   [Directive]
- Language(s): C++
- Purpose: When variant-based semantic values are enabled (see Section 10.1.2.2 [C++ Variants], page 158), request that symbols be handled as a whole (type, value, and possibly location) in the scanner. See Section 10.1.5.2 [Complete Symbols], page 163, for details.
- Accepted Values: Boolean.
- Default Value: `false`
- History: introduced in Bison 3.0

`%define api.token.prefix` *{prefix}*   [Directive]
- Languages(s): all
- Purpose: Add a prefix to the token names when generating their definition in the target language. For instance

```
%token FILE for ERROR
%define api.token.prefix {TOK_}
%%
start: FILE for ERROR;
```

generates the definition of the symbols `TOK_FILE`, `TOK_for`, and `TOK_ERROR` in the generated source files. In particular, the scanner must use these prefixed token names, while the grammar itself may still use the short names (as in the sample rule given above). The generated informational files (`*.output`, `*.xml`, `*.dot`) are not modified by this prefix.

Bison also prefixes the generated member names of the semantic value union. See Section 3.4.3 [Generating the Semantic Value Type], page 62, for more details.

See Section 10.1.6.3 [Calc++ Parser], page 167 and Section 10.1.6.4 [Calc++ Scanner], page 169, for a complete example.

- Accepted Values: Any string. Should be a valid identifier prefix in the target language, in other words, it should typically be an identifier itself (sequence of letters, underscores, and —not at the beginning— digits).

- Default Value: empty

- History: introduced in Bison 3.0

`%define api.value.type` *support*   [Directive]

`%define api.value.type` *{type}*   [Directive]

- Language(s): all

- Purpose: The type for semantic values.

- Accepted Values:

    '`{}`'   This grammar has no semantic value at all. This is not properly supported yet.

    '`union-directive`' (C, C++)
            The type is defined thanks to the `%union` directive. You don't have to define `api.value.type` in that case, using `%union` suffices. See Section 3.4.4 [The Union Declaration], page 63. For instance:

```
%define api.value.type union-directive
%union
{
  int ival;
  char *sval;
}
%token <ival> INT "integer"
%token <sval> STR "string"
```

    '`union`' (C, C++)
            The symbols are defined with type names, from which Bison will generate a `union`. For instance:

```
%define api.value.type union
%token <int> INT "integer"
%token <char *> STR "string"
```

This feature needs user feedback to stabilize. Note that most C++ objects cannot be stored in a union.

'variant' (C++)

This is similar to union, but special storage techniques are used to allow any kind of C++ object to be used. For instance:

```
%define api.value.type variant
%token <int> INT "integer"
%token <std::string> STR "string"
```

This feature needs user feedback to stabilize. See Section 10.1.2.2 [C++ Variants], page 158.

'{type}'   Use this type as semantic value.

```
%code requires
{
  struct my_value
  {
    enum
    {
      is_int, is_str
    } kind;
    union
    {
      int ival;
      char *sval;
    } u;
  };
}
%define api.value.type {struct my_value}
%token <u.ival> INT "integer"
%token <u.sval> STR "string"
```

- Default Value:
  - union-directive if %union is used, otherwise ...
  - int if type tags are used (i.e., '%token <type>...' or '%type <type>...' is used), otherwise ...
  - undefined.
- History: introduced in Bison 3.0. Was introduced for Java only in 2.3b as stype.

%define api.value.union.name *name*   [Directive]
- Language(s): C
- Purpose: The tag of the generated union (*not* the name of the typedef). This variable is set to *id* when '%union *id*' is used. There is no clear reason to give this union a name.
- Accepted Values: Any valid identifier.
- Default Value: YYSTYPE.
- History: Introduced in Bison 3.0.3.

%define location_type   [Directive]
> Obsoleted by `api.location.type` since Bison 2.7.

%define lr.default-reduction *when*   [Directive]
- Language(s): all
- Purpose: Specify the kind of states that are permitted to contain default reductions. See Section 5.8.2 [Default Reductions], page 119. (The ability to specify where default reductions should be used is experimental. More user feedback will help to stabilize it.)
- Accepted Values: `most`, `consistent`, `accepting`
- Default Value:
  - `accepting` if `lr.type` is `canonical-lr`.
  - `most` otherwise.
- History: introduced as `lr.default-reductions` in 2.5, renamed as `lr.default-reduction` in 3.0.

%define lr.keep-unreachable-state   [Directive]
- Language(s): all
- Purpose: Request that Bison allow unreachable parser states to remain in the parser tables. See Section 5.8.4 [Unreachable States], page 122.
- Accepted Values: Boolean
- Default Value: `false`
- History: introduced as `lr.keep_unreachable_states` in 2.3b, renamed as `lr.keep-unreachable-states` in 2.5, and as `lr.keep-unreachable-state` in 3.0.

%define lr.type *type*   [Directive]
- Language(s): all
- Purpose: Specify the type of parser tables within the LR(1) family. See Section 5.8.1 [LR Table Construction], page 118. (This feature is experimental. More user feedback will help to stabilize it.)
- Accepted Values: `lalr`, `ielr`, `canonical-lr`
- Default Value: `lalr`

%define namespace *{namespace}*   [Directive]
> Obsoleted by `api.namespace`

%define parse.assert   [Directive]
- Languages(s): C++
- Purpose: Issue runtime assertions to catch invalid uses. In C++, when variants are used (see Section 10.1.2.2 [C++ Variants], page 158), symbols must be constructed and destroyed properly. This option checks these constraints.
- Accepted Values: Boolean
- Default Value: `false`

%define parse.error *verbosity*   [Directive]
  - Languages(s): all
  - Purpose: Control the kind of error messages passed to the error reporting function. See Section 4.7 [The Error Reporting Function yyerror], page 102.
  - Accepted Values:
    - **simple** Error messages passed to **yyerror** are simply **"syntax error"**.
    - **verbose** Error messages report the unexpected token, and possibly the expected ones. However, this report can often be incorrect when LAC is not enabled (see Section 5.8.3 [LAC], page 121).
  - Default Value: **simple**

%define parse.lac *when*   [Directive]
  - Languages(s): C (deterministic parsers only)
  - Purpose: Enable LAC (lookahead correction) to improve syntax error handling. See Section 5.8.3 [LAC], page 121.
  - Accepted Values: **none**, **full**
  - Default Value: **none**

%define parse.trace   [Directive]
  - Languages(s): C, C++, Java
  - Purpose: Require parser instrumentation for tracing. See Section 8.4 [Tracing Your Parser], page 142.

    In C/C++, define the macro **YYDEBUG** (or *prefix***DEBUG** with '**%define api.prefix {***prefix***}**', see Section 3.8 [Multiple Parsers in the Same Program], page 94) to 1 in the parser implementation file if it is not already defined, so that the debugging facilities are compiled.
  - Accepted Values: Boolean
  - Default Value: **false**

3.7.14 %code Summary

The **%code** directive inserts code verbatim into the output parser source at any of a predefined set of locations. It thus serves as a flexible and user-friendly alternative to the traditional Yacc prologue, **%{***code***%}**. This section summarizes the functionality of **%code** for the various target languages supported by Bison. For a detailed discussion of how to use **%code** in place of **%{***code***%}** for C/C++ and why it is advantageous to do so, see Section 3.1.2 [Prologue Alternatives], page 52.

%code {*code***}**   [Directive]
  This is the unqualified form of the **%code** directive. It inserts *code* verbatim at a language-dependent default location in the parser implementation.

  For C/C++, the default location is the parser implementation file after the usual contents of the parser header file. Thus, the unqualified form replaces **%{***code***%}** for most purposes.

  For Java, the default location is inside the parser class.

`%code qualifier {code}`   [Directive]

This is the qualified form of the `%code` directive. *qualifier* identifies the purpose of *code* and thus the location(s) where Bison should insert it. That is, if you need to specify location-sensitive *code* that does not belong at the default location selected by the unqualified `%code` form, use this form instead.

For any particular qualifier or for the unqualified form, if there are multiple occurrences of the `%code` directive, Bison concatenates the specified code in the order in which it appears in the grammar file.

Not all qualifiers are accepted for all target languages. Unaccepted qualifiers produce an error. Some of the accepted qualifiers are:

`requires`

- Language(s): C, C++
- Purpose: This is the best place to write dependency code required for `YYSTYPE` and `YYLTYPE`. In other words, it's the best place to define types referenced in `%union` directives. If you use `#define` to override Bison's default `YYSTYPE` and `YYLTYPE` definitions, then it is also the best place. However you should rather `%define api.value.type` and `api.location.type`.
- Location(s): The parser header file and the parser implementation file before the Bison-generated `YYSTYPE` and `YYLTYPE` definitions.

`provides`

- Language(s): C, C++
- Purpose: This is the best place to write additional definitions and declarations that should be provided to other modules.
- Location(s): The parser header file and the parser implementation file after the Bison-generated `YYSTYPE`, `YYLTYPE`, and token definitions.

`top`

- Language(s): C, C++
- Purpose: The unqualified `%code` or `%code requires` should usually be more appropriate than `%code top`. However, occasionally it is necessary to insert code much nearer the top of the parser implementation file. For example:

```
%code top {
  #define _GNU_SOURCE
  #include <stdio.h>
}
```

- Location(s): Near the top of the parser implementation file.

`imports`

- Language(s): Java
- Purpose: This is the best place to write Java import directives.
- Location(s): The parser Java file after any Java package directive and before any class definitions.

Though we say the insertion locations are language-dependent, they are technically skeleton-dependent. Writers of non-standard skeletons however should choose their locations consistently with the behavior of the standard Bison skeletons.

3.8 Multiple Parsers in the Same Program

Most programs that use Bison parse only one language and therefore contain only one Bison parser. But what if you want to parse more than one language with the same program? Then you need to avoid name conflicts between different definitions of functions and variables such as yyparse, yylval. To use different parsers from the same compilation unit, you also need to avoid conflicts on types and macros (e.g., YYSTYPE) exported in the generated header.

The easy way to do this is to define the %define variable api.prefix. With different api.prefixs it is guaranteed that headers do not conflict when included together, and that compiled objects can be linked together too. Specifying '%define api.prefix {prefix}' (or passing the option '-Dapi.prefix={prefix}', see Chapter 9 [Invoking Bison], page 149) renames the interface functions and variables of the Bison parser to start with prefix instead of 'yy', and all the macros to start by PREFIX (i.e., prefix upper-cased) instead of 'YY'.

The renamed symbols include yyparse, yylex, yyerror, yynerrs, yylval, yylloc, yychar and yydebug. If you use a push parser, yypush_parse, yypull_parse, yypstate, yypstate_new and yypstate_delete will also be renamed. The renamed macros include YYSTYPE, YYLTYPE, and YYDEBUG, which is treated specifically — more about this below.

For example, if you use '%define api.prefix {c}', the names become cparse, clex, ..., CSTYPE, CLTYPE, and so on.

The %define variable api.prefix works in two different ways. In the implementation file, it works by adding macro definitions to the beginning of the parser implementation file, defining yyparse as prefixparse, and so on:

```
#define YYSTYPE CTYPE
#define yyparse cparse
#define yylval  clval
...
YYSTYPE yylval;
int yyparse (void);
```

This effectively substitutes one name for the other in the entire parser implementation file, thus the "original" names (yylex, YYSTYPE, ...) are also usable in the parser implementation file.

However, in the parser header file, the symbols are defined renamed, for instance:

```
extern CSTYPE clval;
int cparse (void);
```

The macro YYDEBUG is commonly used to enable the tracing support in parsers. To comply with this tradition, when api.prefix is used, YYDEBUG (not renamed) is used as a default value:

```
/* Debug traces.  */
#ifndef CDEBUG
# if defined YYDEBUG
#  if YYDEBUG
```

```
#   define CDEBUG 1
#  else
#   define CDEBUG 0
#  endif
# else
#  define CDEBUG 0
# endif
#endif
#if CDEBUG
extern int cdebug;
#endif
```

Prior to Bison 2.6, a feature similar to `api.prefix` was provided by the obsolete directive `%name-prefix` (see Appendix A [Bison Symbols], page 189) and the option `--name-prefix` (see Section 9.1 [Bison Options], page 149).

4 Parser C-Language Interface

The Bison parser is actually a C function named `yyparse`. Here we describe the interface conventions of `yyparse` and the other functions that it needs to use.

Keep in mind that the parser uses many C identifiers starting with 'yy' and 'YY' for internal purposes. If you use such an identifier (aside from those in this manual) in an action or in epilogue in the grammar file, you are likely to run into trouble.

4.1 The Parser Function `yyparse`

You call the function `yyparse` to cause parsing to occur. This function reads tokens, executes actions, and ultimately returns when it encounters end-of-input or an unrecoverable syntax error. You can also write an action which directs `yyparse` to return immediately without reading further.

`int yyparse (`*void*`)`   [Function]

> The value returned by `yyparse` is 0 if parsing was successful (return is due to end-of-input).
>
> The value is 1 if parsing failed because of invalid input, i.e., input that contains a syntax error or that causes `YYABORT` to be invoked.
>
> The value is 2 if parsing failed due to memory exhaustion.

In an action, you can cause immediate return from `yyparse` by using these macros:

`YYACCEPT`   [Macro]

> Return immediately with value 0 (to report success).

`YYABORT`   [Macro]

> Return immediately with value 1 (to report failure).

If you use a reentrant parser, you can optionally pass additional parameter information to it in a reentrant way. To do so, use the declaration `%parse-param`:

`%parse-param {`*argument-declaration*`} ...`   [Directive]

> Declare that one or more *argument-declaration* are additional `yyparse` arguments. The *argument-declaration* is used when declaring functions or prototypes. The last identifier in *argument-declaration* must be the argument name.

Here's an example. Write this in the parser:

```
%parse-param {int *nastiness} {int *randomness}
```

Then call the parser like this:

```
{
  int nastiness, randomness;
  ...   /* Store proper data in nastiness and randomness.  */
  value = yyparse (&nastiness, &randomness);
  ...
}
```

In the grammar actions, use expressions like this to refer to the data:

```
exp: ...     { ...; *randomness += 1; ... }
```
Using the following:

```
%parse-param {int *randomness}
```

Results in these signatures:

```
void yyerror (int *randomness, const char *msg);
int  yyparse (int *randomness);
```

Or, if both `%define api.pure full` (or just `%define api.pure`) and `%locations` are used:

```
void yyerror (YYLTYPE *llocp, int *randomness, const char *msg);
int  yyparse (int *randomness);
```

4.2 The Push Parser Function `yypush_parse`

(The current push parsing interface is experimental and may evolve. More user feedback will help to stabilize it.)

You call the function `yypush_parse` to parse a single token. This function is available if either the '`%define api.push-pull push`' or '`%define api.push-pull both`' declaration is used. See Section 3.7.11 [A Push Parser], page 81.

int yypush_parse (*yypstate *yyps*)   [Function]
> The value returned by `yypush_parse` is the same as for yyparse with the following exception: it returns `YYPUSH_MORE` if more input is required to finish parsing the grammar.

4.3 The Pull Parser Function `yypull_parse`

(The current push parsing interface is experimental and may evolve. More user feedback will help to stabilize it.)

You call the function `yypull_parse` to parse the rest of the input stream. This function is available if the '`%define api.push-pull both`' declaration is used. See Section 3.7.11 [A Push Parser], page 81.

int yypull_parse (*yypstate *yyps*)   [Function]
> The value returned by `yypull_parse` is the same as for `yyparse`.

4.4 The Parser Create Function `yystate_new`

(The current push parsing interface is experimental and may evolve. More user feedback will help to stabilize it.)

You call the function `yypstate_new` to create a new parser instance. This function is available if either the '`%define api.push-pull push`' or '`%define api.push-pull both`' declaration is used. See Section 3.7.11 [A Push Parser], page 81.

yypstate* yypstate_new (*void*)   [Function]
> The function will return a valid parser instance if there was memory available or 0 if no memory was available. In impure mode, it will also return 0 if a parser instance is currently allocated.

4.5 The Parser Delete Function `yystate_delete`

(The current push parsing interface is experimental and may evolve. More user feedback will help to stabilize it.)

You call the function `yypstate_delete` to delete a parser instance. function is available if either the '`%define api.push-pull push`' or '`%define api.push-pull both`' declaration is used. See Section 3.7.11 [A Push Parser], page 81.

void **yypstate_delete** (*yypstate *yyps*)   [Function]
      This function will reclaim the memory associated with a parser instance. After this
      call, you should no longer attempt to use the parser instance.

4.6 The Lexical Analyzer Function `yylex`

The *lexical analyzer* function, `yylex`, recognizes tokens from the input stream and returns them to the parser. Bison does not create this function automatically; you must write it so that `yyparse` can call it. The function is sometimes referred to as a lexical scanner.

In simple programs, `yylex` is often defined at the end of the Bison grammar file. If `yylex` is defined in a separate source file, you need to arrange for the token-type macro definitions to be available there. To do this, use the '`-d`' option when you run Bison, so that it will write these macro definitions into the separate parser header file, *name*`.tab.h`, which you can include in the other source files that need it. See Chapter 9 [Invoking Bison], page 149.

4.6.1 Calling Convention for `yylex`

The value that `yylex` returns must be the positive numeric code for the type of token it has just found; a zero or negative value signifies end-of-input.

When a token is referred to in the grammar rules by a name, that name in the parser implementation file becomes a C macro whose definition is the proper numeric code for that token type. So `yylex` can use the name to indicate that type. See Section 3.2 [Symbols], page 57.

When a token is referred to in the grammar rules by a character literal, the numeric code for that character is also the code for the token type. So `yylex` can simply return that character code, possibly converted to **unsigned char** to avoid sign-extension. The null character must not be used this way, because its code is zero and that signifies end-of-input.

Here is an example showing these things:

```
int
yylex (void)
{
  ...
  if (c == EOF)    /* Detect end-of-input.  */
    return 0;
  ...
  if (c == '+' || c == '-')
    return c;      /* Assume token type for '+' is '+'.  */
  ...
  return INT;      /* Return the type of the token.  */
  ...
```

```
}
```

This interface has been designed so that the output from the `lex` utility can be used without change as the definition of `yylex`.

If the grammar uses literal string tokens, there are two ways that `yylex` can determine the token type codes for them:

- If the grammar defines symbolic token names as aliases for the literal string tokens, `yylex` can use these symbolic names like all others. In this case, the use of the literal string tokens in the grammar file has no effect on `yylex`.

- `yylex` can find the multicharacter token in the `yytname` table. The index of the token in the table is the token type's code. The name of a multicharacter token is recorded in `yytname` with a double-quote, the token's characters, and another double-quote. The token's characters are escaped as necessary to be suitable as input to Bison.

  Here's code for looking up a multicharacter token in `yytname`, assuming that the characters of the token are stored in `token_buffer`, and assuming that the token does not contain any characters like '"' that require escaping.

```
for (i = 0; i < YYNTOKENS; i++)
  {
    if (yytname[i] != 0
        && yytname[i][0] == '"'
        && ! strncmp (yytname[i] + 1, token_buffer,
                      strlen (token_buffer))
        && yytname[i][strlen (token_buffer) + 1] == '"'
        && yytname[i][strlen (token_buffer) + 2] == 0)
      break;
  }
```

The `yytname` table is generated only if you use the `%token-table` declaration. See Section 3.7.12 [Decl Summary], page 82.

4.6.2 Semantic Values of Tokens

In an ordinary (nonreentrant) parser, the semantic value of the token must be stored into the global variable `yylval`. When you are using just one data type for semantic values, `yylval` has that type. Thus, if the type is `int` (the default), you might write this in `yylex`:

```
...
yylval = value;  /* Put value onto Bison stack.  */
return INT;      /* Return the type of the token.  */
...
```

When you are using multiple data types, `yylval`'s type is a union made from the `%union` declaration (see Section 3.4.4 [The Union Declaration], page 63). So when you store a token's value, you must use the proper member of the union. If the `%union` declaration looks like this:

```
%union {
  int intval;
  double val;
  symrec *tptr;
}
```

then the code in `yylex` might look like this:

```
    ...
    yylval.intval = value; /* Put value onto Bison stack.  */
    return INT;            /* Return the type of the token.  */
    ...
```

4.6.3 Textual Locations of Tokens

If you are using the '`@n`'-feature (see Section 3.5 [Tracking Locations], page 70) in actions to keep track of the textual locations of tokens and groupings, then you must provide this information in `yylex`. The function `yyparse` expects to find the textual location of a token just parsed in the global variable `yylloc`. So `yylex` must store the proper data in that variable.

By default, the value of `yylloc` is a structure and you need only initialize the members that are going to be used by the actions. The four members are called `first_line`, `first_column`, `last_line` and `last_column`. Note that the use of this feature makes the parser noticeably slower.

The data type of `yylloc` has the name `YYLTYPE`.

4.6.4 Calling Conventions for Pure Parsers

When you use the Bison declaration `%define api.pure full` to request a pure, reentrant parser, the global communication variables `yylval` and `yylloc` cannot be used. (See Section 3.7.10 [A Pure (Reentrant) Parser], page 80.) In such parsers the two global variables are replaced by pointers passed as arguments to `yylex`. You must declare them as shown here, and pass the information back by storing it through those pointers.

```
    int
    yylex (YYSTYPE *lvalp, YYLTYPE *llocp)
    {
      ...
      *lvalp = value;  /* Put value onto Bison stack.  */
      return INT;      /* Return the type of the token.  */
      ...
    }
```

If the grammar file does not use the '`@`' constructs to refer to textual locations, then the type `YYLTYPE` will not be defined. In this case, omit the second argument; `yylex` will be called with only one argument.

If you wish to pass additional arguments to `yylex`, use `%lex-param` just like `%parse-param` (see Section 4.1 [Parser Function], page 97). To pass additional arguments to both `yylex` and `yyparse`, use `%param`.

`%lex-param {argument-declaration} ...`   [Directive]
>   Specify that *argument-declaration* are additional `yylex` argument declarations. You may pass one or more such declarations, which is equivalent to repeating `%lex-param`.

`%param {argument-declaration} ...`   [Directive]
>   Specify that *argument-declaration* are additional `yylex`/`yyparse` argument declaration. This is equivalent to '`%lex-param {argument-declaration} ...`

```
%parse-param {argument-declaration} ...'.   You may pass one or more
```
declarations, which is equivalent to repeating %param.

For instance:

```
%lex-param   {scanner_mode *mode}
%parse-param {parser_mode *mode}
%param       {environment_type *env}
```

results in the following signatures:

```
int yylex   (scanner_mode *mode, environment_type *env);
int yyparse (parser_mode *mode, environment_type *env);
```

If '%define api.pure full' is added:

```
int yylex   (YYSTYPE *lvalp, scanner_mode *mode, environment_type *env);
int yyparse (parser_mode *mode, environment_type *env);
```

and finally, if both '%define api.pure full' and %locations are used:

```
int yylex   (YYSTYPE *lvalp, YYLTYPE *llocp,
             scanner_mode *mode, environment_type *env);
int yyparse (parser_mode *mode, environment_type *env);
```

4.7 The Error Reporting Function yyerror

The Bison parser detects a *syntax error* (or *parse error*) whenever it reads a token which
cannot satisfy any syntax rule. An action in the grammar can also explicitly proclaim
an error, using the macro YYERROR (see Section 4.8 [Special Features for Use in Actions],
page 103).

The Bison parser expects to report the error by calling an error reporting function named
yyerror, which you must supply. It is called by yyparse whenever a syntax error is found,
and it receives one argument. For a syntax error, the string is normally "syntax error".

If you invoke '%define parse.error verbose' in the Bison declarations section (see
Section 3.1.3 [The Bison Declarations Section], page 56), then Bison provides a more verbose
and specific error message string instead of just plain "syntax error". However, that
message sometimes contains incorrect information if LAC is not enabled (see Section 5.8.3
[LAC], page 121).

The parser can detect one other kind of error: memory exhaustion. This can happen
when the input contains constructions that are very deeply nested. It isn't likely you will
encounter this, since the Bison parser normally extends its stack automatically up to a very
large limit. But if memory is exhausted, yyparse calls yyerror in the usual fashion, except
that the argument string is "memory exhausted".

In some cases diagnostics like "syntax error" are translated automatically from English
to some other language before they are passed to yyerror. See Section 4.9 [International-
ization], page 105.

The following definition suffices in simple programs:

```
void
yyerror (char const *s)
{
```

```
    fprintf (stderr, "%s\n", s);
  }
```

After yyerror returns to yyparse, the latter will attempt error recovery if you have written suitable error recovery grammar rules (see Chapter 6 [Error Recovery], page 127). If recovery is impossible, yyparse will immediately return 1.

Obviously, in location tracking pure parsers, yyerror should have an access to the current location. With %define api.pure, this is indeed the case for the GLR parsers, but not for the Yacc parser, for historical reasons, and this is the why %define api.pure full should be prefered over %define api.pure.

When %locations %define api.pure full is used, yyerror has the following signature:

```
    void yyerror (YYLTYPE *locp, char const *msg);
```

The prototypes are only indications of how the code produced by Bison uses yyerror. Bison-generated code always ignores the returned value, so yyerror can return any type, including void. Also, yyerror can be a variadic function; that is why the message is always passed last.

Traditionally yyerror returns an int that is always ignored, but this is purely for historical reasons, and void is preferable since it more accurately describes the return type for yyerror.

The variable yynerrs contains the number of syntax errors reported so far. Normally this variable is global; but if you request a pure parser (see Section 3.7.10 [A Pure (Reentrant) Parser], page 80) then it is a local variable which only the actions can access.

4.8 Special Features for Use in Actions

Here is a table of Bison constructs, variables and macros that are useful in actions.

$$ [Variable]

> Acts like a variable that contains the semantic value for the grouping made by the current rule. See Section 3.4.6 [Actions], page 64.

$n   [Variable]

> Acts like a variable that contains the semantic value for the nth component of the current rule. See Section 3.4.6 [Actions], page 64.

$<typealt>$ [Variable]

> Like $$ but specifies alternative typealt in the union specified by the %union declaration. See Section 3.4.7 [Data Types of Values in Actions], page 65.

$<typealt>n   [Variable]

> Like $n but specifies alternative typealt in the union specified by the %union declaration. See Section 3.4.7 [Data Types of Values in Actions], page 65.

YYABORT ;   [Macro]

> Return immediately from yyparse, indicating failure. See Section 4.1 [The Parser Function yyparse], page 97.

YYACCEPT ;   [Macro]

> Return immediately from yyparse, indicating success. See Section 4.1 [The Parser Function yyparse], page 97.

YYBACKUP (*token***, ***value***);**   [Macro]

Unshift a token. This macro is allowed only for rules that reduce a single value, and only when there is no lookahead token. It is also disallowed in GLR parsers. It installs a lookahead token with token type *token* and semantic value *value*; then it discards the value that was going to be reduced by this rule.

If the macro is used when it is not valid, such as when there is a lookahead token already, then it reports a syntax error with a message 'cannot back up' and performs ordinary error recovery.

In either case, the rest of the action is not executed.

YYEMPTY   [Macro]

Value stored in yychar when there is no lookahead token.

YYEOF   [Macro]

Value stored in yychar when the lookahead is the end of the input stream.

YYERROR ;   [Macro]

Cause an immediate syntax error. This statement initiates error recovery just as if the parser itself had detected an error; however, it does not call yyerror, and does not print any message. If you want to print an error message, call yyerror explicitly before the 'YYERROR;' statement. See Chapter 6 [Error Recovery], page 127.

YYRECOVERING   [Macro]

The expression YYRECOVERING () yields 1 when the parser is recovering from a syntax error, and 0 otherwise. See Chapter 6 [Error Recovery], page 127.

yychar   [Variable]

Variable containing either the lookahead token, or YYEOF when the lookahead is the end of the input stream, or YYEMPTY when no lookahead has been performed so the next token is not yet known. Do not modify yychar in a deferred semantic action (see Section 1.5.3 [GLR Semantic Actions], page 25). See Section 5.1 [Lookahead Tokens], page 107.

yyclearin ;   [Macro]

Discard the current lookahead token. This is useful primarily in error rules. Do not invoke yyclearin in a deferred semantic action (see Section 1.5.3 [GLR Semantic Actions], page 25). See Chapter 6 [Error Recovery], page 127.

yyerrok ;   [Macro]

Resume generating error messages immediately for subsequent syntax errors. This is useful primarily in error rules. See Chapter 6 [Error Recovery], page 127.

yylloc   [Variable]

Variable containing the lookahead token location when yychar is not set to YYEMPTY or YYEOF. Do not modify yylloc in a deferred semantic action (see Section 1.5.3 [GLR Semantic Actions], page 25). See Section 3.5.2 [Actions and Locations], page 71.

yylval   [Variable]

Variable containing the lookahead token semantic value when yychar is not set to YYEMPTY or YYEOF. Do not modify yylval in a deferred semantic action (see Section 1.5.3 [GLR Semantic Actions], page 25). See Section 3.4.6 [Actions], page 64.

@$ [Value]

> Acts like a structure variable containing information on the textual location of the
> grouping made by the current rule. See Section 3.5 [Tracking Locations], page 70.

@n   [Value]

> Acts like a structure variable containing information on the textual location of the
> nth component of the current rule. See Section 3.5 [Tracking Locations], page 70.

4.9 Parser Internationalization

A Bison-generated parser can print diagnostics, including error and tracing messages. By
default, they appear in English. However, Bison also supports outputting diagnostics in
the user's native language. To make this work, the user should set the usual environment
variables. See Section "The User's View" in *GNU* gettext *utilities*. For example, the
shell command 'export LC_ALL=fr_CA.UTF-8' might set the user's locale to French Cana-
dian using the UTF-8 encoding. The exact set of available locales depends on the user's
installation.

The maintainer of a package that uses a Bison-generated parser enables the internationalization of the parser's output through the following steps. Here we assume a package that
uses GNU Autoconf and GNU Automake.

1. Into the directory containing the GNU Autoconf macros used by the package
   —often called m4— copy the bison-i18n.m4 file installed by Bison under
   'share/aclocal/bison-i18n.m4' in Bison's installation directory. For example:

   ```
   cp /usr/local/share/aclocal/bison-i18n.m4 m4/bison-i18n.m4
   ```

2. In the top-level configure.ac, after the AM_GNU_GETTEXT invocation, add an invocation
   of BISON_I18N. This macro is defined in the file bison-i18n.m4 that you copied
   earlier. It causes 'configure' to find the value of the BISON_LOCALEDIR variable,
   and it defines the source-language symbol YYENABLE_NLS to enable translations in the
   Bison-generated parser.

3. In the main function of your program, designate the directory containing Bison's
   runtime message catalog, through a call to 'bindtextdomain' with domain name
   'bison-runtime'. For example:

   ```
   bindtextdomain ("bison-runtime", BISON_LOCALEDIR);
   ```

   Typically this appears after any other call bindtextdomain (PACKAGE, LOCALEDIR)
   that your package already has. Here we rely on 'BISON_LOCALEDIR' to be defined as a
   string through the Makefile.

4. In the Makefile.am that controls the compilation of the main function, make
   'BISON_LOCALEDIR' available as a C preprocessor macro, either in 'DEFS' or in
   'AM_CPPFLAGS'. For example:

   ```
   DEFS = @DEFS@ -DBISON_LOCALEDIR='"$(BISON_LOCALEDIR)"'
   ```

   or:

   ```
   AM_CPPFLAGS = -DBISON_LOCALEDIR='"$(BISON_LOCALEDIR)"'
   ```

5. Finally, invoke the command autoreconf to generate the build infrastructure.

5 The Bison Parser Algorithm

As Bison reads tokens, it pushes them onto a stack along with their semantic values. The stack is called the *parser stack*. Pushing a token is traditionally called *shifting*.

For example, suppose the infix calculator has read '1 + 5 *', with a '3' to come. The stack will have four elements, one for each token that was shifted.

But the stack does not always have an element for each token read. When the last n tokens and groupings shifted match the components of a grammar rule, they can be combined according to that rule. This is called *reduction*. Those tokens and groupings are replaced on the stack by a single grouping whose symbol is the result (left hand side) of that rule. Running the rule's action is part of the process of reduction, because this is what computes the semantic value of the resulting grouping.

For example, if the infix calculator's parser stack contains this:

```
1 + 5 * 3
```

and the next input token is a newline character, then the last three elements can be reduced to 15 via the rule:

```
expr: expr '*' expr;
```

Then the stack contains just these three elements:

```
1 + 15
```

At this point, another reduction can be made, resulting in the single value 16. Then the newline token can be shifted.

The parser tries, by shifts and reductions, to reduce the entire input down to a single grouping whose symbol is the grammar's start-symbol (see Section 1.1 [Languages and Context-Free Grammars], page 17).

This kind of parser is known in the literature as a bottom-up parser.

5.1 Lookahead Tokens

The Bison parser does *not* always reduce immediately as soon as the last n tokens and groupings match a rule. This is because such a simple strategy is inadequate to handle most languages. Instead, when a reduction is possible, the parser sometimes "looks ahead" at the next token in order to decide what to do.

When a token is read, it is not immediately shifted; first it becomes the *lookahead token*, which is not on the stack. Now the parser can perform one or more reductions of tokens and groupings on the stack, while the lookahead token remains off to the side. When no more reductions should take place, the lookahead token is shifted onto the stack. This does not mean that all possible reductions have been done; depending on the token type of the lookahead token, some rules may choose to delay their application.

Here is a simple case where lookahead is needed. These three rules define expressions which contain binary addition operators and postfix unary factorial operators ('!'), and allow parentheses for grouping.

```
expr:
  term '+' expr
| term
;
```

```
term:
  '(' expr ')'
| term '!'
| "number"
;
```

Suppose that the tokens '1 + 2' have been read and shifted; what should be done? If the following token is ')', then the first three tokens must be reduced to form an **expr**. This is the only valid course, because shifting the ')' would produce a sequence of symbols **term** ')', and no rule allows this.

If the following token is '!', then it must be shifted immediately so that '2 !' can be reduced to make a **term**. If instead the parser were to reduce before shifting, '1 + 2' would become an **expr**. It would then be impossible to shift the '!' because doing so would produce on the stack the sequence of symbols **expr** '!'. No rule allows that sequence.

The lookahead token is stored in the variable **yychar**. Its semantic value and location, if any, are stored in the variables **yylval** and **yylloc**. See Section 4.8 [Special Features for Use in Actions], page 103.

5.2 Shift/Reduce Conflicts

Suppose we are parsing a language which has if-then and if-then-else statements, with a pair of rules like this:

```
if_stmt:
  "if" expr "then" stmt
| "if" expr "then" stmt "else" stmt
;
```

Here "if", "then" and "else" are terminal symbols for specific keyword tokens.

When the "else" token is read and becomes the lookahead token, the contents of the stack (assuming the input is valid) are just right for reduction by the first rule. But it is also legitimate to shift the "else", because that would lead to eventual reduction by the second rule.

This situation, where either a shift or a reduction would be valid, is called a *shift/reduce conflict*. Bison is designed to resolve these conflicts by choosing to shift, unless otherwise directed by operator precedence declarations. To see the reason for this, let's contrast it with the other alternative.

Since the parser prefers to shift the "else", the result is to attach the else-clause to the innermost if-statement, making these two inputs equivalent:

```
if x then if y then win; else lose;
```

```
if x then do; if y then win; else lose; end;
```

But if the parser chose to reduce when possible rather than shift, the result would be to attach the else-clause to the outermost if-statement, making these two inputs equivalent:

```
if x then if y then win; else lose;
```

```
if x then do; if y then win; end; else lose;
```

The conflict exists because the grammar as written is ambiguous: either parsing of the simple nested if-statement is legitimate. The established convention is that these ambiguities are resolved by attaching the else-clause to the innermost if-statement; this is what Bison accomplishes by choosing to shift rather than reduce. (It would ideally be cleaner to write an unambiguous grammar, but that is very hard to do in this case.) This particular ambiguity was first encountered in the specifications of Algol 60 and is called the "dangling **else**" ambiguity.

To avoid warnings from Bison about predictable, legitimate shift/reduce conflicts, you can use the **%expect n** declaration. There will be no warning as long as the number of shift/reduce conflicts is exactly *n*, and Bison will report an error if there is a different number. See Section 3.7.8 [Suppressing Conflict Warnings], page 80. However, we don't recommend the use of **%expect** (except '**%expect 0**'!), as an equal number of conflicts does not mean that they are the *same*. When possible, you should rather use precedence directives to *fix* the conflicts explicitly (see Section 5.3.6 [Using Precedence For Non Operators], page 112).

The definition of **if_stmt** above is solely to blame for the conflict, but the conflict does not actually appear without additional rules. Here is a complete Bison grammar file that actually manifests the conflict:

```
%%
stmt:
  expr
| if_stmt
;

if_stmt:
  "if" expr "then" stmt
| "if" expr "then" stmt "else" stmt
;

expr:
  "identifier"
;
```

5.3 Operator Precedence

Another situation where shift/reduce conflicts appear is in arithmetic expressions. Here shifting is not always the preferred resolution; the Bison declarations for operator precedence allow you to specify when to shift and when to reduce.

5.3.1 When Precedence is Needed

Consider the following ambiguous grammar fragment (ambiguous because the input '1 - 2 * 3' can be parsed in two different ways):

```
expr:
  expr '-' expr
| expr '*' expr
| expr '<' expr
| '(' expr ')'
...
;
```

Suppose the parser has seen the tokens '1', '-' and '2'; should it reduce them via the rule for the subtraction operator? It depends on the next token. Of course, if the next token is ')', we must reduce; shifting is invalid because no single rule can reduce the token sequence '- 2)' or anything starting with that. But if the next token is '*' or '<', we have a choice: either shifting or reduction would allow the parse to complete, but with different results.

To decide which one Bison should do, we must consider the results. If the next operator token *op* is shifted, then it must be reduced first in order to permit another opportunity to reduce the difference. The result is (in effect) '1 - (2 *op* 3)'. On the other hand, if the subtraction is reduced before shifting *op*, the result is '(1 - 2) *op* 3'. Clearly, then, the choice of shift or reduce should depend on the relative precedence of the operators '-' and *op*: '*' should be shifted first, but not '<'.

What about input such as '1 - 2 - 5'; should this be '(1 - 2) - 5' or should it be '1 - (2 - 5)'? For most operators we prefer the former, which is called *left association*. The latter alternative, *right association*, is desirable for assignment operators. The choice of left or right association is a matter of whether the parser chooses to shift or reduce when the stack contains '1 - 2' and the lookahead token is '-': shifting makes right-associativity.

5.3.2 Specifying Operator Precedence

Bison allows you to specify these choices with the operator precedence declarations %left and %right. Each such declaration contains a list of tokens, which are operators whose precedence and associativity is being declared. The %left declaration makes all those operators left-associative and the %right declaration makes them right-associative. A third alternative is %nonassoc, which declares that it is a syntax error to find the same operator twice "in a row". The last alternative, %precedence, allows to define only precedence and no associativity at all. As a result, any associativity-related conflict that remains will be reported as an compile-time error. The directive %nonassoc creates run-time error: using the operator in a associative way is a syntax error. The directive %precedence creates compile-time errors: an operator *can* be involved in an associativity-related conflict, contrary to what expected the grammar author.

The relative precedence of different operators is controlled by the order in which they are declared. The first precedence/associativity declaration in the file declares the operators whose precedence is lowest, the next such declaration declares the operators whose precedence is a little higher, and so on.

5.3.3 Specifying Precedence Only

Since POSIX Yacc defines only %left, %right, and %nonassoc, which all defines precedence and associativity, little attention is paid to the fact that precedence cannot be defined without defining associativity. Yet, sometimes, when trying to solve a conflict, precedence suffices. In such a case, using `%left`, `%right`, or `%nonassoc` might hide future (associativity related) conflicts that would remain hidden.

The dangling `else` ambiguity (see Section 5.2 [Shift/Reduce Conflicts], page 108) can be solved explicitly. This shift/reduce conflicts occurs in the following situation, where the period denotes the current parsing state:

        if *e1* then if *e2* then *s1* . else *s2*

The conflict involves the reduction of the rule 'IF expr THEN stmt', which precedence is by default that of its last token (THEN), and the shifting of the token ELSE. The usual disambiguation (attach the `else` to the closest `if`), shifting must be preferred, i.e., the precedence of ELSE must be higher than that of THEN. But neither is expected to be involved in an associativity related conflict, which can be specified as follows.

        %precedence THEN
        %precedence ELSE

The unary-minus is another typical example where associativity is usually over-specified, see Section 2.2 [Infix Notation Calculator - `calc`], page 37. The `%left` directive is traditionally used to declare the precedence of NEG, which is more than needed since it also defines its associativity. While this is harmless in the traditional example, who knows how NEG might be used in future evolutions of the grammar...

5.3.4 Precedence Examples

In our example, we would want the following declarations:

        %left '<'
        %left '-'
        %left '*'

In a more complete example, which supports other operators as well, we would declare them in groups of equal precedence. For example, '+' is declared with '-':

        %left '<' '>' '=' "!=" "<=" ">="
        %left '+' '-'
        %left '*' '/'

5.3.5 How Precedence Works

The first effect of the precedence declarations is to assign precedence levels to the terminal symbols declared. The second effect is to assign precedence levels to certain rules: each rule gets its precedence from the last terminal symbol mentioned in the components. (You can also specify explicitly the precedence of a rule. See Section 5.4 [Context-Dependent Precedence], page 112.)

Finally, the resolution of conflicts works by comparing the precedence of the rule being considered with that of the lookahead token. If the token's precedence is higher, the choice is to shift. If the rule's precedence is higher, the choice is to reduce. If they have equal precedence, the choice is made based on the associativity of that precedence level. The verbose output file made by '-v' (see Chapter 9 [Invoking Bison], page 149) says how each conflict was resolved.

Not all rules and not all tokens have precedence. If either the rule or the lookahead token has no precedence, then the default is to shift.

5.3.6 Using Precedence For Non Operators

Using properly precedence and associativity directives can help fixing shift/reduce conflicts that do not involve arithmetics-like operators. For instance, the "dangling **else**" problem (see Section 5.2 [Shift/Reduce Conflicts], page 108) can be solved elegantly in two different ways.

In the present case, the conflict is between the token `"else"` willing to be shifted, and the rule '`if_stmt: "if" expr "then" stmt`', asking for reduction. By default, the precedence of a rule is that of its last token, here `"then"`, so the conflict will be solved appropriately by giving `"else"` a precedence higher than that of `"then"`, for instance as follows:

```
%precedence "then"
%precedence "else"
```

Alternatively, you may give both tokens the same precedence, in which case associativity is used to solve the conflict. To preserve the shift action, use right associativity:

```
%right "then" "else"
```

Neither solution is perfect however. Since Bison does not provide, so far, "scoped" precedence, both force you to declare the precedence of these keywords with respect to the other operators your grammar. Therefore, instead of being warned about new conflicts you would be unaware of (e.g., a shift/reduce conflict due to '`if test then 1 else 2 + 3`' being ambiguous: '`if test then 1 else (2 + 3)`' or '`(if test then 1 else 2) + 3`'?), the conflict will be already "fixed".

5.4 Context-Dependent Precedence

Often the precedence of an operator depends on the context. This sounds outlandish at first, but it is really very common. For example, a minus sign typically has a very high precedence as a unary operator, and a somewhat lower precedence (lower than multiplication) as a binary operator.

The Bison precedence declarations can only be used once for a given token; so a token has only one precedence declared in this way. For context-dependent precedence, you need to use an additional mechanism: the `%prec` modifier for rules.

The `%prec` modifier declares the precedence of a particular rule by specifying a terminal symbol whose precedence should be used for that rule. It's not necessary for that symbol to appear otherwise in the rule. The modifier's syntax is:

```
%prec terminal-symbol
```

and it is written after the components of the rule. Its effect is to assign the rule the precedence of *terminal-symbol*, overriding the precedence that would be deduced for it in the ordinary way. The altered rule precedence then affects how conflicts involving that rule are resolved (see Section 5.3 [Operator Precedence], page 109).

Here is how `%prec` solves the problem of unary minus. First, declare a precedence for a fictitious terminal symbol named `UMINUS`. There are no tokens of this type, but the symbol serves to stand for its precedence:

```
...
%left '+' '-'
%left '*'
```

```
%left UMINUS
```

Now the precedence of UMINUS can be used in specific rules:

```
exp:
  ...
| exp '-' exp
  ...
| '-' exp %prec UMINUS
```

5.5 Parser States

The function yyparse is implemented using a finite-state machine. The values pushed on the parser stack are not simply token type codes; they represent the entire sequence of terminal and nonterminal symbols at or near the top of the stack. The current state collects all the information about previous input which is relevant to deciding what to do next.

Each time a lookahead token is read, the current parser state together with the type of lookahead token are looked up in a table. This table entry can say, "Shift the lookahead token." In this case, it also specifies the new parser state, which is pushed onto the top of the parser stack. Or it can say, "Reduce using rule number n." This means that a certain number of tokens or groupings are taken off the top of the stack, and replaced by one grouping. In other words, that number of states are popped from the stack, and one new state is pushed.

There is one other alternative: the table can say that the lookahead token is erroneous in the current state. This causes error processing to begin (see Chapter 6 [Error Recovery], page 127).

5.6 Reduce/Reduce Conflicts

A reduce/reduce conflict occurs if there are two or more rules that apply to the same sequence of input. This usually indicates a serious error in the grammar.

For example, here is an erroneous attempt to define a sequence of zero or more word groupings.

```
sequence:
  %empty          { printf ("empty sequence\n"); }
| maybeword
| sequence word  { printf ("added word %s\n", $2); }
;

maybeword:
  %empty    { printf ("empty maybeword\n"); }
| word      { printf ("single word %s\n", $1); }
;
```

The error is an ambiguity: there is more than one way to parse a single word into a sequence. It could be reduced to a maybeword and then into a sequence via the second rule. Alternatively, nothing-at-all could be reduced into a sequence via the first rule, and this could be combined with the word using the third rule for sequence.

There is also more than one way to reduce nothing-at-all into a `sequence`. This can be done directly via the first rule, or indirectly via `maybeword` and then the second rule.

You might think that this is a distinction without a difference, because it does not change whether any particular input is valid or not. But it does affect which actions are run. One parsing order runs the second rule's action; the other runs the first rule's action and the third rule's action. In this example, the output of the program changes.

Bison resolves a reduce/reduce conflict by choosing to use the rule that appears first in the grammar, but it is very risky to rely on this. Every reduce/reduce conflict must be studied and usually eliminated. Here is the proper way to define `sequence`:

```
sequence:
  %empty          { printf ("empty sequence\n"); }
| sequence word   { printf ("added word %s\n", $2); }
;
```

Here is another common error that yields a reduce/reduce conflict:

```
sequence:
  %empty
| sequence words
| sequence redirects
;

words:
  %empty
| words word
;

redirects:
  %empty
| redirects redirect
;
```

The intention here is to define a sequence which can contain either `word` or `redirect` groupings. The individual definitions of `sequence`, `words` and `redirects` are error-free, but the three together make a subtle ambiguity: even an empty input can be parsed in infinitely many ways!

Consider: nothing-at-all could be a `words`. Or it could be two `words` in a row, or three, or any number. It could equally well be a `redirects`, or two, or any number. Or it could be a `words` followed by three `redirects` and another `words`. And so on.

Here are two ways to correct these rules. First, to make it a single level of sequence:

```
sequence:
  %empty
| sequence word
| sequence redirect
;
```

Second, to prevent either a `words` or a `redirects` from being empty:

```
sequence:
  %empty
| sequence words
| sequence redirects
;

words:
  word
| words word
;

redirects:
  redirect
| redirects redirect
;
```

Yet this proposal introduces another kind of ambiguity! The input 'word word' can be parsed as a single words composed of two 'word's, or as two one-word words (and likewise for redirect/redirects). However this ambiguity is now a shift/reduce conflict, and therefore it can now be addressed with precedence directives.

To simplify the matter, we will proceed with word and redirect being tokens: "word" and "redirect".

To prefer the longest words, the conflict between the token "word" and the rule 'sequence: sequence words' must be resolved as a shift. To this end, we use the same techniques as exposed above, see Section 5.3.6 [Using Precedence For Non Operators], page 112. One solution relies on precedences: use %prec to give a lower precedence to the rule:

```
%precedence "word"
%precedence "sequence"
%%
sequence:
  %empty
| sequence word      %prec "sequence"
| sequence redirect  %prec "sequence"
;

words:
  word
| words "word"
;
```

Another solution relies on associativity: provide both the token and the rule with the same precedence, but make them right-associative:

```
%right "word" "redirect"
%%
```

```
sequence:
  %empty
| sequence word      %prec "word"
| sequence redirect  %prec "redirect"
;
```

5.7 Mysterious Conflicts

Sometimes reduce/reduce conflicts can occur that don't look warranted. Here is an example:

```
%%
def: param_spec return_spec ',';
param_spec:
  type
| name_list ':' type
;

return_spec:
  type
| name ':' type
;

type: "id";

name: "id";
name_list:
  name
| name ',' name_list
;
```

It would seem that this grammar can be parsed with only a single token of lookahead: when a `param_spec` is being read, an `"id"` is a `name` if a comma or colon follows, or a `type` if another `"id"` follows. In other words, this grammar is LR(1).

However, for historical reasons, Bison cannot by default handle all LR(1) grammars. In this grammar, two contexts, that after an `"id"` at the beginning of a `param_spec` and likewise at the beginning of a `return_spec`, are similar enough that Bison assumes they are the same. They appear similar because the same set of rules would be active—the rule for reducing to a `name` and that for reducing to a `type`. Bison is unable to determine at that stage of processing that the rules would require different lookahead tokens in the two contexts, so it makes a single parser state for them both. Combining the two contexts causes a conflict later. In parser terminology, this occurrence means that the grammar is not LALR(1).

For many practical grammars (specifically those that fall into the non-LR(1) class), the limitations of LALR(1) result in difficulties beyond just mysterious reduce/reduce conflicts. The best way to fix all these problems is to select a different parser table construction algorithm. Either IELR(1) or canonical LR(1) would suffice, but the former is more efficient and easier to debug during development. See Section 5.8.1 [LR Table Construction], page 118, for details. (Bison's IELR(1) and canonical LR(1) implementations are experimental. More user feedback will help to stabilize them.)

If you instead wish to work around LALR(1)'s limitations, you can often fix a mysterious conflict by identifying the two parser states that are being confused, and adding something to make them look distinct. In the above example, adding one rule to `return_spec` as follows makes the problem go away:

```
   . . .
return_spec:
  type
| name ':' type
| "id" "bogus"       /* This rule is never used.  */
;
```

This corrects the problem because it introduces the possibility of an additional active rule in the context after the `"id"` at the beginning of `return_spec`. This rule is not active in the corresponding context in a `param_spec`, so the two contexts receive distinct parser states. As long as the token `"bogus"` is never generated by `yylex`, the added rule cannot alter the way actual input is parsed.

In this particular example, there is another way to solve the problem: rewrite the rule for `return_spec` to use `"id"` directly instead of via `name`. This also causes the two confusing contexts to have different sets of active rules, because the one for `return_spec` activates the altered rule for `return_spec` rather than the one for `name`.

```
param_spec:
  type
| name_list ':' type
;

return_spec:
  type
| "id" ':' type
;
```

For a more detailed exposition of LALR(1) parsers and parser generators, see [DeRemer 1982], page 209.

5.8 Tuning LR

The default behavior of Bison's LR-based parsers is chosen mostly for historical reasons, but that behavior is often not robust. For example, in the previous section, we discussed the mysterious conflicts that can be produced by LALR(1), Bison's default parser table construction algorithm. Another example is Bison's `%define parse.error verbose` directive, which instructs the generated parser to produce verbose syntax error messages, which can sometimes contain incorrect information.

In this section, we explore several modern features of Bison that allow you to tune fundamental aspects of the generated LR-based parsers. Some of these features easily eliminate shortcomings like those mentioned above. Others can be helpful purely for understanding your parser.

Most of the features discussed in this section are still experimental. More user feedback will help to stabilize them.

5.8.1 LR Table Construction

For historical reasons, Bison constructs LALR(1) parser tables by default. However, LALR does not possess the full language-recognition power of LR. As a result, the behavior of parsers employing LALR parser tables is often mysterious. We presented a simple example of this effect in Section 5.7 [Mysterious Conflicts], page 116.

As we also demonstrated in that example, the traditional approach to eliminating such mysterious behavior is to restructure the grammar. Unfortunately, doing so correctly is often difficult. Moreover, merely discovering that LALR causes mysterious behavior in your parser can be difficult as well.

Fortunately, Bison provides an easy way to eliminate the possibility of such mysterious behavior altogether. You simply need to activate a more powerful parser table construction algorithm by using the %define lr.type directive.

%define lr.type *type*   [Directive]
> Specify the type of parser tables within the LR(1) family. The accepted values for *type* are:
>
> - lalr (default)
> - ielr
> - canonical-lr
>
> (This feature is experimental. More user feedback will help to stabilize it.)

For example, to activate IELR, you might add the following directive to you grammar file:

```
%define lr.type ielr
```

For the example in Section 5.7 [Mysterious Conflicts], page 116, the mysterious conflict is then eliminated, so there is no need to invest time in comprehending the conflict or restructuring the grammar to fix it. If, during future development, the grammar evolves such that all mysterious behavior would have disappeared using just LALR, you need not fear that continuing to use IELR will result in unnecessarily large parser tables. That is, IELR generates LALR tables when LALR (using a deterministic parsing algorithm) is sufficient to support the full language-recognition power of LR. Thus, by enabling IELR at the start of grammar development, you can safely and completely eliminate the need to consider LALR's shortcomings.

While IELR is almost always preferable, there are circumstances where LALR or the canonical LR parser tables described by Knuth (see [Knuth 1965], page 209) can be useful. Here we summarize the relative advantages of each parser table construction algorithm within Bison:

- LALR

  There are at least two scenarios where LALR can be worthwhile:

  - GLR without static conflict resolution.

    When employing GLR parsers (see Section 1.5 [GLR Parsers], page 20), if you do not resolve any conflicts statically (for example, with %left or %precedence), then the parser explores all potential parses of any given input. In this case, the choice of parser table construction algorithm is guaranteed not to alter the language accepted by the parser. LALR parser tables are the smallest parser tables Bison can currently construct, so they may then be preferable. Nevertheless, once you begin to resolve conflicts statically, GLR behaves more like a deterministic parser in the syntactic contexts where those conflicts appear, and so either IELR or canonical LR can then be helpful to avoid LALR's mysterious behavior.

- Malformed grammars.

  Occasionally during development, an especially malformed grammar with a major recurring flaw may severely impede the IELR or canonical LR parser table construction algorithm. LALR can be a quick way to construct parser tables in order to investigate such problems while ignoring the more subtle differences from IELR and canonical LR.

- IELR

  IELR (Inadequacy Elimination LR) is a minimal LR algorithm. That is, given any grammar (LR or non-LR), parsers using IELR or canonical LR parser tables always accept exactly the same set of sentences. However, like LALR, IELR merges parser states during parser table construction so that the number of parser states is often an order of magnitude less than for canonical LR. More importantly, because canonical LR's extra parser states may contain duplicate conflicts in the case of non-LR grammars, the number of conflicts for IELR is often an order of magnitude less as well. This effect can significantly reduce the complexity of developing a grammar.

- Canonical LR

  While inefficient, canonical LR parser tables can be an interesting means to explore a grammar because they possess a property that IELR and LALR tables do not. That is, if %nonassoc is not used and default reductions are left disabled (see Section 5.8.2 [Default Reductions], page 119), then, for every left context of every canonical LR state, the set of tokens accepted by that state is guaranteed to be the exact set of tokens that is syntactically acceptable in that left context. It might then seem that an advantage of canonical LR parsers in production is that, under the above constraints, they are guaranteed to detect a syntax error as soon as possible without performing any unnecessary reductions. However, IELR parsers that use LAC are also able to achieve this behavior without sacrificing %nonassoc or default reductions. For details and a few caveats of LAC, see Section 5.8.3 [LAC], page 121.

For a more detailed exposition of the mysterious behavior in LALR parsers and the benefits of IELR, see [Denny 2008 March], page 209, and [Denny 2010 November], page 209.

5.8.2 Default Reductions

After parser table construction, Bison identifies the reduction with the largest lookahead set in each parser state. To reduce the size of the parser state, traditional Bison behavior is to remove that lookahead set and to assign that reduction to be the default parser action. Such a reduction is known as a *default reduction*.

Default reductions affect more than the size of the parser tables. They also affect the behavior of the parser:

- Delayed `yylex` invocations.

  A *consistent state* is a state that has only one possible parser action. If that action is a reduction and is encoded as a default reduction, then that consistent state is called a *defaulted state*. Upon reaching a defaulted state, a Bison-generated parser does not bother to invoke `yylex` to fetch the next token before performing the reduction. In other words, whether default reductions are enabled in consistent states determines how soon a Bison-generated parser invokes `yylex` for a token: immediately when it *reaches* that token in the input or when it eventually *needs* that token as a lookahead to determine the next parser action. Traditionally, default reductions are enabled, and so the parser exhibits the latter behavior.

  The presence of defaulted states is an important consideration when designing `yylex` and the grammar file. That is, if the behavior of `yylex` can influence or be influenced by the semantic actions associated with the reductions in defaulted states, then the delay of the next `yylex` invocation until after those reductions is significant. For example, the semantic actions might pop a scope stack that `yylex` uses to determine what token to return. Thus, the delay might be necessary to ensure that `yylex` does not look up the next token in a scope that should already be considered closed.

- Delayed syntax error detection.

  When the parser fetches a new token by invoking `yylex`, it checks whether there is an action for that token in the current parser state. The parser detects a syntax error if and only if either (1) there is no action for that token or (2) the action for that token is the error action (due to the use of `%nonassoc`). However, if there is a default reduction in that state (which might or might not be a defaulted state), then it is impossible for condition 1 to exist. That is, all tokens have an action. Thus, the parser sometimes fails to detect the syntax error until it reaches a later state.

  While default reductions never cause the parser to accept syntactically incorrect sentences, the delay of syntax error detection can have unexpected effects on the behavior of the parser. However, the delay can be caused anyway by parser state merging and the use of `%nonassoc`, and it can be fixed by another Bison feature, LAC. We discuss the effects of delayed syntax error detection and LAC more in the next section (see Section 5.8.3 [LAC], page 121).

For canonical LR, the only default reduction that Bison enables by default is the accept action, which appears only in the accepting state, which has no other action and is thus a defaulted state. However, the default accept action does not delay any `yylex` invocation or syntax error detection because the accept action ends the parse.

For LALR and IELR, Bison enables default reductions in nearly all states by default. There are only two exceptions. First, states that have a shift action on the **error** token do not have default reductions because delayed syntax error detection could then prevent the **error** token from ever being shifted in that state. However, parser state merging can cause the same effect anyway, and LAC fixes it in both cases, so future versions of Bison might drop this exception when LAC is activated. Second, GLR parsers do not record the default reduction as the action on a lookahead token for which there is a conflict. The correct action in this case is to split the parse instead.

To adjust which states have default reductions enabled, use the `%define` `lr.default-reduction` directive.

%define lr.default-reduction *where* [Directive]

Specify the kind of states that are permitted to contain default reductions. The accepted values of *where* are:

- `most` (default for LALR and IELR)
- `consistent`
- `accepting` (default for canonical LR)

(The ability to specify where default reductions are permitted is experimental. More user feedback will help to stabilize it.)

5.8.3 LAC

Canonical LR, IELR, and LALR can suffer from a couple of problems upon encountering a syntax error. First, the parser might perform additional parser stack reductions before discovering the syntax error. Such reductions can perform user semantic actions that are unexpected because they are based on an invalid token, and they cause error recovery to begin in a different syntactic context than the one in which the invalid token was encountered. Second, when verbose error messages are enabled (see Section 4.7 [Error Reporting], page 102), the expected token list in the syntax error message can both contain invalid tokens and omit valid tokens.

The culprits for the above problems are %nonassoc, default reductions in inconsistent states (see Section 5.8.2 [Default Reductions], page 119), and parser state merging. Because IELR and LALR merge parser states, they suffer the most. Canonical LR can suffer only if %nonassoc is used or if default reductions are enabled for inconsistent states.

LAC (Lookahead Correction) is a new mechanism within the parsing algorithm that solves these problems for canonical LR, IELR, and LALR without sacrificing %nonassoc, default reductions, or state merging. You can enable LAC with the %define parse.lac directive.

%define parse.lac *value* [Directive]

Enable LAC to improve syntax error handling.

- `none` (default)
- `full`

(This feature is experimental. More user feedback will help to stabilize it. Moreover, it is currently only available for deterministic parsers in C.)

Conceptually, the LAC mechanism is straight-forward. Whenever the parser fetches a new token from the scanner so that it can determine the next parser action, it immediately suspends normal parsing and performs an exploratory parse using a temporary copy of the normal parser state stack. During this exploratory parse, the parser does not perform user semantic actions. If the exploratory parse reaches a shift action, normal parsing then resumes on the normal parser stacks. If the exploratory parse reaches an error instead, the parser reports a syntax error. If verbose syntax error messages are enabled, the parser must then discover the list of expected tokens, so it performs a separate exploratory parse for each token in the grammar.

There is one subtlety about the use of LAC. That is, when in a consistent parser state with a default reduction, the parser will not attempt to fetch a token from the scanner because no lookahead is needed to determine the next parser action. Thus, whether default reductions are enabled in consistent states (see Section 5.8.2 [Default Reductions], page 119) affects how soon the parser detects a syntax error: immediately when it *reaches* an erroneous token or when it eventually *needs* that token as a lookahead to determine the next parser action. The latter behavior is probably more intuitive, so Bison currently provides no way to achieve the former behavior while default reductions are enabled in consistent states.

Thus, when LAC is in use, for some fixed decision of whether to enable default reductions in consistent states, canonical LR and IELR behave almost exactly the same for both syntactically acceptable and syntactically unacceptable input. While LALR still does not support the full language-recognition power of canonical LR and IELR, LAC at least enables LALR's syntax error handling to correctly reflect LALR's language-recognition power.

There are a few caveats to consider when using LAC:

- Infinite parsing loops.

  IELR plus LAC does have one shortcoming relative to canonical LR. Some parsers generated by Bison can loop infinitely. LAC does not fix infinite parsing loops that occur between encountering a syntax error and detecting it, but enabling canonical LR or disabling default reductions sometimes does.

- Verbose error message limitations.

  Because of internationalization considerations, Bison-generated parsers limit the size of the expected token list they are willing to report in a verbose syntax error message. If the number of expected tokens exceeds that limit, the list is simply dropped from the message. Enabling LAC can increase the size of the list and thus cause the parser to drop it. Of course, dropping the list is better than reporting an incorrect list.

- Performance.

  Because LAC requires many parse actions to be performed twice, it can have a performance penalty. However, not all parse actions must be performed twice. Specifically, during a series of default reductions in consistent states and shift actions, the parser never has to initiate an exploratory parse. Moreover, the most time-consuming tasks in a parse are often the file I/O, the lexical analysis performed by the scanner, and the user's semantic actions, but none of these are performed during the exploratory parse. Finally, the base of the temporary stack used during an exploratory parse is a pointer into the normal parser state stack so that the stack is never physically copied. In our experience, the performance penalty of LAC has proved insignificant for practical grammars.

While the LAC algorithm shares techniques that have been recognized in the parser community for years, for the publication that introduces LAC, see [Denny 2010 May], page 209.

5.8.4 Unreachable States

If there exists no sequence of transitions from the parser's start state to some state *s*, then Bison considers *s* to be an *unreachable state*. A state can become unreachable during conflict resolution if Bison disables a shift action leading to it from a predecessor state.

By default, Bison removes unreachable states from the parser after conflict resolution because they are useless in the generated parser. However, keeping unreachable states is sometimes useful when trying to understand the relationship between the parser and the grammar.

%define lr.keep-unreachable-state *value*   [Directive]

> Request that Bison allow unreachable states to remain in the parser tables. *value* must be a Boolean. The default is **false**.

There are a few caveats to consider:

- Missing or extraneous warnings.

  Unreachable states may contain conflicts and may use rules not used in any other state. Thus, keeping unreachable states may induce warnings that are irrelevant to your parser's behavior, and it may eliminate warnings that are relevant. Of course, the change in warnings may actually be relevant to a parser table analysis that wants to keep unreachable states, so this behavior will likely remain in future Bison releases.

- Other useless states.

  While Bison is able to remove unreachable states, it is not guaranteed to remove other kinds of useless states. Specifically, when Bison disables reduce actions during conflict resolution, some goto actions may become useless, and thus some additional states may become useless. If Bison were to compute which goto actions were useless and then disable those actions, it could identify such states as unreachable and then remove those states. However, Bison does not compute which goto actions are useless.

5.9 Generalized LR (GLR) Parsing

Bison produces *deterministic* parsers that choose uniquely when to reduce and which reduction to apply based on a summary of the preceding input and on one extra token of lookahead. As a result, normal Bison handles a proper subset of the family of context-free languages. Ambiguous grammars, since they have strings with more than one possible sequence of reductions cannot have deterministic parsers in this sense. The same is true of languages that require more than one symbol of lookahead, since the parser lacks the information necessary to make a decision at the point it must be made in a shift-reduce parser. Finally, as previously mentioned (see Section 5.7 [Mysterious Conflicts], page 116), there are languages where Bison's default choice of how to summarize the input seen so far loses necessary information.

When you use the '%glr-parser' declaration in your grammar file, Bison generates a parser that uses a different algorithm, called Generalized LR (or GLR). A Bison GLR parser uses the same basic algorithm for parsing as an ordinary Bison parser, but behaves differently in cases where there is a shift-reduce conflict that has not been resolved by precedence rules (see Section 5.3 [Precedence], page 109) or a reduce-reduce conflict. When a GLR parser encounters such a situation, it effectively *splits* into a several parsers, one for each possible shift or reduction. These parsers then proceed as usual, consuming tokens in lock-step. Some of the stacks may encounter other conflicts and split further, with the result that instead of a sequence of states, a Bison GLR parsing stack is what is in effect a tree of states.

In effect, each stack represents a guess as to what the proper parse is. Additional input may indicate that a guess was wrong, in which case the appropriate stack silently disappears. Otherwise, the semantics actions generated in each stack are saved, rather than being executed immediately. When a stack disappears, its saved semantic actions never get executed. When a reduction causes two stacks to become equivalent, their sets of semantic actions are both saved with the state that results from the reduction. We say that two stacks are equivalent when they both represent the same sequence of states, and each pair of corresponding states represents a grammar symbol that produces the same segment of the input token stream.

Whenever the parser makes a transition from having multiple states to having one, it reverts to the normal deterministic parsing algorithm, after resolving and executing the saved-up actions. At this transition, some of the states on the stack will have semantic values that are sets (actually multisets) of possible actions. The parser tries to pick one of the actions by first finding one whose rule has the highest dynamic precedence, as set by the '%dprec' declaration. Otherwise, if the alternative actions are not ordered by precedence, but there the same merging function is declared for both rules by the '%merge' declaration, Bison resolves and evaluates both and then calls the merge function on the result. Otherwise, it reports an ambiguity.

It is possible to use a data structure for the GLR parsing tree that permits the processing of any LR(1) grammar in linear time (in the size of the input), any unambiguous (not necessarily LR(1)) grammar in quadratic worst-case time, and any general (possibly ambiguous) context-free grammar in cubic worst-case time. However, Bison currently uses a simpler data structure that requires time proportional to the length of the input times the maximum number of stacks required for any prefix of the input. Thus, really ambiguous or nondeterministic grammars can require exponential time and space to process. Such badly behaving examples, however, are not generally of practical interest. Usually, nondeterminism in a grammar is local—the parser is "in doubt" only for a few tokens at a time. Therefore, the current data structure should generally be adequate. On LR(1) portions of a grammar, in particular, it is only slightly slower than with the deterministic LR(1) Bison parser.

For a more detailed exposition of GLR parsers, see [Scott 2000], page 209.

5.10 Memory Management, and How to Avoid Memory Exhaustion

The Bison parser stack can run out of memory if too many tokens are shifted and not reduced. When this happens, the parser function **yyparse** calls **yyerror** and then returns 2.

Because Bison parsers have growing stacks, hitting the upper limit usually results from using a right recursion instead of a left recursion, see Section 3.3.3 [Recursive Rules], page 60.

By defining the macro **YYMAXDEPTH**, you can control how deep the parser stack can become before memory is exhausted. Define the macro with a value that is an integer. This value is the maximum number of tokens that can be shifted (and not reduced) before overflow.

The stack space allowed is not necessarily allocated. If you specify a large value for **YYMAXDEPTH**, the parser normally allocates a small stack at first, and then makes it bigger by stages as needed. This increasing allocation happens automatically and silently. Therefore, you do not need to make **YYMAXDEPTH** painfully small merely to save space for ordinary inputs that do not need much stack.

However, do not allow `YYMAXDEPTH` to be a value so large that arithmetic overflow could occur when calculating the size of the stack space. Also, do not allow `YYMAXDEPTH` to be less than `YYINITDEPTH`.

The default value of `YYMAXDEPTH`, if you do not define it, is 10000.

You can control how much stack is allocated initially by defining the macro `YYINITDEPTH` to a positive integer. For the deterministic parser in C, this value must be a compile-time constant unless you are assuming C99 or some other target language or compiler that allows variable-length arrays. The default is 200.

Do not allow `YYINITDEPTH` to be greater than `YYMAXDEPTH`.

You can generate a deterministic parser containing C++ user code from the default (C) skeleton, as well as from the C++ skeleton (see Section 10.1 [C++ Parsers], page 157). However, if you do use the default skeleton and want to allow the parsing stack to grow, be careful not to use semantic types or location types that require non-trivial copy constructors. The C skeleton bypasses these constructors when copying data to new, larger stacks.

6 Error Recovery

It is not usually acceptable to have a program terminate on a syntax error. For example, a compiler should recover sufficiently to parse the rest of the input file and check it for errors; a calculator should accept another expression.

In a simple interactive command parser where each input is one line, it may be sufficient to allow **yyparse** to return 1 on error and have the caller ignore the rest of the input line when that happens (and then call **yyparse** again). But this is inadequate for a compiler, because it forgets all the syntactic context leading up to the error. A syntax error deep within a function in the compiler input should not cause the compiler to treat the following line like the beginning of a source file.

You can define how to recover from a syntax error by writing rules to recognize the special token **error**. This is a terminal symbol that is always defined (you need not declare it) and reserved for error handling. The Bison parser generates an **error** token whenever a syntax error happens; if you have provided a rule to recognize this token in the current context, the parse can continue.

For example:

```
stmts:
  %empty
| stmts '\n'
| stmts exp '\n'
| stmts error '\n'
```

The fourth rule in this example says that an error followed by a newline makes a valid addition to any **stmts**.

What happens if a syntax error occurs in the middle of an **exp**? The error recovery rule, interpreted strictly, applies to the precise sequence of a **stmts**, an **error** and a newline. If an error occurs in the middle of an **exp**, there will probably be some additional tokens and subexpressions on the stack after the last **stmts**, and there will be tokens to read before the next newline. So the rule is not applicable in the ordinary way.

But Bison can force the situation to fit the rule, by discarding part of the semantic context and part of the input. First it discards states and objects from the stack until it gets back to a state in which the **error** token is acceptable. (This means that the subexpressions already parsed are discarded, back to the last complete **stmts**.) At this point the **error** token can be shifted. Then, if the old lookahead token is not acceptable to be shifted next, the parser reads tokens and discards them until it finds a token which is acceptable. In this example, Bison reads and discards input until the next newline so that the fourth rule can apply. Note that discarded symbols are possible sources of memory leaks, see Section 3.7.6 [Freeing Discarded Symbols], page 77, for a means to reclaim this memory.

The choice of error rules in the grammar is a choice of strategies for error recovery. A simple and useful strategy is simply to skip the rest of the current input line or current statement if an error is detected:

```
stmt: error ';'  /* On error, skip until ';' is read.  */
```

It is also useful to recover to the matching close-delimiter of an opening-delimiter that has already been parsed. Otherwise the close-delimiter will probably appear to be unmatched, and generate another, spurious error message:

```
primary:
    '(' expr ')'
|   '(' error ')'
...
;
```

Error recovery strategies are necessarily guesses. When they guess wrong, one syntax error often leads to another. In the above example, the error recovery rule guesses that an error is due to bad input within one stmt. Suppose that instead a spurious semicolon is inserted in the middle of a valid stmt. After the error recovery rule recovers from the first error, another syntax error will be found straightaway, since the text following the spurious semicolon is also an invalid stmt.

To prevent an outpouring of error messages, the parser will output no error message for another syntax error that happens shortly after the first; only after three consecutive input tokens have been successfully shifted will error messages resume.

Note that rules which accept the error token may have actions, just as any other rules can.

You can make error messages resume immediately by using the macro yyerrok in an action. If you do this in the error rule's action, no error messages will be suppressed. This macro requires no arguments; 'yyerrok;' is a valid C statement.

The previous lookahead token is reanalyzed immediately after an error. If this is unacceptable, then the macro yyclearin may be used to clear this token. Write the statement 'yyclearin;' in the error rule's action. See Section 4.8 [Special Features for Use in Actions], page 103.

For example, suppose that on a syntax error, an error handling routine is called that advances the input stream to some point where parsing should once again commence. The next symbol returned by the lexical scanner is probably correct. The previous lookahead token ought to be discarded with 'yyclearin;'.

The expression YYRECOVERING () yields 1 when the parser is recovering from a syntax error, and 0 otherwise. Syntax error diagnostics are suppressed while recovering from a syntax error.

7 Handling Context Dependencies

The Bison paradigm is to parse tokens first, then group them into larger syntactic units. In many languages, the meaning of a token is affected by its context. Although this violates the Bison paradigm, certain techniques (known as *kludges*) may enable you to write Bison parsers for such languages.

(Actually, "kludge" means any technique that gets its job done but is neither clean nor robust.)

7.1 Semantic Info in Token Types

The C language has a context dependency: the way an identifier is used depends on what its current meaning is. For example, consider this:

```
foo (x);
```

This looks like a function call statement, but if `foo` is a typedef name, then this is actually a declaration of `x`. How can a Bison parser for C decide how to parse this input?

The method used in GNU C is to have two different token types, `IDENTIFIER` and `TYPENAME`. When `yylex` finds an identifier, it looks up the current declaration of the identifier in order to decide which token type to return: `TYPENAME` if the identifier is declared as a typedef, `IDENTIFIER` otherwise.

The grammar rules can then express the context dependency by the choice of token type to recognize. `IDENTIFIER` is accepted as an expression, but `TYPENAME` is not. `TYPENAME` can start a declaration, but `IDENTIFIER` cannot. In contexts where the meaning of the identifier is *not* significant, such as in declarations that can shadow a typedef name, either `TYPENAME` or `IDENTIFIER` is accepted—there is one rule for each of the two token types.

This technique is simple to use if the decision of which kinds of identifiers to allow is made at a place close to where the identifier is parsed. But in C this is not always so: C allows a declaration to redeclare a typedef name provided an explicit type has been specified earlier:

```
typedef int foo, bar;
int baz (void)
{
  static bar (bar);      /* redeclare bar as static variable */
  extern foo foo (foo);  /* redeclare foo as function */
  return foo (bar);
}
```

Unfortunately, the name being declared is separated from the declaration construct itself by a complicated syntactic structure—the "declarator".

As a result, part of the Bison parser for C needs to be duplicated, with all the nonterminal names changed: once for parsing a declaration in which a typedef name can be redefined, and once for parsing a declaration in which that can't be done. Here is a part of the duplication, with actions omitted for brevity:

```
initdcl:
  declarator maybeasm '=' init
| declarator maybeasm
;
```

```
notype_initdcl:
  notype_declarator maybeasm '=' init
| notype_declarator maybeasm
;
```

Here `initdcl` can redeclare a typedef name, but `notype_initdcl` cannot. The distinction between `declarator` and `notype_declarator` is the same sort of thing.

There is some similarity between this technique and a lexical tie-in (described next), in that information which alters the lexical analysis is changed during parsing by other parts of the program. The difference is here the information is global, and is used for other purposes in the program. A true lexical tie-in has a special-purpose flag controlled by the syntactic context.

7.2 Lexical Tie-ins

One way to handle context-dependency is the *lexical tie-in*: a flag which is set by Bison actions, whose purpose is to alter the way tokens are parsed.

For example, suppose we have a language vaguely like C, but with a special construct 'hex (*hex-expr*)'. After the keyword `hex` comes an expression in parentheses in which all integers are hexadecimal. In particular, the token 'a1b' must be treated as an integer rather than as an identifier if it appears in that context. Here is how you can do it:

```
%{
  int hexflag;
  int yylex (void);
  void yyerror (char const *);
%}
%%
...
expr:
  IDENTIFIER
| constant
| HEX '('        { hexflag = 1; }
    expr ')'     { hexflag = 0; $$ = $4; }
| expr '+' expr  { $$ = make_sum ($1, $3); }
...
;

constant:
  INTEGER
| STRING
;
```

Here we assume that `yylex` looks at the value of `hexflag`; when it is nonzero, all integers are parsed in hexadecimal, and tokens starting with letters are parsed as integers if possible.

The declaration of `hexflag` shown in the prologue of the grammar file is needed to make it accessible to the actions (see Section 3.1.1 [The Prologue], page 51). You must also write the code in `yylex` to obey the flag.

7.3 Lexical Tie-ins and Error Recovery

Lexical tie-ins make strict demands on any error recovery rules you have. See Chapter 6 [Error Recovery], page 127.

The reason for this is that the purpose of an error recovery rule is to abort the parsing of one construct and resume in some larger construct. For example, in C-like languages, a typical error recovery rule is to skip tokens until the next semicolon, and then start a new statement, like this:

```
stmt:
  expr ';'
| IF '(' expr ')' stmt { ... }
...
| error ';'  { hexflag = 0; }
;
```

If there is a syntax error in the middle of a 'hex (*expr*)' construct, this error rule will apply, and then the action for the completed 'hex (*expr*)' will never run. So hexflag would remain set for the entire rest of the input, or until the next hex keyword, causing identifiers to be misinterpreted as integers.

To avoid this problem the error recovery rule itself clears hexflag.

There may also be an error recovery rule that works within expressions. For example, there could be a rule which applies within parentheses and skips to the close-parenthesis:

```
expr:
  ...
| '(' expr ')'  { $$ = $2; }
| '(' error ')'
...
```

If this rule acts within the hex construct, it is not going to abort that construct (since it applies to an inner level of parentheses within the construct). Therefore, it should not clear the flag: the rest of the hex construct should be parsed with the flag still in effect.

What if there is an error recovery rule which might abort out of the hex construct or might not, depending on circumstances? There is no way you can write the action to determine whether a hex construct is being aborted or not. So if you are using a lexical tie-in, you had better make sure your error recovery rules are not of this kind. Each rule must be such that you can be sure that it always will, or always won't, have to clear the flag.

8 Debugging Your Parser

Developing a parser can be a challenge, especially if you don't understand the algorithm (see Chapter 5 [The Bison Parser Algorithm], page 107). This chapter explains how understand and debug a parser.

The first sections focus on the static part of the parser: its structure. They explain how to generate and read the detailed description of the automaton. There are several formats available:

— as text, see Section 8.1 [Understanding Your Parser], page 133;

— as a graph, see Section 8.2 [Visualizing Your Parser], page 139;

— or as a markup report that can be turned, for instance, into HTML, see Section 8.3 [Visualizing your parser in multiple formats], page 142.

The last section focuses on the dynamic part of the parser: how to enable and understand the parser run-time traces (see Section 8.4 [Tracing Your Parser], page 142).

8.1 Understanding Your Parser

As documented elsewhere (see Chapter 5 [The Bison Parser Algorithm], page 107) Bison parsers are *shift/reduce automata*. In some cases (much more frequent than one would hope), looking at this automaton is required to tune or simply fix a parser.

The textual file is generated when the options `--report` or `--verbose` are specified, see Chapter 9 [Invoking Bison], page 149. Its name is made by removing '.tab.c' or '.c' from the parser implementation file name, and adding '.output' instead. Therefore, if the grammar file is `foo.y`, then the parser implementation file is called `foo.tab.c` by default. As a consequence, the verbose output file is called `foo.output`.

The following grammar file, `calc.y`, will be used in the sequel:

```
%token NUM STR
%left '+' '-'
%left '*'
%%
exp:
  exp '+' exp
| exp '-' exp
| exp '*' exp
| exp '/' exp
| NUM
;
useless: STR;
%%
```

bison reports:

```
calc.y: warning: 1 nonterminal useless in grammar
calc.y: warning: 1 rule useless in grammar
calc.y:12.1-7: warning: nonterminal useless in grammar: useless
calc.y:12.10-12: warning: rule useless in grammar: useless: STR
calc.y: conflicts: 7 shift/reduce
```

When given `--report=state`, in addition to `calc.tab.c`, it creates a file `calc.output` with contents detailed below. The order of the output and the exact presentation might vary, but the interpretation is the same.

The first section reports useless tokens, nonterminals and rules. Useless nonterminals and rules are removed in order to produce a smaller parser, but useless tokens are preserved, since they might be used by the scanner (note the difference between "useless" and "unused" below):

```
Nonterminals useless in grammar
    useless

Terminals unused in grammar
    STR

Rules useless in grammar
    6 useless: STR
```

The next section lists states that still have conflicts.

```
State 8 conflicts: 1 shift/reduce
State 9 conflicts: 1 shift/reduce
State 10 conflicts: 1 shift/reduce
State 11 conflicts: 4 shift/reduce
```

Then Bison reproduces the exact grammar it used:

```
Grammar

    0 $accept: exp $end

    1 exp: exp '+' exp
    2    | exp '-' exp
    3    | exp '*' exp
    4    | exp '/' exp
    5    | NUM
```

and reports the uses of the symbols:

```
Terminals, with rules where they appear

$end (0) 0
'*' (42) 3
'+' (43) 1
'-' (45) 2
'/' (47) 4
error (256)
NUM (258) 5
STR (259)
```

```
Nonterminals, with rules where they appear

$accept (9)
    on left: 0
exp (10)
    on left: 1 2 3 4 5, on right: 0 1 2 3 4
```

Bison then proceeds onto the automaton itself, describing each state with its set of *items*, also known as *pointed rules*. Each item is a production rule together with a point ('.') marking the location of the input cursor.

```
State 0

    0 $accept: . exp $end

    NUM  shift, and go to state 1

    exp  go to state 2
```

This reads as follows: "state 0 corresponds to being at the very beginning of the parsing, in the initial rule, right before the start symbol (here, **exp**). When the parser returns to this state right after having reduced a rule that produced an **exp**, the control flow jumps to state 2. If there is no such transition on a nonterminal symbol, and the lookahead is a NUM, then this token is shifted onto the parse stack, and the control flow jumps to state 1. Any other lookahead triggers a syntax error."

Even though the only active rule in state 0 seems to be rule 0, the report lists NUM as a lookahead token because NUM can be at the beginning of any rule deriving an **exp**. By default Bison reports the so-called *core* or *kernel* of the item set, but if you want to see more detail you can invoke **bison** with **--report=itemset** to list the derived items as well:

```
State 0

    0 $accept: . exp $end
    1 exp: . exp '+' exp
    2    | . exp '-' exp
    3    | . exp '*' exp
    4    | . exp '/' exp
    5    | . NUM

    NUM  shift, and go to state 1

    exp  go to state 2
```

In the state 1...

```
State 1

    5 exp: NUM .

    $default  reduce using rule 5 (exp)
```

the rule 5, 'exp: NUM;', is completed. Whatever the lookahead token ('$default'), the parser will reduce it. If it was coming from State 0, then, after this reduction it will return to state 0, and will jump to state 2 ('exp: go to state 2').

```
State 2

    0 $accept: exp . $end
    1 exp: exp . '+' exp
    2    | exp . '-' exp
    3    | exp . '*' exp
    4    | exp . '/' exp

    $end  shift, and go to state 3
    '+'   shift, and go to state 4
    '-'   shift, and go to state 5
    '*'   shift, and go to state 6
    '/'   shift, and go to state 7
```

In state 2, the automaton can only shift a symbol. For instance, because of the item 'exp: exp . '+' exp', if the lookahead is '+' it is shifted onto the parse stack, and the automaton jumps to state 4, corresponding to the item 'exp: exp '+' . exp'. Since there is no default action, any lookahead not listed triggers a syntax error.

The state 3 is named the *final state*, or the *accepting state*:

```
State 3

    0 $accept: exp $end .

    $default  accept
```

the initial rule is completed (the start symbol and the end-of-input were read), the parsing exits successfully.

The interpretation of states 4 to 7 is straightforward, and is left to the reader.

```
State 4

    1 exp: exp '+' . exp

    NUM  shift, and go to state 1

    exp  go to state 8


State 5

    2 exp: exp '-' . exp

    NUM  shift, and go to state 1

    exp  go to state 9
```

```
State 6

    3 exp: exp '*' . exp

    NUM  shift, and go to state 1

    exp  go to state 10


State 7

    4 exp: exp '/' . exp

    NUM  shift, and go to state 1

    exp  go to state 11
```

As was announced in beginning of the report, 'State 8 conflicts: 1 shift/reduce':

```
State 8

    1 exp: exp . '+' exp
    1    | exp '+' exp .
    2    | exp . '-' exp
    3    | exp . '*' exp
    4    | exp . '/' exp

    '*'  shift, and go to state 6
    '/'  shift, and go to state 7

    '/'        [reduce using rule 1 (exp)]
    $default  reduce using rule 1 (exp)
```

Indeed, there are two actions associated to the lookahead '/': either shifting (and going to state 7), or reducing rule 1. The conflict means that either the grammar is ambiguous, or the parser lacks information to make the right decision. Indeed the grammar is ambiguous, as, since we did not specify the precedence of '/', the sentence 'NUM + NUM / NUM' can be parsed as 'NUM + (NUM / NUM)', which corresponds to shifting '/', or as '(NUM + NUM) / NUM', which corresponds to reducing rule 1.

Because in deterministic parsing a single decision can be made, Bison arbitrarily chose to disable the reduction, see Section 5.2 [Shift/Reduce Conflicts], page 108. Discarded actions are reported between square brackets.

Note that all the previous states had a single possible action: either shifting the next token and going to the corresponding state, or reducing a single rule. In the other cases, i.e., when shifting *and* reducing is possible or when *several* reductions are possible, the lookahead is required to select the action. State 8 is one such state: if the lookahead is '*' or '/' then the action is shifting, otherwise the action is reducing rule 1. In other words, the

first two items, corresponding to rule 1, are not eligible when the lookahead token is '*', since
we specified that '*' has higher precedence than '+'. More generally, some items are eligible
only with some set of possible lookahead tokens. When run with `--report=lookahead`,
Bison specifies these lookahead tokens:

```
State 8

    1 exp: exp . '+' exp
    1    | exp '+' exp .  [$end, '+', '-', '/']
    2    | exp . '-' exp
    3    | exp . '*' exp
    4    | exp . '/' exp

    '*'  shift, and go to state 6
    '/'  shift, and go to state 7

    '/'       [reduce using rule 1 (exp)]
    $default  reduce using rule 1 (exp)
```

Note however that while 'NUM + NUM / NUM' is ambiguous (which results in the conflicts on
'/'), 'NUM + NUM * NUM' is not: the conflict was solved thanks to associativity and precedence
directives. If invoked with `--report=solved`, Bison includes information about the solved
conflicts in the report:

```
Conflict between rule 1 and token '+' resolved as reduce (%left '+').
Conflict between rule 1 and token '-' resolved as reduce (%left '-').
Conflict between rule 1 and token '*' resolved as shift ('+' < '*').
```

The remaining states are similar:

```
State 9

    1 exp: exp . '+' exp
    2    | exp . '-' exp
    2    | exp '-' exp .
    3    | exp . '*' exp
    4    | exp . '/' exp

    '*'  shift, and go to state 6
    '/'  shift, and go to state 7

    '/'       [reduce using rule 2 (exp)]
    $default  reduce using rule 2 (exp)
```

```
State 10

    1 exp: exp . '+' exp
    2    | exp . '-' exp
    3    | exp . '*' exp
    3    | exp '*' exp .
    4    | exp . '/' exp


    '/'  shift, and go to state 7

    '/'        [reduce using rule 3 (exp)]
    $default  reduce using rule 3 (exp)

State 11

    1 exp: exp . '+' exp
    2    | exp . '-' exp
    3    | exp . '*' exp
    4    | exp . '/' exp
    4    | exp '/' exp .

    '+'  shift, and go to state 4
    '-'  shift, and go to state 5
    '*'  shift, and go to state 6
    '/'  shift, and go to state 7

    '+'        [reduce using rule 4 (exp)]
    '-'        [reduce using rule 4 (exp)]
    '*'        [reduce using rule 4 (exp)]
    '/'        [reduce using rule 4 (exp)]
    $default  reduce using rule 4 (exp)
```

Observe that state 11 contains conflicts not only due to the lack of precedence of '/' with respect to '+', '-', and '*', but also because the associativity of '/' is not specified.

Bison may also produce an HTML version of this output, via an XML file and XSLT processing (see Section 8.3 [Visualizing your parser in multiple formats], page 142).

8.2 Visualizing Your Parser

As another means to gain better understanding of the shift/reduce automaton corresponding to the Bison parser, a DOT file can be generated. Note that debugging a real grammar with this is tedious at best, and impractical most of the times, because the generated files are huge (the generation of a PDF or PNG file from it will take very long, and more often than not it will fail due to memory exhaustion). This option was rather designed for beginners, to help them understand LR parsers.

This file is generated when the `--graph` option is specified (see Chapter 9 [Invoking Bison], page 149). Its name is made by removing '.tab.c' or '.c' from the parser implementation file name, and adding '.dot' instead. If the grammar file is foo.y, the Graphviz output file is called `foo.dot`. A DOT file may also be produced via an XML file and XSLT processing (see Section 8.3 [Visualizing your parser in multiple formats], page 142).

The following grammar file, `rr.y`, will be used in the sequel:

```
%%
exp: a ";" | b ".";
a: "0";
b: "0";
```

The graphical output (see Figure 8.1) is very similar to the textual one, and as such it is easier understood by making direct comparisons between them. See Chapter 8 [Debugging Your Parser], page 133, for a detailled analysis of the textual report.

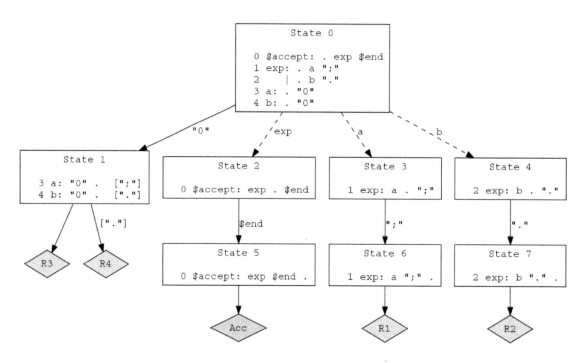

Figure 8.1: A graphical rendering of the parser.

Graphical Representation of States

The items (pointed rules) for each state are grouped together in graph nodes. Their numbering is the same as in the verbose file. See the following points, about transitions, for examples

When invoked with `--report=lookaheads`, the lookahead tokens, when needed, are shown next to the relevant rule between square brackets as a comma separated list. This is the case in the figure for the representation of reductions, below.

The transitions are represented as directed edges between the current and the target states.

Graphical Representation of Shifts

Shifts are shown as solid arrows, labelled with the lookahead token for that shift. The following describes a reduction in the `rr.output` file:

```
State 3

    1 exp: a . ";"

    ";"  shift, and go to state 6
```

A Graphviz rendering of this portion of the graph could be:

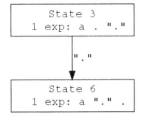

Graphical Representation of Reductions

Reductions are shown as solid arrows, leading to a diamond-shaped node bearing the number of the reduction rule. The arrow is labelled with the appropriate comma separated lookahead tokens. If the reduction is the default action for the given state, there is no such label.

This is how reductions are represented in the verbose file `rr.output`:

```
State 1

    3 a: "0" .  [";"]
    4 b: "0" .  ["."]

    "."      reduce using rule 4 (b)
    $default reduce using rule 3 (a)
```

A Graphviz rendering of this portion of the graph could be:

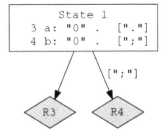

When unresolved conflicts are present, because in deterministic parsing a single decision can be made, Bison can arbitrarily choose to disable a reduction, see Section 5.2 [Shift/Reduce Conflicts], page 108. Discarded actions are distinguished by a red filling color on these nodes, just like how they are reported between square brackets in the verbose file.

The reduction corresponding to the rule number 0 is the acceptation state. It is shown as a blue diamond, labelled "Acc".

Graphical representation of go tos

The 'go to' jump transitions are represented as dotted lines bearing the name of the rule being jumped to.

8.3 Visualizing your parser in multiple formats

Bison supports two major report formats: textual output (see Section 8.1 [Understanding Your Parser], page 133) when invoked with option --verbose, and DOT (see Section 8.2 [Visualizing Your Parser], page 139) when invoked with option --graph. However, another alternative is to output an XML file that may then be, with xsltproc, rendered as either a raw text format equivalent to the verbose file, or as an HTML version of the same file, with clickable transitions, or even as a DOT. The .output and DOT files obtained via XSLT have no difference whatsoever with those obtained by invoking bison with options --verbose or --graph.

The XML file is generated when the options -x or --xml[=FILE] are specified, see Chapter 9 [Invoking Bison], page 149. If not specified, its name is made by removing '.tab.c' or '.c' from the parser implementation file name, and adding '.xml' instead. For instance, if the grammar file is foo.y, the default XML output file is foo.xml.

Bison ships with a data/xslt directory, containing XSL Transformation files to apply to the XML file. Their names are non-ambiguous:

xml2dot.xsl

> Used to output a copy of the DOT visualization of the automaton.

xml2text.xsl

> Used to output a copy of the '.output' file.

xml2xhtml.xsl

> Used to output an xhtml enhancement of the '.output' file.

Sample usage (requires xsltproc):

```
$ bison -x gr.y
$ bison --print-datadir
/usr/local/share/bison
$ xsltproc /usr/local/share/bison/xslt/xml2xhtml.xsl gr.xml >gr.html
```

8.4 Tracing Your Parser

When a Bison grammar compiles properly but parses "incorrectly", the yydebug parser-trace feature helps figuring out why.

8.4.1 Enabling Traces

There are several means to enable compilation of trace facilities:

the macro YYDEBUG

> Define the macro YYDEBUG to a nonzero value when you compile the parser. This is compliant with POSIX Yacc. You could use '-DYYDEBUG=1' as a compiler

option or you could put '#define YYDEBUG 1' in the prologue of the grammar file (see Section 3.1.1 [The Prologue], page 51).

If the %define variable api.prefix is used (see Section 3.8 [Multiple Parsers in the Same Program], page 94), for instance '%define api.prefix x', then if CDEBUG is defined, its value controls the tracing feature (enabled if and only if nonzero); otherwise tracing is enabled if and only if YYDEBUG is nonzero.

the option -t (POSIX Yacc compliant)

the option --debug (Bison extension)

Use the '-t' option when you run Bison (see Chapter 9 [Invoking Bison], page 149). With '%define api.prefix {c}', it defines CDEBUG to 1, otherwise it defines YYDEBUG to 1.

the directive '%debug'

Add the %debug directive (see Section 3.7.12 [Bison Declaration Summary], page 82). This Bison extension is maintained for backward compatibility with previous versions of Bison.

the variable 'parse.trace'

Add the '%define parse.trace' directive (see Section 3.7.13 [parse.trace], page 86), or pass the -Dparse.trace option (see Section 9.1 [Bison Options], page 149). This is a Bison extension, which is especially useful for languages that don't use a preprocessor. Unless POSIX and Yacc portability matter to you, this is the preferred solution.

We suggest that you always enable the trace option so that debugging is always possible.

The trace facility outputs messages with macro calls of the form YYFPRINTF (stderr, *format, args*) where *format* and *args* are the usual printf format and variadic arguments. If you define YYDEBUG to a nonzero value but do not define YYFPRINTF, <stdio.h> is automatically included and YYFPRINTF is defined to fprintf.

Once you have compiled the program with trace facilities, the way to request a trace is to store a nonzero value in the variable yydebug. You can do this by making the C code do it (in main, perhaps), or you can alter the value with a C debugger.

Each step taken by the parser when yydebug is nonzero produces a line or two of trace information, written on stderr. The trace messages tell you these things:

- Each time the parser calls yylex, what kind of token was read.

- Each time a token is shifted, the depth and complete contents of the state stack (see Section 5.5 [Parser States], page 113).

- Each time a rule is reduced, which rule it is, and the complete contents of the state stack afterward.

To make sense of this information, it helps to refer to the automaton description file (see Section 8.1 [Understanding Your Parser], page 133). This file shows the meaning of each state in terms of positions in various rules, and also what each state will do with each possible input token. As you read the successive trace messages, you can see that the parser is functioning according to its specification in the listing file. Eventually you will arrive at the place where something undesirable happens, and you will see which parts of the grammar are to blame.

The parser implementation file is a C/C++/Java program and you can use debuggers on it, but it's not easy to interpret what it is doing. The parser function is a finite-state machine interpreter, and aside from the actions it executes the same code over and over. Only the values of variables show where in the grammar it is working.

8.4.2 Enabling Debug Traces for `mfcalc`

The debugging information normally gives the token type of each token read, but not its semantic value. The `%printer` directive allows specify how semantic values are reported, see Section 3.7.7 [Printing Semantic Values], page 79. For backward compatibility, Yacc like C parsers may also use the `YYPRINT` (see Section 8.4.3 [The `YYPRINT` Macro], page 146), but its use is discouraged.

As a demonstration of `%printer`, consider the multi-function calculator, `mfcalc` (see Section 2.5 [Multi-function Calc], page 42). To enable run-time traces, and semantic value reports, insert the following directives in its prologue:

```
/* Generate the parser description file.  */
%verbose
/* Enable run-time traces (yydebug).  */
%define parse.trace

/* Formatting semantic values.  */
%printer { fprintf (yyoutput, "%s", $$->name); } VAR;
%printer { fprintf (yyoutput, "%s()", $$->name); } FNCT;
%printer { fprintf (yyoutput, "%g", $$); } <double>;
```

The `%define` directive instructs Bison to generate run-time trace support. Then, activation of these traces is controlled at run-time by the `yydebug` variable, which is disabled by default. Because these traces will refer to the "states" of the parser, it is helpful to ask for the creation of a description of that parser; this is the purpose of (admittedly ill-named) `%verbose` directive.

The set of `%printer` directives demonstrates how to format the semantic value in the traces. Note that the specification can be done either on the symbol type (e.g., `VAR` or `FNCT`), or on the type tag: since `<double>` is the type for both `NUM` and `exp`, this printer will be used for them.

Here is a sample of the information provided by run-time traces. The traces are sent onto standard error.

```
$ echo 'sin(1-1)' | ./mfcalc -p
Starting parse
Entering state 0
Reducing stack by rule 1 (line 34):
-> $$ = nterm input ()
Stack now 0
Entering state 1
```

This first batch shows a specific feature of this grammar: the first rule (which is in line 34 of `mfcalc.y` can be reduced without even having to look for the first token. The resulting left-hand symbol ($$) is a valueless ('()') `input` non terminal (`nterm`).

Then the parser calls the scanner.

```
Reading a token: Next token is token FNCT (sin())
Shifting token FNCT (sin())
Entering state 6
```

That token (token) is a function (FNCT) whose value is 'sin' as formatted per our %printer specification: 'sin()'. The parser stores (Shifting) that token, and others, until it can do something about it.

```
Reading a token: Next token is token '(' ()
Shifting token '(' ()
Entering state 14
Reading a token: Next token is token NUM (1.000000)
Shifting token NUM (1.000000)
Entering state 4
Reducing stack by rule 6 (line 44):
   $1 = token NUM (1.000000)
-> $$ = nterm exp (1.000000)
Stack now 0 1 6 14
Entering state 24
```

The previous reduction demonstrates the %printer directive for <double>: both the token NUM and the resulting nonterminal exp have '1' as value.

```
Reading a token: Next token is token '-' ()
Shifting token '-' ()
Entering state 17
Reading a token: Next token is token NUM (1.000000)
Shifting token NUM (1.000000)
Entering state 4
Reducing stack by rule 6 (line 44):
   $1 = token NUM (1.000000)
-> $$ = nterm exp (1.000000)
Stack now 0 1 6 14 24 17
Entering state 26
Reading a token: Next token is token ')' ()
Reducing stack by rule 11 (line 49):
   $1 = nterm exp (1.000000)
   $2 = token '-' ()
   $3 = nterm exp (1.000000)
-> $$ = nterm exp (0.000000)
Stack now 0 1 6 14
Entering state 24
```

The rule for the subtraction was just reduced. The parser is about to discover the end of the call to sin.

```
Next token is token ')' ()
Shifting token ')' ()
Entering state 31
Reducing stack by rule 9 (line 47):
   $1 = token FNCT (sin())
```

```
    $2 = token '(' ()
    $3 = nterm exp (0.000000)
    $4 = token ')' ()
-> $$ = nterm exp (0.000000)
Stack now 0 1
Entering state 11
```

Finally, the end-of-line allow the parser to complete the computation, and display its result.

```
Reading a token: Next token is token '\n' ()
Shifting token '\n' ()
Entering state 22
Reducing stack by rule 4 (line 40):
    $1 = nterm exp (0.000000)
    $2 = token '\n' ()
⇒ 0
-> $$ = nterm line ()
Stack now 0 1
Entering state 10
Reducing stack by rule 2 (line 35):
    $1 = nterm input ()
    $2 = nterm line ()
-> $$ = nterm input ()
Stack now 0
Entering state 1
```

The parser has returned into state 1, in which it is waiting for the next expression to evaluate, or for the end-of-file token, which causes the completion of the parsing.

```
Reading a token: Now at end of input.
Shifting token $end ()
Entering state 2
Stack now 0 1 2
Cleanup: popping token $end ()
Cleanup: popping nterm input ()
```

8.4.3 The YYPRINT Macro

Before %printer support, semantic values could be displayed using the YYPRINT macro, which works only for terminal symbols and only with the yacc.c skeleton.

YYPRINT (*stream*, *token*, *value*);   [Macro]

> If you define YYPRINT, it should take three arguments. The parser will pass a standard I/O stream, the numeric code for the token type, and the token value (from yylval).
>
> For yacc.c only. Obsoleted by %printer.

Here is an example of YYPRINT suitable for the multi-function calculator (see Section 2.5.1 [Declarations for mfcalc], page 43):

```
%{
  static void print_token_value (FILE *, int, YYSTYPE);
  #define YYPRINT(File, Type, Value)                \
```

```
      print_token_value (File, Type, Value)
%}

... %% ... %% ...

static void
print_token_value (FILE *file, int type, YYSTYPE value)
{
  if (type == VAR)
    fprintf (file, "%s", value.tptr->name);
  else if (type == NUM)
    fprintf (file, "%d", value.val);
}
```

9 Invoking Bison

The usual way to invoke Bison is as follows:

```
bison infile
```

Here *infile* is the grammar file name, which usually ends in '`.y`'. The parser implementation file's name is made by replacing the '`.y`' with '`.tab.c`' and removing any leading directory. Thus, the '`bison foo.y`' file name yields `foo.tab.c`, and the '`bison hack/foo.y`' file name yields `foo.tab.c`. It's also possible, in case you are writing C++ code instead of C in your grammar file, to name it `foo.ypp` or `foo.y++`. Then, the output files will take an extension like the given one as input (respectively `foo.tab.cpp` and `foo.tab.c++`). This feature takes effect with all options that manipulate file names like '`-o`' or '`-d`'.

For example :

```
bison -d infile.yxx
```

will produce `infile.tab.cxx` and `infile.tab.hxx`, and

```
bison -d -o output.c++ infile.y
```

will produce `output.c++` and `outfile.h++`.

For compatibility with POSIX, the standard Bison distribution also contains a shell script called `yacc` that invokes Bison with the `-y` option.

9.1 Bison Options

Bison supports both traditional single-letter options and mnemonic long option names. Long option names are indicated with '`--`' instead of '`-`'. Abbreviations for option names are allowed as long as they are unique. When a long option takes an argument, like '`--file-prefix`', connect the option name and the argument with '`=`'.

Here is a list of options that can be used with Bison, alphabetized by short option. It is followed by a cross key alphabetized by long option.

Operations modes:

`-h`
`--help`   Print a summary of the command-line options to Bison and exit.

`-V`
`--version`
        Print the version number of Bison and exit.

`--print-localedir`
        Print the name of the directory containing locale-dependent data.

`--print-datadir`
        Print the name of the directory containing skeletons and XSLT.

`-y`
`--yacc`   Act more like the traditional Yacc command. This can cause different diagnostics to be generated, and may change behavior in other minor ways. Most importantly, imitate Yacc's output file name conventions, so that the parser implementation file is called `y.tab.c`, and the other outputs are called `y.output` and `y.tab.h`. Also, if generating a deterministic parser in C, generate `#define`

statements in addition to an **enum** to associate token numbers with token names. Thus, the following shell script can substitute for Yacc, and the Bison distribution contains such a script for compatibility with POSIX:

```
#! /bin/sh
bison -y "$@"
```

The -y/--yacc option is intended for use with traditional Yacc grammars. If your grammar uses a Bison extension like '%glr-parser', Bison might not be Yacc-compatible even if this option is specified.

-W [*category*]

--warnings[=*category*]

> Output warnings falling in *category*. *category* can be one of:

> **midrule-values**

>> Warn about mid-rule values that are set but not used within any of the actions of the parent rule. For example, warn about unused $2 in:

>>> exp: '1' { $$ = 1; } '+' exp { $$ = $1 + $4; };

>> Also warn about mid-rule values that are used but not set. For example, warn about unset $$ in the mid-rule action in:

>>> exp: '1' { $1 = 1; } '+' exp { $$ = $2 + $4; };

>> These warnings are not enabled by default since they sometimes prove to be false alarms in existing grammars employing the Yacc constructs $0 or $-*n* (where *n* is some positive integer).

> **yacc**   Incompatibilities with POSIX Yacc.

> **conflicts-sr**

> **conflicts-rr**

>> S/R and R/R conflicts. These warnings are enabled by default. However, if the %expect or %expect-rr directive is specified, an unexpected number of conflicts is an error, and an expected number of conflicts is not reported, so -W and --warning then have no effect on the conflict report.

> **deprecated**

>> Deprecated constructs whose support will be removed in future versions of Bison.

> **empty-rule**

>> Empty rules without %empty. See Section 3.3.2 [Empty Rules], page 60. Disabled by default, but enabled by uses of %empty, unless -Wno-empty-rule was specified.

> **precedence**

>> Useless precedence and associativity directives. Disabled by default.

>> Consider for instance the following grammar:

```
%nonassoc "="
%left "+"
%left "*"
%precedence "("
%%
stmt:
  exp
| "var" "=" exp
;

exp:
  exp "+" exp
| exp "*" "num"
| "(" exp ")"
| "num"
;
```

Bison reports:

```
warning: useless precedence and associativity for "="
 %nonassoc "="
           ^^^
warning: useless associativity for "*", use %precedence
 %left "*"
       ^^^
warning: useless precedence for "("
 %precedence "("
             ^^^
```

One would get the exact same parser with the following directives instead:

```
%left "+"
%precedence "*"
```

other   All warnings not categorized above. These warnings are enabled by default.

           This category is provided merely for the sake of completeness. Future releases of Bison may move warnings from this category to new, more specific categories.

all   All the warnings except yacc.

none   Turn off all the warnings.

error   See -Werror, below.

A category can be turned off by prefixing its name with 'no-'. For instance, -Wno-yacc will hide the warnings about POSIX Yacc incompatibilities.

-Werror   Turn enabled warnings for every *category* into errors, unless they are explicitly disabled by -Wno-error=*category*.

`-Werror=`*category*

> Enable warnings falling in *category*, and treat them as errors.
>
> *category* is the same as for `--warnings`, with the exception that it may not be prefixed with 'no-' (see above).
>
> Note that the precedence of the '=' and ',' operators is such that the following commands are *not* equivalent, as the first will not treat S/R conflicts as errors.
>
> $ bison -Werror=yacc,conflicts-sr input.y
> $ bison -Werror=yacc,error=conflicts-sr input.y

`-Wno-error`

> Do not turn enabled warnings for every *category* into errors, unless they are explicitly enabled by `-Werror=`*category*.

`-Wno-error=`*category*

> Deactivate the error treatment for this *category*. However, the warning itself won't be disabled, or enabled, by this option.

`-f [`*feature*`]`

`--feature[=`*feature*`]`

> Activate miscellaneous *feature*. *feature* can be one of:
>
> `caret`
>
> `diagnostics-show-caret`
>
> > Show caret errors, in a manner similar to GCC's `-fdiagnostics-show-caret`, or Clang's `-fcaret-diagnotics`. The location provided with the message is used to quote the corresponding line of the source file, underlining the important part of it with carets (^). Here is an example, using the following file `in.y`:
> >
> >   %type <ival> exp
> >   %%
> >   exp: exp '+' exp { $exp = $1 + $2; };
> >
> > When invoked with `-fcaret` (or nothing), Bison will report:
> >
> >   in.y:3.20-23: error: ambiguous reference: '$exp'
> >   exp: exp '+' exp { $exp = $1 + $2; };
> >   ^^^^
> >
> >   in.y:3.1-3:   refers to: $exp at $$
> >   exp: exp '+' exp { $exp = $1 + $2; };
> >   ^^^
> >
> >   in.y:3.6-8:   refers to: $exp at $1
> >   exp: exp '+' exp { $exp = $1 + $2; };
> >   ^^^
> >
> >   in.y:3.14-16:   refers to: $exp at $3
> >   exp: exp '+' exp { $exp = $1 + $2; };
> >   ^^^
> >
> >   in.y:3.32-33: error: $2 of 'exp' has no declared type
> >   exp: exp '+' exp { $exp = $1 + $2; };
> >   ^^

Whereas, when invoked with `-fno-caret`, Bison will only report:

```
in.y:3.20-23: error: ambiguous reference: '$exp'
in.y:3.1-3:       refers to: $exp at $$
in.y:3.6-8:       refers to: $exp at $1
in.y:3.14-16:     refers to: $exp at $3
in.y:3.32-33: error: $2 of 'exp' has no declared type
```

This option is activated by default.

Tuning the parser:

-t

--debug   In the parser implementation file, define the macro YYDEBUG to 1 if it is not already defined, so that the debugging facilities are compiled. See Section 8.4 [Tracing Your Parser], page 142.

-D name[=value]
--define=name[=value]
-F name[=value]
--force-define=name[=value]

Each of these is equivalent to '%define name "value"' (see Section 3.7.13 [%define Summary], page 86) except that Bison processes multiple definitions for the same name as follows:

- Bison quietly ignores all command-line definitions for name except the last.

- If that command-line definition is specified by a -D or --define, Bison reports an error for any %define definition for name.

- If that command-line definition is specified by a -F or --force-define instead, Bison quietly ignores all %define definitions for name.

- Otherwise, Bison reports an error if there are multiple %define definitions for name.

You should avoid using -F and --force-define in your make files unless you are confident that it is safe to quietly ignore any conflicting %define that may be added to the grammar file.

-L language
--language=language

Specify the programming language for the generated parser, as if %language was specified (see Section 3.7.12 [Bison Declaration Summary], page 82). Currently supported languages include C, C++, and Java. language is case-insensitive.

--locations

Pretend that %locations was specified. See Section 3.7.12 [Decl Summary], page 82.

-p prefix
--name-prefix=prefix

Pretend that %name-prefix "prefix" was specified (see Section 3.7.12 [Decl Summary], page 82). Obsoleted by -Dapi.prefix=prefix. See Section 3.8 [Multiple Parsers in the Same Program], page 94.

`-l`

`--no-lines`

>Don't put any `#line` preprocessor commands in the parser implementation file. Ordinarily Bison puts them in the parser implementation file so that the C compiler and debuggers will associate errors with your source file, the grammar file. This option causes them to associate errors with the parser implementation file, treating it as an independent source file in its own right.

`-S file`

`--skeleton=file`

>Specify the skeleton to use, similar to `%skeleton` (see Section 3.7.12 [Bison Declaration Summary], page 82).

>If *file* does not contain a `/`, *file* is the name of a skeleton file in the Bison installation directory. If it does, *file* is an absolute file name or a file name relative to the current working directory. This is similar to how most shells resolve commands.

`-k`

`--token-table`

>Pretend that `%token-table` was specified. See Section 3.7.12 [Decl Summary], page 82.

Adjust the output:

`--defines[=file]`

>Pretend that `%defines` was specified, i.e., write an extra output file containing macro definitions for the token type names defined in the grammar, as well as a few other declarations. See Section 3.7.12 [Decl Summary], page 82.

`-d`   This is the same as `--defines` except `-d` does not accept a *file* argument since POSIX Yacc requires that `-d` can be bundled with other short options.

`-b file-prefix`

`--file-prefix=prefix`

>Pretend that `%file-prefix` was specified, i.e., specify prefix to use for all Bison output file names. See Section 3.7.12 [Decl Summary], page 82.

`-r things`

`--report=things`

>Write an extra output file containing verbose description of the comma separated list of *things* among:

>>`state`   Description of the grammar, conflicts (resolved and unresolved), and parser's automaton.

>>`itemset`   Implies `state` and augments the description of the automaton with the full set of items for each state, instead of its core only.

>>`lookahead`
>>>Implies `state` and augments the description of the automaton with each rule's lookahead set.

>>`solved`   Implies `state`. Explain how conflicts were solved thanks to precedence and associativity directives.

        `all`   Enable all the items.

        `none`   Do not generate the report.

`--report-file=file`
> Specify the *file* for the verbose description.

`-v`
`--verbose`
> Pretend that `%verbose` was specified, i.e., write an extra output file containing verbose descriptions of the grammar and parser. See Section 3.7.12 [Decl Summary], page 82.

`-o file`
`--output=file`
> Specify the *file* for the parser implementation file.
>
> The other output files' names are constructed from *file* as described under the '-v' and '-d' options.

`-g [file]`
`--graph[=file]`
> Output a graphical representation of the parser's automaton computed by Bison, in Graphviz DOT format. `file` is optional. If omitted and the grammar file is `foo.y`, the output file will be `foo.dot`.

`-x [file]`
`--xml[=file]`
> Output an XML report of the parser's automaton computed by Bison. `file` is optional. If omitted and the grammar file is `foo.y`, the output file will be `foo.xml`. (The current XML schema is experimental and may evolve. More user feedback will help to stabilize it.)

9.2 Option Cross Key

Here is a list of options, alphabetized by long option, to help you find the corresponding short option and directive.

Long Option	Short Option	Bison Directive
`--debug`	`-t`	`%debug`
`--define=name[=value]`	`-D name[=value]`	`%define name ["value"]`
`--defines[=file]`	`-d`	`%defines ["file"]`
`--feature[=feature]`	`-f [feature]`	
`--file-prefix=prefix`	`-b prefix`	`%file-prefix "prefix"`
`--force-define=name[=value]`	`-F name[=value]`	`%define name ["value"]`
`--graph[=file]`	`-g [file]`	

```
--help                          -h
--language=language             -L language      %language "language"

--locations                                      %locations

--name-prefix=prefix            -p prefix        %name-prefix "prefix"

--no-lines                      -l               %no-lines

--output=file                   -o file          %output "file"

--print-datadir
--print-localedir
--report-file=file
--report=things                 -r things
--skeleton=file                 -S file          %skeleton "file"

--token-table                   -k               %token-table

--verbose                       -v               %verbose

--version                       -V
--warnings[=category]           -W [category]
--xml[=file]                    -x [file]
--yacc                          -y               %yacc
```

9.3 Yacc Library

The Yacc library contains default implementations of the **yyerror** and **main** functions. These default implementations are normally not useful, but POSIX requires them. To use the Yacc library, link your program with the **-ly** option. Note that Bison's implementation of the Yacc library is distributed under the terms of the GNU General Public License (see [Copying], page 5).

If you use the Yacc library's **yyerror** function, you should declare **yyerror** as follows:

```
int yyerror (char const *);
```

The **int** value returned by this **yyerror** is ignored.

The implementation of Yacc library's **main** function is:

```
int main (void)
{
  setlocale (LC_ALL, "");
  return yyparse ();
}
```

so if you use it, the internationalization support is enabled (e.g., error messages are translated), and your **yyparse** function should have the following type signature:

```
int yyparse (void);
```

10 Parsers Written In Other Languages

10.1 C++ Parsers

10.1.1 C++ Bison Interface

The C++ deterministic parser is selected using the skeleton directive, '`%skeleton "lalr1.cc"`', or the synonymous command-line option `--skeleton=lalr1.cc`. See Section 3.7.12 [Decl Summary], page 82.

When run, `bison` will create several entities in the 'yy' namespace. Use the '`%define api.namespace`' directive to change the namespace name, see Section 3.7.13 [api.namespace], page 86. The various classes are generated in the following files:

`position.hh`
`location.hh`
> The definition of the classes `position` and `location`, used for location tracking when enabled. These files are not generated if the `%define` variable `api.location.type` is defined. See Section 10.1.3 [C++ Location Values], page 159.

`stack.hh`   An auxiliary class `stack` used by the parser.

file`.hh`
file`.cc`   (Assuming the extension of the grammar file was '.yy'.) The declaration and implementation of the C++ parser class. The basename and extension of these two files follow the same rules as with regular C parsers (see Chapter 9 [Invocation], page 149).

> The header is *mandatory*; you must either pass `-d`/`--defines` to `bison`, or use the '`%defines`' directive.

All these files are documented using Doxygen; run `doxygen` for a complete and accurate documentation.

10.1.2 C++ Semantic Values

Bison supports two different means to handle semantic values in C++. One is alike the C interface, and relies on unions (see Section 10.1.2.1 [C++ Unions], page 157). As C++ practitioners know, unions are inconvenient in C++, therefore another approach is provided, based on variants (see Section 10.1.2.2 [C++ Variants], page 158).

10.1.2.1 C++ Unions

The `%union` directive works as for C, see Section 3.4.4 [The Union Declaration], page 63. In particular it produces a genuine `union`, which have a few specific features in C++.

- The type `YYSTYPE` is defined but its use is discouraged: rather you should refer to the parser's encapsulated type `yy::parser::semantic_type`.

- Non POD (Plain Old Data) types cannot be used. C++ forbids any instance of classes with constructors in unions: only *pointers* to such objects are allowed.

Because objects have to be stored via pointers, memory is not reclaimed automatically: using the `%destructor` directive is the only means to avoid leaks. See Section 3.7.6 [Freeing Discarded Symbols], page 77.

10.1.2.2 C++ Variants

Bison provides a *variant* based implementation of semantic values for C++. This alleviates all the limitations reported in the previous section, and in particular, object types can be used without pointers.

To enable variant-based semantic values, set `%define` variable `variant` (see Section 3.7.13 [variant], page 86). Once this defined, `%union` is ignored, and instead of using the name of the fields of the `%union` to "type" the symbols, use genuine types.

For instance, instead of

```
%union
{
  int ival;
  std::string* sval;
}
%token <ival> NUMBER;
%token <sval> STRING;
```

write

```
%token <int> NUMBER;
%token <std::string> STRING;
```

`STRING` is no longer a pointer, which should fairly simplify the user actions in the grammar and in the scanner (in particular the memory management).

Since C++ features destructors, and since it is customary to specialize `operator<<` to support uniform printing of values, variants also typically simplify Bison printers and destructors.

Variants are stricter than unions. When based on unions, you may play any dirty game with `yylval`, say storing an `int`, reading a `char*`, and then storing a `double` in it. This is no longer possible with variants: they must be initialized, then assigned to, and eventually, destroyed.

T& build<T> ()   [Method on `semantic_type`]
    Initialize, but leave empty. Returns the address where the actual value may be stored.
    Requires that the variant was not initialized yet.

T& build<T> (*const T& t*)   [Method on `semantic_type`]
    Initialize, and copy-construct from *t*.

Warning: We do not use Boost.Variant, for two reasons. First, it appeared unacceptable to require Boost on the user's machine (i.e., the machine on which the generated parser will be compiled, not the machine on which `bison` was run). Second, for each possible semantic value, Boost.Variant not only stores the value, but also a tag specifying its type. But the parser already "knows" the type of the semantic value, so that would be duplicating the information.

Therefore we developed light-weight variants whose type tag is external (so they are really like `unions` for C++ actually). But our code is much less mature that Boost.Variant. So there is a number of limitations in (the current implementation of) variants:

- Alignment must be enforced: values should be aligned in memory according to the most demanding type. Computing the smallest alignment possible requires meta-programming techniques that are not currently implemented in Bison, and therefore, since, as far as we know, `double` is the most demanding type on all platforms, alignments are enforced for `double` whatever types are actually used. This may waste space in some cases.

- There might be portability issues we are not aware of.

As far as we know, these limitations *can* be alleviated. All it takes is some time and/or some talented C++ hacker willing to contribute to Bison.

10.1.3 C++ Location Values

When the directive `%locations` is used, the C++ parser supports location tracking, see Section 3.5 [Tracking Locations], page 70.

By default, two auxiliary classes define a `position`, a single point in a file, and a `location`, a range composed of a pair of `positions` (possibly spanning several files). But if the `%define` variable `api.location.type` is defined, then these classes will not be generated, and the user defined type will be used.

In this section `uint` is an abbreviation for `unsigned int`: in genuine code only the latter is used.

10.1.3.1 C++ position

`position` (*std::string* `file` = 0, uint `line` = 1, uint `col`*   [Constructor on `position`]
   = 1)
   Create a `position` denoting a given point. Note that `file` is not reclaimed when the `position` is destroyed: memory managed must be handled elsewhere.

`void initialize` (*std::string* `file` = 0, uint `line` = 1,*   [Method on `position`]
   uint `col` = 1)
   Reset the position to the given values.

`std::string* file`   [Instance Variable of `position`]
   The name of the file. It will always be handled as a pointer, the parser will never duplicate nor deallocate it. As an experimental feature you may change it to '`type*`' using '`%define filename_type "type"`'.

`uint line`   [Instance Variable of `position`]
   The line, starting at 1.

`void lines` (*int `height` = 1*)   [Method on `position`]
   If *height* is not null, advance by *height* lines, resetting the column number. The resulting line number cannot be less than 1.

`uint column`   [Instance Variable of `position`]
   The column, starting at 1.

void columns (*int* **width** = *1*)   [Method on **position**]
> Advance by *width* columns, without changing the line number. The resulting column number cannot be less than 1.

position& operator+= (*int* **width**)   [Method on **position**]
position operator+ (*int* **width**)   [Method on **position**]
position& operator-= (*int* **width**)   [Method on **position**]
position operator- (*int* **width**)   [Method on **position**]
> Various forms of syntactic sugar for **columns**.

bool operator== (*const position&* **that**)   [Method on **position**]
bool operator!= (*const position&* **that**)   [Method on **position**]
> Whether ***this** and **that** denote equal/different positions.

std::ostream& operator<< (*std::ostream&* *o*, *const position&* *p*)   [Function]
> Report *p* on *o* like this: '**file:line.column**', or '**line.column**' if *file* is null.

10.1.3.2 C++ **location**

location (*const position&* **begin**, *const position&* **end**)   [Constructor on **location**]
> Create a **Location** from the endpoints of the range.

location (*const position&* **pos** = *position()*)   [Constructor on **location**]
location (*std::string** **file**, *uint* **line**, *uint* **col**)   [Constructor on **location**]
> Create a **Location** denoting an empty range located at a given point.

void initialize (*std::string** **file** = *0*, *uint* **line** = *1*,   [Method on **location**]
> *uint* **col** = *1*)
> Reset the location to an empty range at the given values.

position begin   [Instance Variable of **location**]
position end   [Instance Variable of **location**]
> The first, inclusive, position of the range, and the first beyond.

void columns (*int* **width** = *1*)   [Method on **location**]
void lines (*int* **height** = *1*)   [Method on **location**]
> Forwarded to the **end** position.

location operator+ (*int* **width**)   [Method on **location**]
location operator+= (*int* **width**)   [Method on **location**]
location operator- (*int* **width**)   [Method on **location**]
location operator-= (*int* **width**)   [Method on **location**]
> Various forms of syntactic sugar for **columns**.

location operator+ (*const location&* **end**)   [Method on **location**]
location operator+= (*const location&* **end**)   [Method on **location**]
> Join two locations: starts at the position of the first one, and ends at the position of the second.

void step ()   [Method on **location**]
> Move **begin** onto **end**.

bool operator== (*const location&* **that**)   [Method on `location`]
bool operator!= (*const location&* **that**)   [Method on `location`]
> Whether ***this** and **that** denote equal/different ranges of positions.

std::ostream& operator<< (*std::ostream&* *o*, *const location&* *p*)   [Function]
> Report *p* on *o*, taking care of special cases such as: no `filename` defined, or equal
> filename/line or column.

10.1.3.3 User Defined Location Type

Instead of using the built-in types you may use the `%define` variable `api.location.type`
to specify your own type:

```
%define api.location.type {LocationType}
```

The requirements over your *LocationType* are:

- it must be copyable;

- in order to compute the (default) value of `@$` in a reduction, the parser basically runs

  ```
  @$.begin = @1.begin;
  @$.end   = @N.end; // The location of last right-hand side symbol.
  ```

  so there must be copyable `begin` and `end` members;

- alternatively you may redefine the computation of the default location, in which case
  these members are not required (see Section 3.5.3 [Location Default Action], page 72);

- if traces are enabled, then there must exist an 'std::ostream& operator<<
  (std::ostream& o, const *LocationType*& s)' function.

In programs with several C++ parsers, you may also use the `%define` variable
`api.location.type` to share a common set of built-in definitions for `position` and
`location`. For instance, one parser `master/parser.yy` might use:

```
%defines
%locations
%define api.namespace {master::}
```

to generate the `master/position.hh` and `master/location.hh` files, reused by other
parsers as follows:

```
%define api.location.type {master::location}
%code requires { #include <master/location.hh> }
```

10.1.4 C++ Parser Interface

The output files *output.hh* and *output.cc* declare and define the parser class in the
namespace yy. The class name defaults to **parser**, but may be changed using '`%define
parser_class_name {name}`'. The interface of this class is detailed below. It can be ex-
tended using the `%parse-param` feature: its semantics is slightly changed since it describes
an additional member of the parser class, and an additional argument for its constructor.

semantic_type   [Type of `parser`]
location_type   [Type of `parser`]
> The types for semantic values and locations (if enabled).

token   [Type of parser]

> A structure that contains (only) the yytokentype enumeration, which defines the tokens. To refer to the token FOO, use yy::parser::token::FOO. The scanner can use 'typedef yy::parser::token token;' to "import" the token enumeration (see Section 10.1.6.4 [Calc++ Scanner], page 169).

syntax_error   [Type of parser]

> This class derives from std::runtime_error. Throw instances of it from the scanner or from the user actions to raise parse errors. This is equivalent with first invoking error to report the location and message of the syntax error, and then to invoke YYERROR to enter the error-recovery mode. But contrary to YYERROR which can only be invoked from user actions (i.e., written in the action itself), the exception can be thrown from function invoked from the user action.

parser (*type1 arg1*, ...)   [Method on parser]

> Build a new parser object. There are no arguments by default, unless '%parse-param {*type1 arg1*}' was used.

syntax_error (*const location_type& 1, const*   [Method on syntax_error]
           std::string& m)
syntax_error (*const std::string& m*)   [Method on syntax_error]

> Instantiate a syntax-error exception.

int parse ()   [Method on parser]

> Run the syntactic analysis, and return 0 on success, 1 otherwise.

> The whole function is wrapped in a try/catch block, so that when an exception is thrown, the %destructors are called to release the lookahead symbol, and the symbols pushed on the stack.

std::ostream& debug_stream ()   [Method on parser]
void set_debug_stream (*std::ostream& o*)   [Method on parser]

> Get or set the stream used for tracing the parsing. It defaults to std::cerr.

debug_level_type debug_level ()   [Method on parser]
void set_debug_level (*debug_level l*)   [Method on parser]

> Get or set the tracing level. Currently its value is either 0, no trace, or nonzero, full tracing.

void error (*const location_type& l, const std::string& m*) [Method on parser]
void error (*const std::string& m*)   [Method on parser]

> The definition for this member function must be supplied by the user: the parser uses it to report a parser error occurring at *l*, described by *m*. If location tracking is not enabled, the second signature is used.

10.1.5 C++ Scanner Interface

The parser invokes the scanner by calling yylex. Contrary to C parsers, C++ parsers are always pure: there is no point in using the '%define api.pure' directive. The actual interface with yylex depends whether you use unions, or variants.

10.1.5.1 Split Symbols

The interface is as follows.

int yylex (*semantic_type* yylval, location_type* yylloc,*   [Method on **parser**]
      type1 arg1, ...)

int yylex (*semantic_type* yylval, type1 arg1, ...*)   [Method on **parser**]
      Return the next token. Its type is the return value, its semantic value and location
      (if enabled) being *yylval* and *yylloc*. Invocations of '%lex-param {*type1 arg1*}' yield
      additional arguments.

Note that when using variants, the interface for yylex is the same, but yylval is handled
differently.

Regular union-based code in Lex scanner typically look like:

```
[0-9]+    {
              yylval.ival = text_to_int (yytext);
              return yy::parser::INTEGER;
          }
[a-z]+    {
              yylval.sval = new std::string (yytext);
              return yy::parser::IDENTIFIER;
          }
```

Using variants, yylval is already constructed, but it is not initialized. So the code would
look like:

```
[0-9]+    {
              yylval.build<int>() = text_to_int (yytext);
              return yy::parser::INTEGER;
          }
[a-z]+    {
              yylval.build<std::string> = yytext;
              return yy::parser::IDENTIFIER;
          }
```

or

```
[0-9]+    {
              yylval.build(text_to_int (yytext));
              return yy::parser::INTEGER;
          }
[a-z]+    {
              yylval.build(yytext);
              return yy::parser::IDENTIFIER;
          }
```

10.1.5.2 Complete Symbols

If you specified both %define api.value.type variant and %define api.token.constructor,
the **parser** class also defines the class parser::symbol_type which defines a *complete*
symbol, aggregating its type (i.e., the traditional value returned by yylex), its semantic
value (i.e., the value passed in yylval, and possibly its location (yylloc).

symbol_type (*token_type* **type**, *const semantic_type&*   [Method on symbol_type]
          value, *const location_type&* **location**)
> Build a complete terminal symbol which token type is *type*, and which semantic value
> is *value*. If location tracking is enabled, also pass the *location*.

This interface is low-level and should not be used for two reasons. First, it is inconvenient, as you still have to build the semantic value, which is a variant, and second, because consistency is not enforced: as with unions, it is still possible to give an integer as semantic value for a string.

So for each token type, Bison generates named constructors as follows.

make_token (*const* **value_type&** **value**, *const*   [Method on symbol_type]
          location_type& **location**)
make_token (*const location_type&* **location**)   [Method on symbol_type]
> Build a complete terminal symbol for the token type *token* (not including the
> **api.token.prefix**) whose possible semantic value is *value* of adequate *value_type*.
> If location tracking is enabled, also pass the *location*.

For instance, given the following declarations:

```
%define api.token.prefix {TOK_}
%token <std::string> IDENTIFIER;
%token <int> INTEGER;
%token COLON;
```

Bison generates the following functions:

```
symbol_type make_IDENTIFIER(const std::string& v,
                            const location_type& l);
symbol_type make_INTEGER(const int& v,
                         const location_type& loc);
symbol_type make_COLON(const location_type& loc);
```

which should be used in a Lex-scanner as follows.

```
[0-9]+    return yy::parser::make_INTEGER(text_to_int (yytext), loc);
[a-z]+    return yy::parser::make_IDENTIFIER(yytext, loc);
":"       return yy::parser::make_COLON(loc);
```

Tokens that do not have an identifier are not accessible: you cannot simply use characters such as ':', they must be declared with %token.

10.1.6 A Complete C++ Example

This section demonstrates the use of a C++ parser with a simple but complete example. This example should be available on your system, ready to compile, in the directory *.../bison/examples/calc++*. It focuses on the use of Bison, therefore the design of the various C++ classes is very naive: no accessors, no encapsulation of members etc. We will use a Lex scanner, and more precisely, a Flex scanner, to demonstrate the various interactions. A hand-written scanner is actually easier to interface with.

10.1.6.1 Calc++ — C++ Calculator

Of course the grammar is dedicated to arithmetics, a single expression, possibly preceded by variable assignments. An environment containing possibly predefined variables such as one and two, is exchanged with the parser. An example of valid input follows.

```
three := 3
seven := one + two * three
seven * seven
```

10.1.6.2 Calc++ Parsing Driver

To support a pure interface with the parser (and the scanner) the technique of the "parsing context" is convenient: a structure containing all the data to exchange. Since, in addition to simply launch the parsing, there are several auxiliary tasks to execute (open the file for parsing, instantiate the parser etc.), we recommend transforming the simple parsing context structure into a fully blown *parsing driver* class.

The declaration of this driver class, calc++-driver.hh, is as follows. The first part includes the CPP guard and imports the required standard library components, and the declaration of the parser class.

```
#ifndef CALCXX_DRIVER_HH
# define CALCXX_DRIVER_HH
# include <string>
# include <map>
# include "calc++-parser.hh"
```

Then comes the declaration of the scanning function. Flex expects the signature of yylex to be defined in the macro YY_DECL, and the C++ parser expects it to be declared. We can factor both as follows.

```
// Tell Flex the lexer's prototype ...
# define YY_DECL \
  yy::calcxx_parser::symbol_type yylex (calcxx_driver& driver)
// ... and declare it for the parser's sake.
YY_DECL;
```

The calcxx_driver class is then declared with its most obvious members.

```
// Conducting the whole scanning and parsing of Calc++.
class calcxx_driver
{
public:
  calcxx_driver ();
  virtual ~calcxx_driver ();

  std::map<std::string, int> variables;

  int result;
```

To encapsulate the coordination with the Flex scanner, it is useful to have member functions to open and close the scanning phase.

```
// Handling the scanner.
```

```
void scan_begin ();
void scan_end ();
bool trace_scanning;
```

Similarly for the parser itself.

```
// Run the parser on file F.
// Return 0 on success.
int parse (const std::string& f);
// The name of the file being parsed.
// Used later to pass the file name to the location tracker.
std::string file;
// Whether parser traces should be generated.
bool trace_parsing;
```

To demonstrate pure handling of parse errors, instead of simply dumping them on the standard error output, we will pass them to the compiler driver using the following two member functions. Finally, we close the class declaration and CPP guard.

```
// Error handling.
void error (const yy::location& l, const std::string& m);
void error (const std::string& m);
};
#endif // ! CALCXX_DRIVER_HH
```

The implementation of the driver is straightforward. The **parse** member function deserves some attention. The **error** functions are simple stubs, they should actually register the located error messages and set error state.

```
#include "calc++-driver.hh"
#include "calc++-parser.hh"

calcxx_driver::calcxx_driver ()
  : trace_scanning (false), trace_parsing (false)
{
  variables["one"] = 1;
  variables["two"] = 2;
}

calcxx_driver::~calcxx_driver ()
{
}

int
calcxx_driver::parse (const std::string &f)
{
  file = f;
  scan_begin ();
  yy::calcxx_parser parser (*this);
  parser.set_debug_level (trace_parsing);
  int res = parser.parse ();
```

```
    scan_end ();
    return res;
}


void
calcxx_driver::error (const yy::location& l, const std::string& m)
{
    std::cerr << l << ": " << m << std::endl;
}


void
calcxx_driver::error (const std::string& m)
{
    std::cerr << m << std::endl;
}
```

10.1.6.3 Calc++ Parser

The grammar file calc++-parser.yy starts by asking for the C++ deterministic parser skeleton, the creation of the parser header file, and specifies the name of the parser class. Because the C++ skeleton changed several times, it is safer to require the version you designed the grammar for.

```
%skeleton "lalr1.cc" /* -*- C++ -*- */
%require "3.0.4"
%defines
%define parser_class_name {calcxx_parser}
```

This example will use genuine C++ objects as semantic values, therefore, we require the variant-based interface. To make sure we properly use it, we enable assertions. To fully benefit from type-safety and more natural definition of "symbol", we enable api.token.constructor.

```
%define api.token.constructor
%define api.value.type variant
%define parse.assert
```

Then come the declarations/inclusions needed by the semantic values. Because the parser uses the parsing driver and reciprocally, both would like to include the header of the other, which is, of course, insane. This mutual dependency will be broken using forward declarations. Because the driver's header needs detailed knowledge about the parser class (in particular its inner types), it is the parser's header which will use a forward declaration of the driver. See Section 3.7.14 [%code Summary], page 92.

```
%code requires
{
# include <string>
class calcxx_driver;
}
```

The driver is passed by reference to the parser and to the scanner. This provides a simple but effective pure interface, not relying on global variables.

```
// The parsing context.
%param { calcxx_driver& driver }
```

Then we request location tracking, and initialize the first location's file name. Afterward new locations are computed relatively to the previous locations: the file name will be propagated.

```
%locations
%initial-action
{
  // Initialize the initial location.
  @$.begin.filename = @$.end.filename = &driver.file;
};
```

Use the following two directives to enable parser tracing and verbose error messages. However, verbose error messages can contain incorrect information (see Section 5.8.3 [LAC], page 121).

```
%define parse.trace
%define parse.error verbose
```

The code between '%code {' and '}' is output in the *.cc file; it needs detailed knowledge about the driver.

```
%code
{
# include "calc++-driver.hh"
}
```

The token numbered as 0 corresponds to end of file; the following line allows for nicer error messages referring to "end of file" instead of "$end". Similarly user friendly names are provided for each symbol. To avoid name clashes in the generated files (see Section 10.1.6.4 [Calc++ Scanner], page 169), prefix tokens with TOK_ (see Section 3.7.13 [api.token.prefix], page 86).

```
%define api.token.prefix {TOK_}
%token
  END    0  "end of file"
  ASSIGN    ":="
  MINUS     "-"
  PLUS      "+"
  STAR      "*"
  SLASH     "/"
  LPAREN    "("
  RPAREN    ")"
;
```

Since we use variant-based semantic values, %union is not used, and both %type and %token expect genuine types, as opposed to type tags.

```
%token <std::string> IDENTIFIER "identifier"
%token <int> NUMBER "number"
%type  <int> exp
```

No `%destructor` is needed to enable memory deallocation during error recovery; the memory, for strings for instance, will be reclaimed by the regular destructors. All the values are printed using their `operator<<` (see Section 3.7.7 [Printing Semantic Values], page 79).

```
%printer { yyoutput << $$; } <*>;
```

The grammar itself is straightforward (see Section 2.4 [Location Tracking Calculator - ltcalc], page 39).

```
%%
%start unit;
unit: assignments exp  { driver.result = $2; };

assignments:
  %empty                 {}
| assignments assignment {};

assignment:
  "identifier" ":=" exp { driver.variables[$1] = $3; };

%left "+" "-";
%left "*" "/";
exp:
  exp "+" exp   { $$ = $1 + $3; }
| exp "-" exp   { $$ = $1 - $3; }
| exp "*" exp   { $$ = $1 * $3; }
| exp "/" exp   { $$ = $1 / $3; }
| "(" exp ")"   { std::swap ($$, $2); }
| "identifier"  { $$ = driver.variables[$1]; }
| "number"      { std::swap ($$, $1); };
%%
```

Finally the `error` member function registers the errors to the driver.

```
void
yy::calcxx_parser::error (const location_type& l,
                          const std::string& m)
{
  driver.error (l, m);
}
```

10.1.6.4 Calc++ Scanner

The Flex scanner first includes the driver declaration, then the parser's to get the set of defined tokens.

```
%{ /* -*- C++ -*- */
# include <cerrno>
# include <climits>
# include <cstdlib>
# include <string>
# include "calc++-driver.hh"
```

```
# include "calc++-parser.hh"

// Work around an incompatibility in flex (at least versions
// 2.5.31 through 2.5.33): it generates code that does
// not conform to C89.  See Debian bug 333231
// <http://bugs.debian.org/cgi-bin/bugreport.cgi?bug=333231>.
# undef yywrap
# define yywrap() 1


// The location of the current token.
static yy::location loc;
%}
```

Because there is no #include-like feature we don't need yywrap, we don't need unput
either, and we parse an actual file, this is not an interactive session with the user. Finally,
we enable scanner tracing.

```
%option noyywrap nounput batch debug noinput
```

Abbreviations allow for more readable rules.

```
id    [a-zA-Z][a-zA-Z_0-9]*
int   [0-9]+
blank [ \t]
```

The following paragraph suffices to track locations accurately. Each time yylex is invoked,
the begin position is moved onto the end position. Then when a pattern is matched, its width
is added to the end column. When matching ends of lines, the end cursor is adjusted, and
each time blanks are matched, the begin cursor is moved onto the end cursor to effectively
ignore the blanks preceding tokens. Comments would be treated equally.

```
%{
  // Code run each time a pattern is matched.
  # define YY_USER_ACTION  loc.columns (yyleng);
%}
%%
%{
  // Code run each time yylex is called.
  loc.step ();
%}
{blank}+   loc.step ();
[\n]+      loc.lines (yyleng); loc.step ();
```

The rules are simple. The driver is used to report errors.

```
"-"        return yy::calcxx_parser::make_MINUS(loc);
"+"        return yy::calcxx_parser::make_PLUS(loc);
"*"        return yy::calcxx_parser::make_STAR(loc);
"/"        return yy::calcxx_parser::make_SLASH(loc);
"("        return yy::calcxx_parser::make_LPAREN(loc);
")"        return yy::calcxx_parser::make_RPAREN(loc);
":="       return yy::calcxx_parser::make_ASSIGN(loc);
```

```
{int}      {
  errno = 0;
  long n = strtol (yytext, NULL, 10);
  if (! (INT_MIN <= n && n <= INT_MAX && errno != ERANGE))
    driver.error (loc, "integer is out of range");
  return yy::calcxx_parser::make_NUMBER(n, loc);
}
{id}       return yy::calcxx_parser::make_IDENTIFIER(yytext, loc);
.          driver.error (loc, "invalid character");
<<EOF>>    return yy::calcxx_parser::make_END(loc);
%%
```

Finally, because the scanner-related driver's member-functions depend on the scanner's data, it is simpler to implement them in this file.

```
void
calcxx_driver::scan_begin ()
{
  yy_flex_debug = trace_scanning;
  if (file.empty () || file == "-")
    yyin = stdin;
  else if (!(yyin = fopen (file.c_str (), "r")))
    {
      error ("cannot open " + file + ": " + strerror(errno));
      exit (EXIT_FAILURE);
    }
}

void
calcxx_driver::scan_end ()
{
  fclose (yyin);
}
```

10.1.6.5 Calc++ Top Level

The top level file, calc++.cc, poses no problem.

```
#include <iostream>
#include "calc++-driver.hh"
```

```
int
main (int argc, char *argv[])
{
  int res = 0;
  calcxx_driver driver;
  for (int i = 1; i < argc; ++i)
    if (argv[i] == std::string ("-p"))
      driver.trace_parsing = true;
    else if (argv[i] == std::string ("-s"))
      driver.trace_scanning = true;
    else if (!driver.parse (argv[i]))
      std::cout << driver.result << std::endl;
    else
      res = 1;
  return res;
}
```

10.2 Java Parsers

10.2.1 Java Bison Interface

(The current Java interface is experimental and may evolve. More user feedback will help to stabilize it.)

The Java parser skeletons are selected using the %language "Java" directive or the -L java/--language=java option.

When generating a Java parser, bison *basename*.y will create a single Java source file named *basename*.java containing the parser implementation. Using a grammar file without a .y suffix is currently broken. The basename of the parser implementation file can be changed by the %file-prefix directive or the -p/--name-prefix option. The entire parser implementation file name can be changed by the %output directive or the -o/--output option. The parser implementation file contains a single class for the parser.

You can create documentation for generated parsers using Javadoc.

Contrary to C parsers, Java parsers do not use global variables; the state of the parser is always local to an instance of the parser class. Therefore, all Java parsers are "pure", and the %pure-parser and %define api.pure directives do nothing when used in Java.

Push parsers are currently unsupported in Java and %define api.push-pull have no effect.

GLR parsers are currently unsupported in Java. Do not use the glr-parser directive.

No header file can be generated for Java parsers. Do not use the %defines directive or the -d/--defines options.

Currently, support for tracing is always compiled in. Thus the '%define parse.trace' and '%token-table' directives and the -t/--debug and -k/--token-table options have no effect. This may change in the future to eliminate unused code in the generated parser, so use '%define parse.trace' explicitly if needed. Also, in the future the %token-table directive might enable a public interface to access the token names and codes.

Getting a "code too large" error from the Java compiler means the code hit the 64KB bytecode per method limitation of the Java class file. Try reducing the amount of code in actions and static initializers; otherwise, report a bug so that the parser skeleton will be improved.

10.2.2 Java Semantic Values

There is no %union directive in Java parsers. Instead, the semantic values' types (class names) should be specified in the %type or %token directive:

```
%type <Expression> expr assignment_expr term factor
%type <Integer> number
```

By default, the semantic stack is declared to have Object members, which means that the class types you specify can be of any class. To improve the type safety of the parser, you can declare the common superclass of all the semantic values using the '%define api.value.type' directive. For example, after the following declaration:

```
%define api.value.type {ASTNode}
```

any %type or %token specifying a semantic type which is not a subclass of ASTNode, will cause a compile-time error.

Types used in the directives may be qualified with a package name. Primitive data types are accepted for Java version 1.5 or later. Note that in this case the autoboxing feature of Java 1.5 will be used. Generic types may not be used; this is due to a limitation in the implementation of Bison, and may change in future releases.

Java parsers do not support %destructor, since the language adopts garbage collection. The parser will try to hold references to semantic values for as little time as needed.

Java parsers do not support %printer, as toString() can be used to print the semantic values. This however may change (in a backwards-compatible way) in future versions of Bison.

10.2.3 Java Location Values

When the directive %locations is used, the Java parser supports location tracking, see Section 3.5 [Tracking Locations], page 70. An auxiliary user-defined class defines a *position*, a single point in a file; Bison itself defines a class representing a *location*, a range composed of a pair of positions (possibly spanning several files). The location class is an inner class of the parser; the name is Location by default, and may also be renamed using %define api.location.type {*class-name*}.

The location class treats the position as a completely opaque value. By default, the class name is Position, but this can be changed with %define api.position.type {*class-name*}. This class must be supplied by the user.

Position begin   [Instance Variable of Location]
Position end   [Instance Variable of Location]
    The first, inclusive, position of the range, and the first beyond.

Location (*Position loc*)   [Constructor on Location]
    Create a Location denoting an empty range located at a given point.

Location (*Position* **begin**, *Position* **end**)   [Constructor on **Location**]

  Create a **Location** from the endpoints of the range.

String toString ()   [Method on **Location**]

  Prints the range represented by the location. For this to work properly, the position
  class should override the **equals** and **toString** methods appropriately.

10.2.4 Java Parser Interface

The name of the generated parser class defaults to **YYParser**. The YY prefix may be changed
using the **%name-prefix** directive or the **-p/--name-prefix** option. Alternatively, use
'**%define parser_class_name** {*name*}' to give a custom name to the class. The interface
of this class is detailed below.

By default, the parser class has package visibility. A declaration '**%define public**' will
change to public visibility. Remember that, according to the Java language specification,
the name of the .**java** file should match the name of the class in this case. Similarly, you can
use **abstract**, **final** and **strictfp** with the **%define** declaration to add other modifiers
to the parser class. A single '**%define annotations** {*annotations*}' directive can be used
to add any number of annotations to the parser class.

The Java package name of the parser class can be specified using the '**%define package**'
directive. The superclass and the implemented interfaces of the parser class can be specified
with the **%define extends** and '**%define implements**' directives.

The parser class defines an inner class, **Location**, that is used for location tracking
(see Section 10.2.3 [Java Location Values], page 173), and a inner interface, **Lexer** (see
Section 10.2.5 [Java Scanner Interface], page 175). Other than these inner class/interface,
and the members described in the interface below, all the other members and fields are
preceded with a **yy** or **YY** prefix to avoid clashes with user code.

The parser class can be extended using the **%parse-param** directive. Each occurrence of
the directive will add a **protected final** field to the parser class, and an argument to its
constructor, which initialize them automatically.

YYParser (*lex_param*, ..., *parse_param*, ...)   [Constructor on **YYParser**]

  Build a new parser object with embedded **%code lexer**. There are no parameters,
  unless **%params** and/or **%parse-params** and/or **%lex-params** are used.

  Use **%code init** for code added to the start of the constructor body. This is especially
  useful to initialize superclasses. Use '**%define init_throws**' to specify any uncaught
  exceptions.

YYParser (*Lexer* **lexer**, *parse_param*, ...)   [Constructor on **YYParser**]

  Build a new parser object using the specified scanner. There are no additional parameters unless **%params** and/or **%parse-params** are used.

  If the scanner is defined by **%code lexer**, this constructor is declared **protected**
  and is called automatically with a scanner created with the correct **%params** and/or
  %lex-params.

  Use **%code init** for code added to the start of the constructor body. This is especially
  useful to initialize superclasses. Use '**%define init_throws**' to specify any uncaught
  exceptions.

boolean parse () [Method on YYParser]
> Run the syntactic analysis, and return **true** on success, **false** otherwise.

boolean getErrorVerbose () [Method on YYParser]
void setErrorVerbose (*boolean verbose***)** [Method on YYParser]
> Get or set the option to produce verbose error messages. These are only available with '**%define parse.error verbose**', which also turns on verbose error messages.

void yyerror (*String msg***)** [Method on YYParser]
void yyerror (*Position pos, String msg***)** [Method on YYParser]
void yyerror (*Location loc, String msg***)** [Method on YYParser]
> Print an error message using the **yyerror** method of the scanner instance in use. The **Location** and **Position** parameters are available only if location tracking is active.

boolean recovering () [Method on YYParser]
> During the syntactic analysis, return **true** if recovering from a syntax error. See Chapter 6 [Error Recovery], page 127.

java.io.PrintStream getDebugStream () [Method on YYParser]
void setDebugStream (*java.io.printStream o***)** [Method on YYParser]
> Get or set the stream used for tracing the parsing. It defaults to **System.err**.

int getDebugLevel () [Method on YYParser]
void setDebugLevel (*int l***)** [Method on YYParser]
> Get or set the tracing level. Currently its value is either 0, no trace, or nonzero, full tracing.

String bisonVersion [Constant of YYParser]
String bisonSkeleton [Constant of YYParser]
> Identify the Bison version and skeleton used to generate this parser.

10.2.5 Java Scanner Interface

There are two possible ways to interface a Bison-generated Java parser with a scanner: the scanner may be defined by **%code lexer**, or defined elsewhere. In either case, the scanner has to implement the **Lexer** inner interface of the parser class. This interface also contain constants for all user-defined token names and the predefined **EOF** token.

In the first case, the body of the scanner class is placed in **%code lexer** blocks. If you want to pass parameters from the parser constructor to the scanner constructor, specify them with **%lex-param**; they are passed before **%parse-params** to the constructor.

In the second case, the scanner has to implement the **Lexer** interface, which is defined within the parser class (e.g., **YYParser.Lexer**). The constructor of the parser object will then accept an object implementing the interface; **%lex-param** is not used in this case.

In both cases, the scanner has to implement the following methods.

void yyerror (*Location loc, String msg***)** [Method on Lexer]
> This method is defined by the user to emit an error message. The first parameter is omitted if location tracking is not active. Its type can be changed using **%define api.location.type {***class-name***}**.

`int yylex ()`   [Method on `Lexer`]

>   Return the next token. Its type is the return value, its semantic value and location
>   are saved and returned by the their methods in the interface.
>
>   Use '`%define lex_throws`' to specify any uncaught exceptions.   Default is
>   `java.io.IOException`.

`Position getStartPos ()`   [Method on `Lexer`]
`Position getEndPos ()`   [Method on `Lexer`]

>   Return respectively the first position of the last token that `yylex` returned, and the
>   first position beyond it. These methods are not needed unless location tracking is
>   active.
>
>   The return type can be changed using `%define api.position.type {class-name}`.

`Object getLVal ()`   [Method on `Lexer`]

>   Return the semantic value of the last token that yylex returned.
>
>   The return type can be changed using '`%define api.value.type {class-name}`'.

10.2.6 Special Features for Use in Java Actions

The following special constructs can be uses in Java actions. Other analogous C action
features are currently unavailable for Java.

Use '`%define throws`' to specify any uncaught exceptions from parser actions, and initial
actions specified by `%initial-action`.

`$n`   [Variable]

>   The semantic value for the nth component of the current rule. This may not be
>   assigned to. See Section 10.2.2 [Java Semantic Values], page 173.

`$<typealt>n`   [Variable]

>   Like `$n` but specifies a alternative type *typealt*. See Section 10.2.2 [Java Semantic
>   Values], page 173.

`$$`   [Variable]

>   The semantic value for the grouping made by the current rule. As a value, this is
>   in the base type (`Object` or as specified by '`%define api.value.type`') as in not
>   cast to the declared subtype because casts are not allowed on the left-hand side of
>   Java assignments. Use an explicit Java cast if the correct subtype is needed. See
>   Section 10.2.2 [Java Semantic Values], page 173.

`$<typealt>$`   [Variable]

>   Same as `$$` since Java always allow assigning to the base type. Perhaps we should
>   use this and `$<>$` for the value and `$$` for setting the value but there is currently no
>   easy way to distinguish these constructs. See Section 10.2.2 [Java Semantic Values],
>   page 173.

`@n`   [Variable]

>   The location information of the nth component of the current rule. This may not be
>   assigned to. See Section 10.2.3 [Java Location Values], page 173.

`@$`   [Variable]
> The location information of the grouping made by the current rule. See Section 10.2.3 [Java Location Values], page 173.

`return YYABORT ;`   [Statement]
> Return immediately from the parser, indicating failure. See Section 10.2.4 [Java Parser Interface], page 174.

`return YYACCEPT ;`   [Statement]
> Return immediately from the parser, indicating success. See Section 10.2.4 [Java Parser Interface], page 174.

`return YYERROR ;`   [Statement]
> Start error recovery (without printing an error message). See Chapter 6 [Error Recovery], page 127.

`boolean recovering ()`   [Function]
> Return whether error recovery is being done. In this state, the parser reads token until it reaches a known state, and then restarts normal operation. See Chapter 6 [Error Recovery], page 127.

`void yyerror (`*String* `msg)`   [Function]
`void yyerror (`*Position* `loc,` *String* `msg)`   [Function]
`void yyerror (`*Location* `loc,` *String* `msg)`   [Function]
> Print an error message using the `yyerror` method of the scanner instance in use. The `Location` and `Position` parameters are available only if location tracking is active.

10.2.7 Java Push Parser Interface

(The current push parsing interface is experimental and may evolve. More user feedback will help to stabilize it.)

Normally, Bison generates a pull parser for Java. The following Bison declaration says that you want the parser to be a push parser (see Section 3.7.13 [api.push-pull], page 86):

    %define api.push-pull push

Most of the discussion about the Java pull Parser Interface, (see Section 10.2.4 [Java Parser Interface], page 174) applies to the push parser interface as well.

When generating a push parser, the method `push_parse` is created with the following signature (depending on if locations are enabled).

`void push_parse (`*int* `token,` *Object* `yylval)`   [Method on `YYParser`]
`void push_parse (`*int* `token,` *Object* `yylval, Location`   [Method on `YYParser`]
> `yyloc)`
`void push_parse (`*int* `token,` *Object* `yylval, Position`   [Method on `YYParser`]
> `yypos)`

The primary difference with respect to a pull parser is that the parser method `push_parse` is invoked repeatedly to parse each token. This function is available if either the `"%define api.push-pull push"` or `"%define api.push-pull both"` declaration is used (see Section 3.7.13 [api.push-pull], page 86). The `Location` and `Position` parameters are available only if location tracking is active.

The value returned by the push_parse method is one of the following four constants: YYABORT, YYACCEPT, YYERROR, or YYPUSH_MORE. This new value, YYPUSH_MORE, may be returned if more input is required to finish parsing the grammar.

If api.push-pull is declared as both, then the generated parser class will also implement the parse method. This method's body is a loop that repeatedly invokes the scanner and then passes the values obtained from the scanner to the push_parse method.

There is one additional complication. Technically, the push parser does not need to know about the scanner (i.e. an object implementing the YYParser.Lexer interface), but it does need access to the yyerror method. Currently, the yyerror method is defined in the YYParser.Lexer interface. Hence, an implementation of that interface is still required in order to provide an implementation of yyerror. The current approach (and subject to change) is to require the YYParser constructor to be given an object implementing the YYParser.Lexer interface. This object need only implement the yyerror method; the other methods can be stubbed since they will never be invoked. The simplest way to do this is to add a trivial scanner implementation to your grammar file using whatever implementation of yyerror is desired. The following code sample shows a simple way to accomplish this.

```
%code lexer
{
  public Object getLVal () {return null;}
  public int yylex () {return 0;}
  public void yyerror (String s) {System.err.println(s);}
}
```

10.2.8 Differences between C/C++ and Java Grammars

The different structure of the Java language forces several differences between C/C++ grammars, and grammars designed for Java parsers. This section summarizes these differences.

- Java lacks a preprocessor, so the YYERROR, YYACCEPT, YYABORT symbols (see Appendix A [Table of Symbols], page 189) cannot obviously be macros. Instead, they should be preceded by return when they appear in an action. The actual definition of these symbols is opaque to the Bison grammar, and it might change in the future. The only meaningful operation that you can do, is to return them. See Section 10.2.6 [Java Action Features], page 176.

  Note that of these three symbols, only YYACCEPT and YYABORT will cause a return from the yyparse method[1].

- Java lacks unions, so %union has no effect. Instead, semantic values have a common base type: Object or as specified by '%define api.value.type'. Angle brackets on %token, type, $n and $$ specify subtypes rather than fields of an union. The type of $$, even with angle brackets, is the base type since Java casts are not allow on the left-hand side of assignments. Also, $n and @n are not allowed on the left-hand side of assignments. See Section 10.2.2 [Java Semantic Values], page 173, and Section 10.2.6 [Java Action Features], page 176.

- The prologue declarations have a different meaning than in C/C++ code.

---

[1] Java parsers include the actions in a separate method than yyparse in order to have an intuitive syntax that corresponds to these C macros.

`%code imports`
> blocks are placed at the beginning of the Java source code. They may include copyright notices. For a `package` declarations, it is suggested to use '`%define package`' instead.

unqualified `%code`
> blocks are placed inside the parser class.

`%code lexer`
> blocks, if specified, should include the implementation of the scanner. If there is no such block, the scanner can be any class that implements the appropriate interface (see Section 10.2.5 [Java Scanner Interface], page 175).

Other `%code` blocks are not supported in Java parsers. In particular, `%{ ... %}` blocks should not be used and may give an error in future versions of Bison.

The epilogue has the same meaning as in C/C++ code and it can be used to define other classes used by the parser *outside* the parser class.

10.2.9 Java Declarations Summary

This summary only include declarations specific to Java or have special meaning when used in a Java parser.

`%language "Java"`   [Directive]
> Generate a Java class for the parser.

`%lex-param {type name}`   [Directive]
> A parameter for the lexer class defined by `%code lexer` *only*, added as parameters to the lexer constructor and the parser constructor that *creates* a lexer. Default is none. See Section 10.2.5 [Java Scanner Interface], page 175.

`%name-prefix "prefix"`   [Directive]
> The prefix of the parser class name `prefixParser` if '`%define parser_class_name`' is not used. Default is YY. See Section 10.2.1 [Java Bison Interface], page 172.

`%parse-param {type name}`   [Directive]
> A parameter for the parser class added as parameters to constructor(s) and as fields initialized by the constructor(s). Default is none. See Section 10.2.4 [Java Parser Interface], page 174.

`%token <type> token ...`   [Directive]
> Declare tokens. Note that the angle brackets enclose a Java *type*. See Section 10.2.2 [Java Semantic Values], page 173.

`%type <type> nonterminal ...`   [Directive]
> Declare the type of nonterminals. Note that the angle brackets enclose a Java *type*. See Section 10.2.2 [Java Semantic Values], page 173.

`%code { code ... }`   [Directive]
> Code appended to the inside of the parser class. See Section 10.2.8 [Java Differences], page 178.

%code imports *{ code ... }*   [Directive]

Code inserted just after the **package** declaration. See Section 10.2.8 [Java Differences], page 178.

%code init *{ code ... }*   [Directive]

Code inserted at the beginning of the parser constructor body. See Section 10.2.4 [Java Parser Interface], page 174.

%code lexer *{ code ... }*   [Directive]

Code added to the body of a inner lexer class within the parser class. See Section 10.2.5 [Java Scanner Interface], page 175.

%% code ...   [Directive]

Code (after the second **%%**) appended to the end of the file, *outside* the parser class. See Section 10.2.8 [Java Differences], page 178.

%{ code ... %}   [Directive]

Not supported. Use **%code imports** instead. See Section 10.2.8 [Java Differences], page 178.

%define abstract   [Directive]

Whether the parser class is declared **abstract**. Default is false. See Section 10.2.1 [Java Bison Interface], page 172.

%define annotations *{annotations}*   [Directive]

The Java annotations for the parser class. Default is none. See Section 10.2.1 [Java Bison Interface], page 172.

%define extends *{superclass}*   [Directive]

The superclass of the parser class. Default is none. See Section 10.2.1 [Java Bison Interface], page 172.

%define final   [Directive]

Whether the parser class is declared **final**. Default is false. See Section 10.2.1 [Java Bison Interface], page 172.

%define implements *{interfaces}*   [Directive]

The implemented interfaces of the parser class, a comma-separated list. Default is none. See Section 10.2.1 [Java Bison Interface], page 172.

%define init_throws *{exceptions}*   [Directive]

The exceptions thrown by **%code init** from the parser class constructor. Default is none. See Section 10.2.4 [Java Parser Interface], page 174.

%define lex_throws *{exceptions}*   [Directive]

The exceptions thrown by the **yylex** method of the lexer, a comma-separated list. Default is **java.io.IOException**. See Section 10.2.5 [Java Scanner Interface], page 175.

%define api.location.type *{class}*   [Directive]

The name of the class used for locations (a range between two positions). This class is generated as an inner class of the parser class by **bison**. Default is **Location**. Formerly named **location_type**. See Section 10.2.3 [Java Location Values], page 173.

`%define package {package}`   [Directive]

> The package to put the parser class in. Default is none. See Section 10.2.1 [Java Bison Interface], page 172.

`%define parser_class_name {name}`   [Directive]

> The name of the parser class. Default is `YYParser` or *name-prefix*`Parser`. See Section 10.2.1 [Java Bison Interface], page 172.

`%define api.position.type {class}`   [Directive]

> The name of the class used for positions. This class must be supplied by the user. Default is `Position`. Formerly named `position_type`. See Section 10.2.3 [Java Location Values], page 173.

`%define public`   [Directive]

> Whether the parser class is declared `public`. Default is false. See Section 10.2.1 [Java Bison Interface], page 172.

`%define api.value.type {class}`   [Directive]

> The base type of semantic values. Default is `Object`. See Section 10.2.2 [Java Semantic Values], page 173.

`%define strictfp`   [Directive]

> Whether the parser class is declared `strictfp`. Default is false. See Section 10.2.1 [Java Bison Interface], page 172.

`%define throws {exceptions}`   [Directive]

> The exceptions thrown by user-supplied parser actions and `%initial-action`, a comma-separated list. Default is none. See Section 10.2.4 [Java Parser Interface], page 174.

11 Frequently Asked Questions

Several questions about Bison come up occasionally. Here some of them are addressed.

11.1 Memory Exhausted

My parser returns with error with a 'memory exhausted' message. What can I do?

This question is already addressed elsewhere, see Section 3.3.3 [Recursive Rules], page 60.

11.2 How Can I Reset the Parser

The following phenomenon has several symptoms, resulting in the following typical questions:

I invoke yyparse several times, and on correct input it works properly; but when a parse error is found, all the other calls fail too. How can I reset the error flag of yyparse?

or

My parser includes support for an '#include'-like feature, in which case I run yyparse from yyparse. This fails although I did specify '%define api.pure full'.

These problems typically come not from Bison itself, but from Lex-generated scanners. Because these scanners use large buffers for speed, they might not notice a change of input file. As a demonstration, consider the following source file, first-line.l:

```
%{
#include <stdio.h>
#include <stdlib.h>
%}
%%
.*\n    ECHO; return 1;
%%
int
yyparse (char const *file)
{
  yyin = fopen (file, "r");
  if (!yyin)
    {
      perror ("fopen");
      exit (EXIT_FAILURE);
    }
```

```
      /* One token only.  */
      yylex ();
      if (fclose (yyin) != 0)
        {
          perror ("fclose");
          exit (EXIT_FAILURE);
        }
      return 0;
    }

    int
    main (void)
    {
      yyparse ("input");
      yyparse ("input");
      return 0;
    }
```

If the file `input` contains

```
      input:1: Hello,
      input:2: World!
```

then instead of getting the first line twice, you get:

```
      $ flex -ofirst-line.c first-line.l
      $ gcc  -ofirst-line   first-line.c -ll
      $ ./first-line
      input:1: Hello,
      input:2: World!
```

Therefore, whenever you change `yyin`, you must tell the Lex-generated scanner to discard its current buffer and switch to the new one. This depends upon your implementation of Lex; see its documentation for more. For Flex, it suffices to call 'YY_FLUSH_BUFFER' after each change to `yyin`. If your Flex-generated scanner needs to read from several input streams to handle features like include files, you might consider using Flex functions like 'yy_switch_to_buffer' that manipulate multiple input buffers.

If your Flex-generated scanner uses start conditions (see Section "Start conditions" in *The Flex Manual*), you might also want to reset the scanner's state, i.e., go back to the initial start condition, through a call to 'BEGIN (0)'.

11.3 Strings are Destroyed

My parser seems to destroy old strings, or maybe it loses track of them. Instead of reporting '"foo", "bar"', it reports '"bar", "bar"', or even '"foo\nbar", "bar"'.

This error is probably the single most frequent "bug report" sent to Bison lists, but is only concerned with a misunderstanding of the role of the scanner. Consider the following Lex code:

```
%{
#include <stdio.h>
char *yylval = NULL;
%}
%%
.*      yylval = yytext; return 1;
\n      /* IGNORE */
%%
int
main ()
{
  /* Similar to using $1, $2 in a Bison action.  */
  char *fst = (yylex (), yylval);
  char *snd = (yylex (), yylval);
  printf ("\"%s\", \"%s\"\n", fst, snd);
  return 0;
}
```

If you compile and run this code, you get:

```
$ flex -osplit-lines.c split-lines.l
$ gcc  -osplit-lines  split-lines.c -ll
$ printf 'one\ntwo\n' | ./split-lines
"one
two", "two"
```

this is because **yytext** is a buffer provided for *reading* in the action, but if you want to keep it, you have to duplicate it (e.g., using **strdup**). Note that the output may depend on how your implementation of Lex handles **yytext**. For instance, when given the Lex compatibility option −l (which triggers the option '**%array**') Flex generates a different behavior:

```
$ flex -l -osplit-lines.c split-lines.l
$ gcc    -osplit-lines  split-lines.c -ll
$ printf 'one\ntwo\n' | ./split-lines
"two", "two"
```

11.4 Implementing Gotos/Loops

> My simple calculator supports variables, assignments, and functions, but how can I implement gotos, or loops?

Although very pedagogical, the examples included in the document blur the distinction to make between the parser—whose job is to recover the structure of a text and to transmit it to subsequent modules of the program—and the processing (such as the execution) of this structure. This works well with so called straight line programs, i.e., precisely those that have a straightforward execution model: execute simple instructions one after the others.

If you want a richer model, you will probably need to use the parser to construct a tree that does represent the structure it has recovered; this tree is usually called the *abstract syntax tree*, or *AST* for short. Then, walking through this tree, traversing it in various ways, will enable treatments such as its execution or its translation, which will result in an interpreter or a compiler.

This topic is way beyond the scope of this manual, and the reader is invited to consult the dedicated literature.

11.5 Multiple start-symbols

I have several closely related grammars, and I would like to share their implementations. In fact, I could use a single grammar but with multiple entry points.

Bison does not support multiple start-symbols, but there is a very simple means to simulate them. If foo and bar are the two pseudo start-symbols, then introduce two new tokens, say START_FOO and START_BAR, and use them as switches from the real start-symbol:

```
%token START_FOO START_BAR;
%start start;
start:
  START_FOO foo
| START_BAR bar;
```

These tokens prevents the introduction of new conflicts. As far as the parser goes, that is all that is needed.

Now the difficult part is ensuring that the scanner will send these tokens first. If your scanner is hand-written, that should be straightforward. If your scanner is generated by Lex, them there is simple means to do it: recall that anything between '%{ ... %}' after the first %% is copied verbatim in the top of the generated yylex function. Make sure a variable start_token is available in the scanner (e.g., a global variable or using %lex-param etc.), and use the following:

```
    /* Prologue.  */
%%
%{
  if (start_token)
    {
      int t = start_token;
      start_token = 0;
      return t;
    }
%}
    /* The rules.  */
```

11.6 Secure? Conform?

Is Bison secure? Does it conform to POSIX?

If you're looking for a guarantee or certification, we don't provide it. However, Bison is intended to be a reliable program that conforms to the POSIX specification for Yacc. If you run into problems, please send us a bug report.

11.7 I can't build Bison

I can't build Bison because make complains that msgfmt is not found. What should I do?

Like most GNU packages with internationalization support, that feature is turned on by default. If you have problems building in the `po` subdirectory, it indicates that your system's internationalization support is lacking. You can re-configure Bison with `--disable-nls` to turn off this support, or you can install GNU gettext from `ftp://ftp.gnu.org/gnu/gettext/` and re-configure Bison. See the file `ABOUT-NLS` for more information.

11.8 Where can I find help?

I'm having trouble using Bison. Where can I find help?

First, read this fine manual. Beyond that, you can send mail to `help-bison@gnu.org`. This mailing list is intended to be populated with people who are willing to answer questions about using and installing Bison. Please keep in mind that (most of) the people on the list have aspects of their lives which are not related to Bison (!), so you may not receive an answer to your question right away. This can be frustrating, but please try not to honk them off; remember that any help they provide is purely voluntary and out of the kindness of their hearts.

11.9 Bug Reports

I found a bug. What should I include in the bug report?

Before you send a bug report, make sure you are using the latest version. Check `ftp://ftp.gnu.org/pub/gnu/bison/` or one of its mirrors. Be sure to include the version number in your bug report. If the bug is present in the latest version but not in a previous version, try to determine the most recent version which did not contain the bug.

If the bug is parser-related, you should include the smallest grammar you can which demonstrates the bug. The grammar file should also be complete (i.e., I should be able to run it through Bison without having to edit or add anything). The smaller and simpler the grammar, the easier it will be to fix the bug.

Include information about your compilation environment, including your operating system's name and version and your compiler's name and version. If you have trouble compiling, you should also include a transcript of the build session, starting with the invocation of 'configure'. Depending on the nature of the bug, you may be asked to send additional files as well (such as `config.h` or `config.cache`).

Patches are most welcome, but not required. That is, do not hesitate to send a bug report just because you cannot provide a fix.

Send bug reports to `bug-bison@gnu.org`.

11.10 More Languages

Will Bison ever have C++ and Java support? How about *insert your favorite language here*?

C++ and Java support is there now, and is documented. We'd love to add other languages; contributions are welcome.

11.11 Beta Testing

What is involved in being a beta tester?

It's not terribly involved. Basically, you would download a test release, compile it, and use it to build and run a parser or two. After that, you would submit either a bug report or a message saying that everything is okay. It is important to report successes as well as failures because test releases eventually become mainstream releases, but only if they are adequately tested. If no one tests, development is essentially halted.

Beta testers are particularly needed for operating systems to which the developers do not have easy access. They currently have easy access to recent GNU/Linux and Solaris versions. Reports about other operating systems are especially welcome.

11.12 Mailing Lists

How do I join the help-bison and bug-bison mailing lists?

See `http://lists.gnu.org/`.

Appendix A Bison Symbols

@$ [Variable]

In an action, the location of the left-hand side of the rule. See Section 3.5 [Tracking Locations], page 70.

@n   [Variable]
@n   [Symbol]

In an action, the location of the *n*-th symbol of the right-hand side of the rule. See Section 3.5 [Tracking Locations], page 70.

In a grammar, the Bison-generated nonterminal symbol for a mid-rule action with a semantical value. See Section 3.4.8.2 [Mid-Rule Action Translation], page 68.

@name   [Variable]
@[name]   [Variable]

In an action, the location of a symbol addressed by *name*. See Section 3.5 [Tracking Locations], page 70.

$@n   [Symbol]

In a grammar, the Bison-generated nonterminal symbol for a mid-rule action with no semantical value. See Section 3.4.8.2 [Mid-Rule Action Translation], page 68.

$$ [Variable]

In an action, the semantic value of the left-hand side of the rule. See Section 3.4.6 [Actions], page 64.

$n   [Variable]

In an action, the semantic value of the *n*-th symbol of the right-hand side of the rule. See Section 3.4.6 [Actions], page 64.

$name   [Variable]
$[name]   [Variable]

In an action, the semantic value of a symbol addressed by *name*. See Section 3.4.6 [Actions], page 64.

%%   [Delimiter]

Delimiter used to separate the grammar rule section from the Bison declarations section or the epilogue. See Section 1.9 [The Overall Layout of a Bison Grammar], page 29.

%{code%}   [Delimiter]

All code listed between '%{' and '%}' is copied verbatim to the parser implementation file. Such code forms the prologue of the grammar file. See Section 3.1 [Outline of a Bison Grammar], page 51.

%?{expression}   [Directive]

Predicate actions. This is a type of action clause that may appear in rules. The expression is evaluated, and if false, causes a syntax error. In GLR parsers during nondeterministic operation, this silently causes an alternative parse to die. During deterministic operation, it is the same as the effect of YYERROR. See Section 1.5.4 [Semantic Predicates], page 26.

This feature is experimental. More user feedback will help to determine whether it should become a permanent feature.

/ ... */*   [Construct]
// ...   [Construct]
    Comments, as in C/C++.

:   [Delimiter]
    Separates a rule's result from its components. See Section 3.3 [Syntax of Grammar Rules], page 59.

;   [Delimiter]
    Terminates a rule. See Section 3.3 [Syntax of Grammar Rules], page 59.

| [Delimiter]
    Separates alternate rules for the same result nonterminal. See Section 3.3 [Syntax of Grammar Rules], page 59.

<*>   [Directive]
    Used to define a default tagged **%destructor** or default tagged **%printer**.

    This feature is experimental. More user feedback will help to determine whether it should become a permanent feature.

    See Section 3.7.6 [Freeing Discarded Symbols], page 77.

<>   [Directive]
    Used to define a default tagless **%destructor** or default tagless **%printer**.

    This feature is experimental. More user feedback will help to determine whether it should become a permanent feature.

    See Section 3.7.6 [Freeing Discarded Symbols], page 77.

$accept   [Symbol]
    The predefined nonterminal whose only rule is '$accept: *start* $end', where *start* is the start symbol. See Section 3.7.9 [The Start-Symbol], page 80. It cannot be used in the grammar.

%code *{code}*   [Directive]
%code *qualifier {code}*   [Directive]
    Insert *code* verbatim into the output parser source at the default location or at the location specified by *qualifier*. See Section 3.7.14 [%code Summary], page 92.

%debug   [Directive]
    Equip the parser for debugging. See Section 3.7.12 [Decl Summary], page 82.

%define *variable*   [Directive]
%define *variable value*   [Directive]
%define *variable {value}*   [Directive]
%define *variable* "*value*"   [Directive]
    Define a variable to adjust Bison's behavior. See Section 3.7.13 [%define Summary], page 86.

%defines [Directive]

Bison declaration to create a parser header file, which is usually meant for the scanner. See Section 3.7.12 [Decl Summary], page 82.

%defines *defines-file* [Directive]

Same as above, but save in the file *defines-file*. See Section 3.7.12 [Decl Summary], page 82.

%destructor [Directive]

Specify how the parser should reclaim the memory associated to discarded symbols. See Section 3.7.6 [Freeing Discarded Symbols], page 77.

%dprec [Directive]

Bison declaration to assign a precedence to a rule that is used at parse time to resolve reduce/reduce conflicts. See Section 1.5 [Writing GLR Parsers], page 20.

%empty [Directive]

Bison declaration to declare make explicit that a rule has an empty right-hand side. See Section 3.3.2 [Empty Rules], page 60.

$end [Symbol]

The predefined token marking the end of the token stream. It cannot be used in the grammar.

error [Symbol]

A token name reserved for error recovery. This token may be used in grammar rules so as to allow the Bison parser to recognize an error in the grammar without halting the process. In effect, a sentence containing an error may be recognized as valid. On a syntax error, the token **error** becomes the current lookahead token. Actions corresponding to **error** are then executed, and the lookahead token is reset to the token that originally caused the violation. See Chapter 6 [Error Recovery], page 127.

%error-verbose [Directive]

An obsolete directive standing for '%define parse.error verbose' (see Section 4.7 [The Error Reporting Function yyerror], page 102).

%file-prefix "*prefix*" [Directive]

Bison declaration to set the prefix of the output files. See Section 3.7.12 [Decl Summary], page 82.

%glr-parser [Directive]

Bison declaration to produce a GLR parser. See Section 1.5 [Writing GLR Parsers], page 20.

%initial-action [Directive]

Run user code before parsing. See Section 3.7.5 [Performing Actions before Parsing], page 77.

%language [Directive]

Specify the programming language for the generated parser. See Section 3.7.12 [Decl Summary], page 82.

%left   [Directive]
> Bison declaration to assign precedence and left associativity to token(s). See Section 3.7.3 [Operator Precedence], page 76.

%lex-param {*argument-declaration*} ...   [Directive]
> Bison declaration to specifying additional arguments that `yylex` should accept. See Section 4.6.4 [Calling Conventions for Pure Parsers], page 101.

%merge   [Directive]
> Bison declaration to assign a merging function to a rule. If there is a reduce/reduce conflict with a rule having the same merging function, the function is applied to the two semantic values to get a single result. See Section 1.5 [Writing GLR Parsers], page 20.

%name-prefix "*prefix*"   [Directive]
> Obsoleted by the `%define` variable `api.prefix` (see Section 3.8 [Multiple Parsers in the Same Program], page 94).
>
> Rename the external symbols (variables and functions) used in the parser so that they start with *prefix* instead of 'yy'. Contrary to `api.prefix`, do no rename types and macros.
>
> The precise list of symbols renamed in C parsers is `yyparse`, `yylex`, `yyerror`, `yynerrs`, `yylval`, `yychar`, `yydebug`, and (if locations are used) `yylloc`. If you use a push parser, `yypush_parse`, `yypull_parse`, `yypstate`, `yypstate_new` and `yypstate_delete` will also be renamed. For example, if you use '%name-prefix "c_"', the names become `c_parse`, `c_lex`, and so on. For C++ parsers, see the `%define api.namespace` documentation in this section.

%no-lines   [Directive]
> Bison declaration to avoid generating `#line` directives in the parser implementation file. See Section 3.7.12 [Decl Summary], page 82.

%nonassoc   [Directive]
> Bison declaration to assign precedence and nonassociativity to token(s). See Section 3.7.3 [Operator Precedence], page 76.

%output "*file*"   [Directive]
> Bison declaration to set the name of the parser implementation file. See Section 3.7.12 [Decl Summary], page 82.

%param {*argument-declaration*} ...   [Directive]
> Bison declaration to specify additional arguments that both `yylex` and `yyparse` should accept. See Section 4.1 [The Parser Function yyparse], page 97.

%parse-param {*argument-declaration*} ...   [Directive]
> Bison declaration to specify additional arguments that `yyparse` should accept. See Section 4.1 [The Parser Function yyparse], page 97.

%prec   [Directive]
> Bison declaration to assign a precedence to a specific rule. See Section 5.4 [Context-Dependent Precedence], page 112.

%precedence   [Directive]

Bison declaration to assign precedence to token(s), but no associativity See Section 3.7.3 [Operator Precedence], page 76.

%pure-parser   [Directive]

Deprecated version of '**%define api.pure**' (see Section 3.7.13 [api.pure], page 86), for which Bison is more careful to warn about unreasonable usage.

%require "*version*"   [Directive]

Require version *version* or higher of Bison. See Section 3.7.1 [Require a Version of Bison], page 74.

%right   [Directive]

Bison declaration to assign precedence and right associativity to token(s). See Section 3.7.3 [Operator Precedence], page 76.

%skeleton   [Directive]

Specify the skeleton to use; usually for development. See Section 3.7.12 [Decl Summary], page 82.

%start   [Directive]

Bison declaration to specify the start symbol. See Section 3.7.9 [The Start-Symbol], page 80.

%token   [Directive]

Bison declaration to declare token(s) without specifying precedence. See Section 3.7.2 [Token Type Names], page 75.

%token-table   [Directive]

Bison declaration to include a token name table in the parser implementation file. See Section 3.7.12 [Decl Summary], page 82.

%type   [Directive]

Bison declaration to declare nonterminals. See Section 3.7.4 [Nonterminal Symbols], page 76.

$undefined   [Symbol]

The predefined token onto which all undefined values returned by **yylex** are mapped. It cannot be used in the grammar, rather, use **error**.

%union   [Directive]

Bison declaration to specify several possible data types for semantic values. See Section 3.4.4 [The Union Declaration], page 63.

YYABORT   [Macro]

Macro to pretend that an unrecoverable syntax error has occurred, by making **yyparse** return 1 immediately. The error reporting function **yyerror** is not called. See Section 4.1 [The Parser Function **yyparse**], page 97.

For Java parsers, this functionality is invoked using **return YYABORT;** instead.

YYACCEPT   [Macro]

Macro to pretend that a complete utterance of the language has been read, by making **yyparse** return 0 immediately. See Section 4.1 [The Parser Function yyparse], page 97.

For Java parsers, this functionality is invoked using **return YYACCEPT;** instead.

YYBACKUP   [Macro]

Macro to discard a value from the parser stack and fake a lookahead token. See Section 4.8 [Special Features for Use in Actions], page 103.

yychar   [Variable]

External integer variable that contains the integer value of the lookahead token. (In a pure parser, it is a local variable within **yyparse**.) Error-recovery rule actions may examine this variable. See Section 4.8 [Special Features for Use in Actions], page 103.

yyclearin   [Variable]

Macro used in error-recovery rule actions. It clears the previous lookahead token. See Chapter 6 [Error Recovery], page 127.

YYDEBUG   [Macro]

Macro to define to equip the parser with tracing code. See Section 8.4 [Tracing Your Parser], page 142.

yydebug   [Variable]

External integer variable set to zero by default. If **yydebug** is given a nonzero value, the parser will output information on input symbols and parser action. See Section 8.4 [Tracing Your Parser], page 142.

yyerrok   [Macro]

Macro to cause parser to recover immediately to its normal mode after a syntax error. See Chapter 6 [Error Recovery], page 127.

YYERROR   [Macro]

Cause an immediate syntax error. This statement initiates error recovery just as if the parser itself had detected an error; however, it does not call **yyerror**, and does not print any message. If you want to print an error message, call **yyerror** explicitly before the 'YYERROR;' statement. See Chapter 6 [Error Recovery], page 127.

For Java parsers, this functionality is invoked using **return YYERROR;** instead.

yyerror   [Function]

User-supplied function to be called by **yyparse** on error. See Section 4.7 [The Error Reporting Function yyerror], page 102.

YYERROR_VERBOSE   [Macro]

An obsolete macro used in the **yacc.c** skeleton, that you define with **#define** in the prologue to request verbose, specific error message strings when **yyerror** is called. It doesn't matter what definition you use for YYERROR_VERBOSE, just whether you define it. Using '**%define parse.error verbose**' is preferred (see Section 4.7 [The Error Reporting Function yyerror], page 102).

YYFPRINTF   [Macro]

Macro used to output run-time traces. See Section 8.4.1 [Enabling Traces], page 142.

YYINITDEPTH   [Macro]

Macro for specifying the initial size of the parser stack. See Section 5.10 [Memory Management], page 124.

`yylex`   [Function]

User-supplied lexical analyzer function, called with no arguments to get the next token. See Section 4.6 [The Lexical Analyzer Function `yylex`], page 99.

`yylloc`   [Variable]

External variable in which `yylex` should place the line and column numbers associated with a token. (In a pure parser, it is a local variable within `yyparse`, and its address is passed to `yylex`.) You can ignore this variable if you don't use the '`@`' feature in the grammar actions. See Section 4.6.3 [Textual Locations of Tokens], page 101. In semantic actions, it stores the location of the lookahead token. See Section 3.5.2 [Actions and Locations], page 71.

YYLTYPE   [Type]

Data type of `yylloc`; by default, a structure with four members. See Section 3.5.1 [Data Types of Locations], page 70.

`yylval`   [Variable]

External variable in which `yylex` should place the semantic value associated with a token. (In a pure parser, it is a local variable within `yyparse`, and its address is passed to `yylex`.) See Section 4.6.2 [Semantic Values of Tokens], page 100. In semantic actions, it stores the semantic value of the lookahead token. See Section 3.4.6 [Actions], page 64.

YYMAXDEPTH   [Macro]

Macro for specifying the maximum size of the parser stack. See Section 5.10 [Memory Management], page 124.

`yynerrs`   [Variable]

Global variable which Bison increments each time it reports a syntax error. (In a pure parser, it is a local variable within `yyparse`. In a pure push parser, it is a member of `yypstate`.) See Section 4.7 [The Error Reporting Function `yyerror`], page 102.

`yyparse`   [Function]

The parser function produced by Bison; call this function to start parsing. See Section 4.1 [The Parser Function `yyparse`], page 97.

YYPRINT   [Macro]

Macro used to output token semantic values. For `yacc.c` only. Obsoleted by `%printer`. See Section 8.4.3 [The `YYPRINT` Macro], page 146.

`yypstate_delete`   [Function]

The function to delete a parser instance, produced by Bison in push mode; call this function to delete the memory associated with a parser. See Section 4.5 [The Parser Delete Function `yypstate_delete`], page 99. (The current push parsing interface is experimental and may evolve. More user feedback will help to stabilize it.)

yypstate_new   [Function]
The function to create a parser instance, produced by Bison in push mode; call this function to create a new parser. See Section 4.4 [The Parser Create Function yypstate_new], page 98. (The current push parsing interface is experimental and may evolve. More user feedback will help to stabilize it.)

yypull_parse   [Function]
The parser function produced by Bison in push mode; call this function to parse the rest of the input stream. See Section 4.3 [The Pull Parser Function yypull_parse], page 98. (The current push parsing interface is experimental and may evolve. More user feedback will help to stabilize it.)

yypush_parse   [Function]
The parser function produced by Bison in push mode; call this function to parse a single token. See Section 4.2 [The Push Parser Function yypush_parse], page 98. (The current push parsing interface is experimental and may evolve. More user feedback will help to stabilize it.)

YYRECOVERING   [Macro]
The expression YYRECOVERING () yields 1 when the parser is recovering from a syntax error, and 0 otherwise. See Section 4.8 [Special Features for Use in Actions], page 103.

YYSTACK_USE_ALLOCA   [Macro]
Macro used to control the use of alloca when the deterministic parser in C needs to extend its stacks. If defined to 0, the parser will use malloc to extend its stacks. If defined to 1, the parser will use alloca. Values other than 0 and 1 are reserved for future Bison extensions. If not defined, YYSTACK_USE_ALLOCA defaults to 0.

In the all-too-common case where your code may run on a host with a limited stack and with unreliable stack-overflow checking, you should set YYMAXDEPTH to a value that cannot possibly result in unchecked stack overflow on any of your target hosts when alloca is called. You can inspect the code that Bison generates in order to determine the proper numeric values. This will require some expertise in low-level implementation details.

YYSTYPE   [Type]
Deprecated in favor of the %define variable api.value.type. Data type of semantic values; int by default. See Section 3.4.1 [Data Types of Semantic Values], page 61.

Appendix B Glossary

Accepting state

A state whose only action is the accept action. The accepting state is thus a consistent state. See Section 8.1 [Understanding Your Parser], page 133.

Backus-Naur Form (BNF; also called "Backus Normal Form")

Formal method of specifying context-free grammars originally proposed by John Backus, and slightly improved by Peter Naur in his 1960-01-02 committee document contributing to what became the Algol 60 report. See Section 1.1 [Languages and Context-Free Grammars], page 17.

Consistent state

A state containing only one possible action. See Section 5.8.2 [Default Reductions], page 119.

Context-free grammars

Grammars specified as rules that can be applied regardless of context. Thus, if there is a rule which says that an integer can be used as an expression, integers are allowed *anywhere* an expression is permitted. See Section 1.1 [Languages and Context-Free Grammars], page 17.

Default reduction

The reduction that a parser should perform if the current parser state contains no other action for the lookahead token. In permitted parser states, Bison declares the reduction with the largest lookahead set to be the default reduction and removes that lookahead set. See Section 5.8.2 [Default Reductions], page 119.

Defaulted state

A consistent state with a default reduction. See Section 5.8.2 [Default Reductions], page 119.

Dynamic allocation

Allocation of memory that occurs during execution, rather than at compile time or on entry to a function.

Empty string

Analogous to the empty set in set theory, the empty string is a character string of length zero.

Finite-state stack machine

A "machine" that has discrete states in which it is said to exist at each instant in time. As input to the machine is processed, the machine moves from state to state as specified by the logic of the machine. In the case of the parser, the input is the language being parsed, and the states correspond to various stages in the grammar rules. See Chapter 5 [The Bison Parser Algorithm], page 107.

Generalized LR (GLR)

A parsing algorithm that can handle all context-free grammars, including those that are not LR(1). It resolves situations that Bison's deterministic parsing algorithm cannot by effectively splitting off multiple parsers, trying all possible parsers, and discarding those that fail in the light of additional right context. See Section 5.9 [Generalized LR Parsing], page 123.

Grouping   A language construct that is (in general) grammatically divisible; for example, 'expression' or 'declaration' in C. See Section 1.1 [Languages and Context-Free Grammars], page 17.

IELR(1) (Inadequacy Elimination LR(1))
           A minimal LR(1) parser table construction algorithm. That is, given any context-free grammar, IELR(1) generates parser tables with the full language-recognition power of canonical LR(1) but with nearly the same number of parser states as LALR(1). This reduction in parser states is often an order of magnitude. More importantly, because canonical LR(1)'s extra parser states may contain duplicate conflicts in the case of non-LR(1) grammars, the number of conflicts for IELR(1) is often an order of magnitude less as well. This can significantly reduce the complexity of developing a grammar. See Section 5.8.1 [LR Table Construction], page 118.

Infix operator
           An arithmetic operator that is placed between the operands on which it performs some operation.

Input stream
           A continuous flow of data between devices or programs.

LAC (Lookahead Correction)
           A parsing mechanism that fixes the problem of delayed syntax error detection, which is caused by LR state merging, default reductions, and the use of %nonassoc. Delayed syntax error detection results in unexpected semantic actions, initiation of error recovery in the wrong syntactic context, and an incorrect list of expected tokens in a verbose syntax error message. See Section 5.8.3 [LAC], page 121.

Language construct
           One of the typical usage schemas of the language. For example, one of the constructs of the C language is the if statement. See Section 1.1 [Languages and Context-Free Grammars], page 17.

Left associativity
           Operators having left associativity are analyzed from left to right: 'a+b+c' first computes 'a+b' and then combines with 'c'. See Section 5.3 [Operator Precedence], page 109.

Left recursion
           A rule whose result symbol is also its first component symbol; for example, 'expseq1 : expseq1 ',' exp;'. See Section 3.3.3 [Recursive Rules], page 60.

Left-to-right parsing
           Parsing a sentence of a language by analyzing it token by token from left to right. See Chapter 5 [The Bison Parser Algorithm], page 107.

Lexical analyzer (scanner)

> A function that reads an input stream and returns tokens one by one. See Section 4.6 [The Lexical Analyzer Function yylex], page 99.

Lexical tie-in

> A flag, set by actions in the grammar rules, which alters the way tokens are parsed. See Section 7.2 [Lexical Tie-ins], page 130.

Literal string token

> A token which consists of two or more fixed characters. See Section 3.2 [Symbols], page 57.

Lookahead token

> A token already read but not yet shifted. See Section 5.1 [Lookahead Tokens], page 107.

LALR(1)   The class of context-free grammars that Bison (like most other parser generators) can handle by default; a subset of LR(1). See Section 5.7 [Mysterious Conflicts], page 116.

LR(1)   The class of context-free grammars in which at most one token of lookahead is needed to disambiguate the parsing of any piece of input.

Nonterminal symbol

> A grammar symbol standing for a grammatical construct that can be expressed through rules in terms of smaller constructs; in other words, a construct that is not a token. See Section 3.2 [Symbols], page 57.

Parser   A function that recognizes valid sentences of a language by analyzing the syntax structure of a set of tokens passed to it from a lexical analyzer.

Postfix operator

> An arithmetic operator that is placed after the operands upon which it performs some operation.

Reduction   Replacing a string of nonterminals and/or terminals with a single nonterminal, according to a grammar rule. See Chapter 5 [The Bison Parser Algorithm], page 107.

Reentrant   A reentrant subprogram is a subprogram which can be in invoked any number of times in parallel, without interference between the various invocations. See Section 3.7.10 [A Pure (Reentrant) Parser], page 80.

Reverse polish notation

> A language in which all operators are postfix operators.

Right recursion

> A rule whose result symbol is also its last component symbol; for example, 'expseq1: exp ',' expseq1;'. See Section 3.3.3 [Recursive Rules], page 60.

Semantics   In computer languages, the semantics are specified by the actions taken for each instance of the language, i.e., the meaning of each statement. See Section 3.4 [Defining Language Semantics], page 61.

Shift   A parser is said to shift when it makes the choice of analyzing further input from
               the stream rather than reducing immediately some already-recognized rule. See
               Chapter 5 [The Bison Parser Algorithm], page 107.

Single-character literal
               A single character that is recognized and interpreted as is. See Section 1.2
               [From Formal Rules to Bison Input], page 18.

Start symbol
               The nonterminal symbol that stands for a complete valid utterance in the lan-
               guage being parsed. The start symbol is usually listed as the first nontermi-
               nal symbol in a language specification. See Section 3.7.9 [The Start-Symbol],
               page 80.

Symbol table
               A data structure where symbol names and associated data are stored during
               parsing to allow for recognition and use of existing information in repeated uses
               of a symbol. See Section 2.5 [Multi-function Calc], page 42.

Syntax error
               An error encountered during parsing of an input stream due to invalid syntax.
               See Chapter 6 [Error Recovery], page 127.

Token   A basic, grammatically indivisible unit of a language. The symbol that describes
               a token in the grammar is a terminal symbol. The input of the Bison parser
               is a stream of tokens which comes from the lexical analyzer. See Section 3.2
               [Symbols], page 57.

Terminal symbol
               A grammar symbol that has no rules in the grammar and therefore is gram-
               matically indivisible. The piece of text it represents is a token. See Section 1.1
               [Languages and Context-Free Grammars], page 17.

Unreachable state
               A parser state to which there does not exist a sequence of transitions from the
               parser's start state. A state can become unreachable during conflict resolution.
               See Section 5.8.4 [Unreachable States], page 122.

Appendix C Copying This Manual

Version 1.3, 3 November 2008

Copyright © 2000, 2001, 2002, 2007, 2008 Free Software Foundation, Inc.
http://fsf.org/

Everyone is permitted to copy and distribute verbatim copies
of this license document, but changing it is not allowed.

0. PREAMBLE

The purpose of this License is to make a manual, textbook, or other functional and
useful document *free* in the sense of freedom: to assure everyone the effective freedom
to copy and redistribute it, with or without modifying it, either commercially or noncommercially. Secondarily, this License preserves for the author and publisher a way
to get credit for their work, while not being considered responsible for modifications
made by others.

This License is a kind of "copyleft", which means that derivative works of the document
must themselves be free in the same sense. It complements the GNU General Public
License, which is a copyleft license designed for free software.

We have designed this License in order to use it for manuals for free software, because
free software needs free documentation: a free program should come with manuals
providing the same freedoms that the software does. But this License is not limited to
software manuals; it can be used for any textual work, regardless of subject matter or
whether it is published as a printed book. We recommend this License principally for
works whose purpose is instruction or reference.

1. APPLICABILITY AND DEFINITIONS

This License applies to any manual or other work, in any medium, that contains a
notice placed by the copyright holder saying it can be distributed under the terms
of this License. Such a notice grants a world-wide, royalty-free license, unlimited in
duration, to use that work under the conditions stated herein. The "Document",
below, refers to any such manual or work. Any member of the public is a licensee, and
is addressed as "you". You accept the license if you copy, modify or distribute the work
in a way requiring permission under copyright law.

A "Modified Version" of the Document means any work containing the Document or
a portion of it, either copied verbatim, or with modifications and/or translated into
another language.

A "Secondary Section" is a named appendix or a front-matter section of the Document
that deals exclusively with the relationship of the publishers or authors of the Document
to the Document's overall subject (or to related matters) and contains nothing that
could fall directly within that overall subject. (Thus, if the Document is in part a
textbook of mathematics, a Secondary Section may not explain any mathematics.) The
relationship could be a matter of historical connection with the subject or with related
matters, or of legal, commercial, philosophical, ethical or political position regarding
them.

The "Invariant Sections" are certain Secondary Sections whose titles are designated, as
being those of Invariant Sections, in the notice that says that the Document is released

under this License. If a section does not fit the above definition of Secondary then it is not allowed to be designated as Invariant. The Document may contain zero Invariant Sections. If the Document does not identify any Invariant Sections then there are none.

The "Cover Texts" are certain short passages of text that are listed, as Front-Cover Texts or Back-Cover Texts, in the notice that says that the Document is released under this License. A Front-Cover Text may be at most 5 words, and a Back-Cover Text may be at most 25 words.

A "Transparent" copy of the Document means a machine-readable copy, represented in a format whose specification is available to the general public, that is suitable for revising the document straightforwardly with generic text editors or (for images composed of pixels) generic paint programs or (for drawings) some widely available drawing editor, and that is suitable for input to text formatters or for automatic translation to a variety of formats suitable for input to text formatters. A copy made in an otherwise Transparent file format whose markup, or absence of markup, has been arranged to thwart or discourage subsequent modification by readers is not Transparent. An image format is not Transparent if used for any substantial amount of text. A copy that is not "Transparent" is called "Opaque".

Examples of suitable formats for Transparent copies include plain ASCII without markup, Texinfo input format, LaTeX input format, SGML or XML using a publicly available DTD, and standard-conforming simple HTML, PostScript or PDF designed for human modification. Examples of transparent image formats include PNG, XCF and JPG. Opaque formats include proprietary formats that can be read and edited only by proprietary word processors, SGML or XML for which the DTD and/or processing tools are not generally available, and the machine-generated HTML, PostScript or PDF produced by some word processors for output purposes only.

The "Title Page" means, for a printed book, the title page itself, plus such following pages as are needed to hold, legibly, the material this License requires to appear in the title page. For works in formats which do not have any title page as such, "Title Page" means the text near the most prominent appearance of the work's title, preceding the beginning of the body of the text.

The "publisher" means any person or entity that distributes copies of the Document to the public.

A section "Entitled XYZ" means a named subunit of the Document whose title either is precisely XYZ or contains XYZ in parentheses following text that translates XYZ in another language. (Here XYZ stands for a specific section name mentioned below, such as "Acknowledgements", "Dedications", "Endorsements", or "History".) To "Preserve the Title" of such a section when you modify the Document means that it remains a section "Entitled XYZ" according to this definition.

The Document may include Warranty Disclaimers next to the notice which states that this License applies to the Document. These Warranty Disclaimers are considered to be included by reference in this License, but only as regards disclaiming warranties: any other implication that these Warranty Disclaimers may have is void and has no effect on the meaning of this License.

2. VERBATIM COPYING

You may copy and distribute the Document in any medium, either commercially or noncommercially, provided that this License, the copyright notices, and the license notice saying this License applies to the Document are reproduced in all copies, and that you add no other conditions whatsoever to those of this License. You may not use technical measures to obstruct or control the reading or further copying of the copies you make or distribute. However, you may accept compensation in exchange for copies. If you distribute a large enough number of copies you must also follow the conditions in section 3.

You may also lend copies, under the same conditions stated above, and you may publicly display copies.

3. COPYING IN QUANTITY

If you publish printed copies (or copies in media that commonly have printed covers) of the Document, numbering more than 100, and the Document's license notice requires Cover Texts, you must enclose the copies in covers that carry, clearly and legibly, all these Cover Texts: Front-Cover Texts on the front cover, and Back-Cover Texts on the back cover. Both covers must also clearly and legibly identify you as the publisher of these copies. The front cover must present the full title with all words of the title equally prominent and visible. You may add other material on the covers in addition. Copying with changes limited to the covers, as long as they preserve the title of the Document and satisfy these conditions, can be treated as verbatim copying in other respects.

If the required texts for either cover are too voluminous to fit legibly, you should put the first ones listed (as many as fit reasonably) on the actual cover, and continue the rest onto adjacent pages.

If you publish or distribute Opaque copies of the Document numbering more than 100, you must either include a machine-readable Transparent copy along with each Opaque copy, or state in or with each Opaque copy a computer-network location from which the general network-using public has access to download using public-standard network protocols a complete Transparent copy of the Document, free of added material. If you use the latter option, you must take reasonably prudent steps, when you begin distribution of Opaque copies in quantity, to ensure that this Transparent copy will remain thus accessible at the stated location until at least one year after the last time you distribute an Opaque copy (directly or through your agents or retailers) of that edition to the public.

It is requested, but not required, that you contact the authors of the Document well before redistributing any large number of copies, to give them a chance to provide you with an updated version of the Document.

4. MODIFICATIONS

You may copy and distribute a Modified Version of the Document under the conditions of sections 2 and 3 above, provided that you release the Modified Version under precisely this License, with the Modified Version filling the role of the Document, thus licensing distribution and modification of the Modified Version to whoever possesses a copy of it. In addition, you must do these things in the Modified Version:

A. Use in the Title Page (and on the covers, if any) a title distinct from that of the Document, and from those of previous versions (which should, if there were any, be listed in the History section of the Document). You may use the same title as a previous version if the original publisher of that version gives permission.

B. List on the Title Page, as authors, one or more persons or entities responsible for authorship of the modifications in the Modified Version, together with at least five of the principal authors of the Document (all of its principal authors, if it has fewer than five), unless they release you from this requirement.

C. State on the Title page the name of the publisher of the Modified Version, as the publisher.

D. Preserve all the copyright notices of the Document.

E. Add an appropriate copyright notice for your modifications adjacent to the other copyright notices.

F. Include, immediately after the copyright notices, a license notice giving the public permission to use the Modified Version under the terms of this License, in the form shown in the Addendum below.

G. Preserve in that license notice the full lists of Invariant Sections and required Cover Texts given in the Document's license notice.

H. Include an unaltered copy of this License.

I. Preserve the section Entitled "History", Preserve its Title, and add to it an item stating at least the title, year, new authors, and publisher of the Modified Version as given on the Title Page. If there is no section Entitled "History" in the Document, create one stating the title, year, authors, and publisher of the Document as given on its Title Page, then add an item describing the Modified Version as stated in the previous sentence.

J. Preserve the network location, if any, given in the Document for public access to a Transparent copy of the Document, and likewise the network locations given in the Document for previous versions it was based on. These may be placed in the "History" section. You may omit a network location for a work that was published at least four years before the Document itself, or if the original publisher of the version it refers to gives permission.

K. For any section Entitled "Acknowledgements" or "Dedications", Preserve the Title of the section, and preserve in the section all the substance and tone of each of the contributor acknowledgements and/or dedications given therein.

L. Preserve all the Invariant Sections of the Document, unaltered in their text and in their titles. Section numbers or the equivalent are not considered part of the section titles.

M. Delete any section Entitled "Endorsements". Such a section may not be included in the Modified Version.

N. Do not retitle any existing section to be Entitled "Endorsements" or to conflict in title with any Invariant Section.

O. Preserve any Warranty Disclaimers.

If the Modified Version includes new front-matter sections or appendices that qualify as Secondary Sections and contain no material copied from the Document, you may at your option designate some or all of these sections as invariant. To do this, add their titles to the list of Invariant Sections in the Modified Version's license notice. These titles must be distinct from any other section titles.

You may add a section Entitled "Endorsements", provided it contains nothing but endorsements of your Modified Version by various parties—for example, statements of peer review or that the text has been approved by an organization as the authoritative definition of a standard.

You may add a passage of up to five words as a Front-Cover Text, and a passage of up to 25 words as a Back-Cover Text, to the end of the list of Cover Texts in the Modified Version. Only one passage of Front-Cover Text and one of Back-Cover Text may be added by (or through arrangements made by) any one entity. If the Document already includes a cover text for the same cover, previously added by you or by arrangement made by the same entity you are acting on behalf of, you may not add another; but you may replace the old one, on explicit permission from the previous publisher that added the old one.

The author(s) and publisher(s) of the Document do not by this License give permission to use their names for publicity for or to assert or imply endorsement of any Modified Version.

5. COMBINING DOCUMENTS

You may combine the Document with other documents released under this License, under the terms defined in section 4 above for modified versions, provided that you include in the combination all of the Invariant Sections of all of the original documents, unmodified, and list them all as Invariant Sections of your combined work in its license notice, and that you preserve all their Warranty Disclaimers.

The combined work need only contain one copy of this License, and multiple identical Invariant Sections may be replaced with a single copy. If there are multiple Invariant Sections with the same name but different contents, make the title of each such section unique by adding at the end of it, in parentheses, the name of the original author or publisher of that section if known, or else a unique number. Make the same adjustment to the section titles in the list of Invariant Sections in the license notice of the combined work.

In the combination, you must combine any sections Entitled "History" in the various original documents, forming one section Entitled "History"; likewise combine any sections Entitled "Acknowledgements", and any sections Entitled "Dedications". You must delete all sections Entitled "Endorsements."

6. COLLECTIONS OF DOCUMENTS

You may make a collection consisting of the Document and other documents released under this License, and replace the individual copies of this License in the various documents with a single copy that is included in the collection, provided that you follow the rules of this License for verbatim copying of each of the documents in all other respects.

You may extract a single document from such a collection, and distribute it individually under this License, provided you insert a copy of this License into the extracted document, and follow this License in all other respects regarding verbatim copying of that document.

7. AGGREGATION WITH INDEPENDENT WORKS

A compilation of the Document or its derivatives with other separate and independent documents or works, in or on a volume of a storage or distribution medium, is called an "aggregate" if the copyright resulting from the compilation is not used to limit the legal rights of the compilation's users beyond what the individual works permit. When the Document is included in an aggregate, this License does not apply to the other works in the aggregate which are not themselves derivative works of the Document.

If the Cover Text requirement of section 3 is applicable to these copies of the Document, then if the Document is less than one half of the entire aggregate, the Document's Cover Texts may be placed on covers that bracket the Document within the aggregate, or the electronic equivalent of covers if the Document is in electronic form. Otherwise they must appear on printed covers that bracket the whole aggregate.

8. TRANSLATION

Translation is considered a kind of modification, so you may distribute translations of the Document under the terms of section 4. Replacing Invariant Sections with translations requires special permission from their copyright holders, but you may include translations of some or all Invariant Sections in addition to the original versions of these Invariant Sections. You may include a translation of this License, and all the license notices in the Document, and any Warranty Disclaimers, provided that you also include the original English version of this License and the original versions of those notices and disclaimers. In case of a disagreement between the translation and the original version of this License or a notice or disclaimer, the original version will prevail.

If a section in the Document is Entitled "Acknowledgements", "Dedications", or "History", the requirement (section 4) to Preserve its Title (section 1) will typically require changing the actual title.

9. TERMINATION

You may not copy, modify, sublicense, or distribute the Document except as expressly provided under this License. Any attempt otherwise to copy, modify, sublicense, or distribute it is void, and will automatically terminate your rights under this License.

However, if you cease all violation of this License, then your license from a particular copyright holder is reinstated (a) provisionally, unless and until the copyright holder explicitly and finally terminates your license, and (b) permanently, if the copyright holder fails to notify you of the violation by some reasonable means prior to 60 days after the cessation.

Moreover, your license from a particular copyright holder is reinstated permanently if the copyright holder notifies you of the violation by some reasonable means, this is the first time you have received notice of violation of this License (for any work) from that copyright holder, and you cure the violation prior to 30 days after your receipt of the notice.

Termination of your rights under this section does not terminate the licenses of parties who have received copies or rights from you under this License. If your rights have been terminated and not permanently reinstated, receipt of a copy of some or all of the same material does not give you any rights to use it.

10. FUTURE REVISIONS OF THIS LICENSE

The Free Software Foundation may publish new, revised versions of the GNU Free Documentation License from time to time. Such new versions will be similar in spirit to the present version, but may differ in detail to address new problems or concerns. See `http://www.gnu.org/copyleft/`.

Each version of the License is given a distinguishing version number. If the Document specifies that a particular numbered version of this License "or any later version" applies to it, you have the option of following the terms and conditions either of that specified version or of any later version that has been published (not as a draft) by the Free Software Foundation. If the Document does not specify a version number of this License, you may choose any version ever published (not as a draft) by the Free Software Foundation. If the Document specifies that a proxy can decide which future versions of this License can be used, that proxy's public statement of acceptance of a version permanently authorizes you to choose that version for the Document.

11. RELICENSING

"Massive Multiauthor Collaboration Site" (or "MMC Site") means any World Wide Web server that publishes copyrightable works and also provides prominent facilities for anybody to edit those works. A public wiki that anybody can edit is an example of such a server. A "Massive Multiauthor Collaboration" (or "MMC") contained in the site means any set of copyrightable works thus published on the MMC site.

"CC-BY-SA" means the Creative Commons Attribution-Share Alike 3.0 license published by Creative Commons Corporation, a not-for-profit corporation with a principal place of business in San Francisco, California, as well as future copyleft versions of that license published by that same organization.

"Incorporate" means to publish or republish a Document, in whole or in part, as part of another Document.

An MMC is "eligible for relicensing" if it is licensed under this License, and if all works that were first published under this License somewhere other than this MMC, and subsequently incorporated in whole or in part into the MMC, (1) had no cover texts or invariant sections, and (2) were thus incorporated prior to November 1, 2008.

The operator of an MMC Site may republish an MMC contained in the site under CC-BY-SA on the same site at any time before August 1, 2009, provided the MMC is eligible for relicensing.

ADDENDUM: How to use this License for your documents

To use this License in a document you have written, include a copy of the License in the
document and put the following copyright and license notices just after the title page:

```
Copyright (C)  year  your name.
Permission is granted to copy, distribute and/or modify this document
under the terms of the GNU Free Documentation License, Version 1.3
or any later version published by the Free Software Foundation;
with no Invariant Sections, no Front-Cover Texts, and no Back-Cover
Texts.  A copy of the license is included in the section entitled ``GNU
Free Documentation License''.
```

If you have Invariant Sections, Front-Cover Texts and Back-Cover Texts, replace the
"with...Texts." line with this:

```
with the Invariant Sections being list their titles, with
the Front-Cover Texts being list, and with the Back-Cover Texts
being list.
```

If you have Invariant Sections without Cover Texts, or some other combination of the
three, merge those two alternatives to suit the situation.

If your document contains nontrivial examples of program code, we recommend releasing
these examples in parallel under your choice of free software license, such as the GNU
General Public License, to permit their use in free software.

Bibliography

[Denny 2008]
> Joel E. Denny and Brian A. Malloy, IELR(1): Practical LR(1) Parser Tables for Non-LR(1) Grammars with Conflict Resolution, in *Proceedings of the 2008 ACM Symposium on Applied Computing* (SAC'08), ACM, New York, NY, USA, pp. 240–245. http://dx.doi.org/10.1145/1363686.1363747

[Denny 2010 May]
> Joel E. Denny, PSLR(1): Pseudo-Scannerless Minimal LR(1) for the Deterministic Parsing of Composite Languages, Ph.D. Dissertation, Clemson University, Clemson, SC, USA (May 2010). http://proquest.umi.com/pqdlink?did=2041473591&Fmt=7&clientId=79356&RQT=309&VName=PQD

[Denny 2010 November]
> Joel E. Denny and Brian A. Malloy, The IELR(1) Algorithm for Generating Minimal LR(1) Parser Tables for Non-LR(1) Grammars with Conflict Resolution, in *Science of Computer Programming*, Vol. 75, Issue 11 (November 2010), pp. 943–979. http://dx.doi.org/10.1016/j.scico.2009.08.001

[DeRemer 1982]
> Frank DeRemer and Thomas Pennello, Efficient Computation of LALR(1) Look-Ahead Sets, in *ACM Transactions on Programming Languages and Systems*, Vol. 4, No. 4 (October 1982), pp. 615–649. http://dx.doi.org/10.1145/69622.357187

[Knuth 1965]
> Donald E. Knuth, On the Translation of Languages from Left to Right, in *Information and Control*, Vol. 8, Issue 6 (December 1965), pp. 607–639. http://dx.doi.org/10.1016/S0019-9958(65)90426-2

[Scott 2000]
> Elizabeth Scott, Adrian Johnstone, and Shamsa Sadaf Hussain, *Tomita-Style Generalised LR Parsers*, Royal Holloway, University of London, Department of Computer Science, TR-00-12 (December 2000). http://www.cs.rhul.ac.uk/research/languages/publications/tomita_style_1.ps

Index of Terms